MORE PRAISE FOR *WHEN WE FIGHT, WE WIN!*

"[A] beautiful book. . . . At this moment in history, it's more important than ever that young people recognize how their futures are tied to the vitality of social movements. *When We Fight, We Win!* is a valuable resource for educators as we help students come to see themselves as activists."

—*Rethinking Schools*

"As protests and demonstrations sprout across the land, young organizers and activists need to know why and how movements are sustained and how they grow. That resource has arrived. It's a slim volume, chockfull of artwork, entitled *When We Fight, We Win!* . . . It discusses victories and losses, high points and depths, lessons learned, and missed opportunities. The core of its message is that social movements really matter, and when they are smart, adaptive, determined, and focused, they can win against tremendous odds. For such movements change minds, they transform consciousness, and they build social power that their opponents cannot resist. They echo, in action, the words of one of the greatest black leaders in American history, Frederick Douglass, who said, 'Without struggle, there is no progress.'"

—**Mumia Abu-Jamal**, author and prison activist

"Remarkable. . . . One of the things that makes this book so unusual is the stunning artwork throughout."

—**Amy Goodman**, host of *Democracy Now!*

WHEN WE FIGHT WE WIN!

Twenty-First-Century
Social Movements and the Activists
That Are Transforming Our World

**Greg Jobin-Leeds
and AgitArte**

**Foreword by Rinku Sen
Afterword by Antonia Darder**

THE NEW PRESS

NEW YORK
LONDON

"Hard Time Out" by David Goodman (pages 63–64) was
previously published in *Mother Jones*, August 2008.
Reprinted by permission of the author.

Photographs on pages 171–173 by Osvaldo Budet

Requests for permission to reproduce selections from this
book should be mailed to: Permissions Department, The
New Press, 120 Wall Street, 31st floor, New York, NY 10005.

Published in the United States by
The New Press, New York, 2016
Distributed by Two Rivers Distribution

LIBRARY OF CONGRESS CATALOGING-IN-PUBLICATION DATA

Jobin-Leeds, Greg, author.
When we fight, we win!: twenty-first-century
social movements and the activists that are
transforming our world / Greg Jobin-Leeds,
pages cm
Includes bibliographical references and index.
ISBN 978-1-62097-093-5 (paperback) -- ISBN 978-1-
62097-140-6 (e-book) 1. Social reformers--United
States. 2. Political activists--United States. 3. Social
action--United States--History--21st century. 4. Social
movements--United States--History--21st century. I. Title.
HN59.2.J625 2016
303.48'40973--dc23
2015022368

The New Press publishes books that promote and
enrich public discussion and understanding of the
issues vital to our democracy and to a more equitable
world. These books are made possible by the enthusiasm
of our readers; the support of a committed group of
donors, large and small; the collaboration of our many
partners in the independent media and the not-for-
profit sector; booksellers, who often hand-sell New
Press books; librarians; and above all by our authors.

www.thenewpress.com

Book design by AgitArte

Printed in the United States of America

10 9 8 7 6 5

To all the activists and artists in this book,

and my parents,

Lilo Leeds

and

Gerry Leeds (1922–2014),

for showing us how to fight for what we love,

and,

no matter how dark the times, how to win our humanity

"Radicals are in many ways social artists. They restate the hidden truths of society through working with people and social movements. . . . They teach people to see with a fresh vision . . . laying bare the full absurdities of treasured hypocrisies."

Judith Nies, author of *Nine Women: Portraits from the American Radical Tradition*

"If there is no struggle, there is no progress. Those who profess to favor freedom, and yet deprecate agitation, are men who want crops without plowing up the ground. They want rain without thunder and lightning. They want the ocean without the awful roar of its many waters. . . . Power concedes nothing without a demand. It never did and it never will."

Frederick Douglass, author and slavery abolitionist, 1857

CONTENTS

FORE-
WORD

RINKU SEN

By the time I discovered racial justice organizing at the age of seventeen, the social movements of the 1960s had waned. Sit-ins and protests had given way to the work that comes after victory: implementing the many changes brought into being by the civil rights, black power, women's, and peace movements. My generation was the first to benefit from those changes. Indeed, I owe my very presence in the United States, and thus my identity as an American, to a historic piece of legislation reflecting the anti-discrimination ethos that pushed this country forward in 1965. The civil rights movement and power movements among black, brown, red, and yellow people had successfully asserted equal treatment as an American value. I've devoted my whole adult life to figuring out how to create social movements of a similar scope and depth.

When I started on this road in the mid-1980s, I didn't realize that a mere twenty years had been more than enough to craft a distorted popular retelling of movement history, and to establish that distortion as fact. The political stories I heard as a child featured deeply misleading "lessons" about massive social progress sparked by individual acts of heroic resistance. Before I knew better, what people called "movements" often seemed to have been led by exceptional charismatic men, working in concert with other exceptional charismatic men.

These were fantasy versions of movements, in which the mundane was deleted in favor of the dramatic, and the collective in favor of the individual. Popular movement stories also frequently delete the poor, the female, the queer, and the nonwhite. To get access to the full range of questions and answers, to the reflections that would actually help me act in ways that fostered movement, I had to push past revision to get to reality. I busted through this fiction in no small part by reading books like *When We Fight, We Win!*

The world and the United States are unquestionably in a turbulent time, as communities rise up to assert their right not only to exist but also to thrive with every expectation of safety and self-determination. In 2014 and 2015, thousands of demonstrators have taken to the streets in Ferguson, Baltimore, and too many other places to count, facing down tear gas and tanks while protesting the systemic inaction that enabled yet another police killing of an unarmed black teenager.

In these pages, we see Native Americans reminding the nation that they are still here and still fighting. We meet people who are stretching and bending the gender binary in ways that make its abolition seem certain. We encounter both the difficulties and the joys of fighting to save humanity by reviving our stewardship of the earth.

In *When We Fight, We Win!*, contemporary movements become the sources of the lessons I sought as a young organizer—lessons that I still seek.

Some of the efforts featured here are so nascent that they have yet to win their ultimate prize. Some of these efforts are pre-movements, still in those years of toiling that create the organizations, the consciousness, and the platform for change that undergirds any successful movement. We don't have comprehensive immigration reform, even after more than a decade of fighting. As a global society, we have not yet committed to the sacrifices required to stop climate change. We still incarcerate people, the vast majority black and Latino, at the highest rates of any industrialized country in the world.

Whether or not we win will be based on many things other than our own strategy and strength. Even strong, huge movements sometimes fail. There is, however, no path to victory without trying.

The real-time lessons of movements, whatever their current shape, are critical if we want more movement. At the cliff edge of history is as good a place as any from which to mine insights that can help all those brave enough to attempt making the kinds of changes that can seem impossible.

This is the true beauty of this book: its offering of movements in progress, long before they are co-opted into the endless narrative of American individualism. The voices of veteran organizers and emerging leaders alike reveal the ingredients that make modern movements inclusive, radical, and effective. These voices can fuel our growing vision, improve our daily practice, and, most important, make us feel hopeful for the future of our world.

From there, all we need to do is act.

New York City, May 2015

Rinku Sen is the president and executive director of Race Forward: The Center for Racial Justice Innovation and the publisher of the award-winning news site Colorlines. *Sen co-chairs the Schott Foundation for Public Education with the author, Greg Jobin-Leeds.*

■ **HANDS UP DON'T SHOOT. Molly Crabapple, Brooklyn, New York, 2014**
"Hands up, don't shoot!" became the people's cry for justice and accountability in the aftermath of several killings of unarmed black people by police and vigilantes across the United States. The phrase was coined by Ferguson and St. Louis protesters in the wake of Michael Brown's murder in 2014 to illustrate the circumstances of his death. As reported in the news and later in grand jury testimony, Brown was shot while his hands were in the air. Currently, both the gesture and the phrase are widely used across the nation as powerful protest symbols against racism and police brutality.

INTRO-
DUCTION
INSPIRATION FROM STORIES

Same-sex marriage, #BlackLivesMatter, the DREAM Act, the People's Climate March, End the New Jim Crow, Occupy Wall Street . . . today, ordinary people are taking on extraordinary problems, gaining traction, and making the impossible possible. For five years, I asked leaders of these and other thriving social movements: "What are the lessons you've learned that you would like to pass on to new activists?" Themes began to emerge. Their answers became captivating stories that told of their visions and victories, communities and allies, adversaries and disappointments, and unique practices and strategies for change.

Storytelling—in words, song, and art —is one of the vital practices that activists use. Storytelling is a connective tissue of social movements used to teach each other how to fight. Through stories we identify what we are fighting against, what we are fighting for, and how to take action. Stories ground us and inspire activists to keep fighting. Through the tradition of telling stories, we create a collective powerful "we" to build courage and take on entrenched and often alarming adversaries who are blocking change. Stories are used to share visions and reshape language and political debates. Stories in words and art are the medium we use in this book.

We think differently about what is possible when we learn of activists' victories large and small and when we hear their successful and inspiring visions that offer alternatives to the inequities of our economy, climate destruction, the school testing mania, deportations, and the exploding police and prison systems. Twenty-first-century activists offer inspiring conceptualizations of families and gender, new language and ways of thinking, teaching, and acting. These visionary movement leaders share how they created their successes and recovered from their failures. *When We Fight, We Win!* is about their transformations and twenty-first-century movements that are shaping and inspiring a generation across the globe.

Real people are making change right now. We can too.

This book spans from 2000–2015, the beginning of the twenty-first century, a fertile era of activism. *When We Fight, We Win!* is part of a multigenerational struggle for liberation, for the democratization of power, so all of us can participate in deciding the fate of our lives and communities.

WHY I WROTE THIS BOOK

In 2006, I was working on a successful fifteen-year campaign for New York's children. A network of organizations was helping to nurture a strong statewide parent crusade focused on building the public and political will to provide every child an opportunity to learn. We were on the cusp of winning systemic change that resulted in the largest historical increase in public school funding. The equitable funding would support preschools, teacher professional development, library books, class-size reduction, and other proven and desperately needed educational resources in struggling communities and low-income school districts. Parents were succeeding in the media, the community, the courts, and the legislature.

Through political pressure, New York governor Eliot Spitzer—who had opposed the parents and kids on funding issues when he was the state attorney general, two years before—now became our champion. The New York State Legislature (one of whose members had sworn that these parents would not win "in our lifetime") voted for billions of dollars to flow to the highest-need children and schools.

The multipronged legal, media, legislative, community organizing, and donor campaign was effective. It received the Champion Award from the Center for Community Change and the Critical Impact Award from the Council on Foundations. Case studies were written about this victory that had been won by determined parents, students, teachers, and their allies.

Just a few years later, schools would be in worse shape in almost every urban setting in New York State and around the country.

In 2010, the New York State legislature voted to cut back funding and resources for inner-city schools. In 2011, New York's Democratic governor, Andrew Cuomo, reduced taxes for the extremely wealthy and, with New York City's Republican mayor, Michael Bloomberg, halted the advances. The progress we had made over many years was quickly reversed. In my beloved New York City, as well as Chicago, Philadelphia, Boston, and other cities across the country, teachers were fired, art and gym programs cut, and class sizes increased. President Barack Obama, governors, legislators, school boards, and mayors increased punitive testing and closed more and more schools, mostly in already devastated communities of color. They demonized teachers, students, and parents as the cause of our educational problems.

I had been a high school teacher; seeing the rapid disinvestment in and decline of public schools was heartbreaking. I watched in horror as the political and public conversation moved from providing kids with the opportunities they needed to focusing on school closures, high-stakes testing, and unproven, billionaire-promoted charter schools. The devastating impact of New York education cuts and all the budget cuts throughout the country still horrifies me as I think of the millions of children who are being denied a fair opportunity to learn and will suffer a lifetime of consequences.

Why did we lose momentum? What could we have done differently? Was our analysis of the political reality that far off?

Many people working on other issues were raising these same questions. I began to examine how we could more effectively do our work of changing political and public will and the day-to-day reality for children and families. I took a step back to investigate the historical roots, deepen my analysis, and study successful strategies for change. During this time I searched for a book of cross-cutting lessons, culled from past social movements. I asked one of my favorite authors if such a book existed. She replied, "No. Why don't you write it?"

With the help of a few friends and fellow organizers, I examined broad-scale social change, focusing on three key questions:

- How do we create real and enduring change?
- What have successful organizers done that works, and what doesn't work?
- How can anyone get involved and make a difference?

I posed these questions to hundreds of activists, academics, political organizers, and movement leaders. They offered gripping stories and surprising answers. I found crosscutting lessons that helped me understand how transformative change happened and is happening today. These leaders talked of practices, traditions, and attributes of movement building that cut across each of today's struggles and those of the past. This led me to rethink and reprioritize. Colleagues asked me to write and speak about these lessons. From that beginning, this book took shape.

This is neither a comprehensive study nor an instruction manual; it is stories and observations based on interviews and experiences in the United States.

THE *WHEN WE FIGHT, WE WIN!* TEAM

When We Fight, We Win! emerged from a partnership with a design and editorial team that has evolved through many years of friendship and shared struggles with Antonia Darder, José Jorge Díaz, David Goodman, Deymirie Hernández, and Rinku Sen. This book reflects their clear thinking and visionary voices. They all shared their organizing knowledge, introduced us to remarkable activists, and read and challenged me on every chapter.

AgitArte created the art narrative through images, captions, artist interviews, and the overall design, which amplifies the stories and gives light to the breadth, power, and vision of movements. AgitArte is an organization of artists and organizers whose mission is to create cultural projects and practices in solidarity with grassroots struggles of the working class and communities of color for social and economic justice. Deymirie Hernández, an educator, architect, and puppeteer, designed the book, curated the art, and researched and wrote the captions. José Jorge Díaz, the artistic director and founder of AgitArte, led the artist interviews and edited the entire book. Jorge and I have worked with each other for more than twenty years and he helped me write the first version of this book as a letter to colleagues and I have helped him with AgitArte since its early days. José "Primo" Hernández designed the cover and partnered with Dey on the layout.

The Foreword is the voice of Rinku Sen, author of the organizing manual *Stir It Up*, publisher of *Colorlines*, and executive director of Race Forward. Rinku has co-chaired the board of the Schott Foundation for Public Education with me for eight years, and we have toiled together for many more.

The Afterword is by Antonia Darder, author of the books *A Dissident Voice*, *After Race*, *Freire and Education*, and many other inspiring writings. She is a dear friend and longtime activist and holds an endowed chair in ethics and moral leadership at Loyola Marymount University.

I created the story narrative, using the voices of cutting-edge leaders who are addressing the root causes of inequities and injustices as well as voices from the larger movements that are building the infrastructure of change. These stories, based on interviews, are from organizers who are actively involved in some of today's most flourishing social change organizations. David Goodman, a master storyteller, was my writing advisor and helped create these tales. An award-winning journalist for national publications, David is the author of ten books.

While these five certainly do not agree with everything written here, they have been my editorial and artistic guides.

THE GATHERING

In August 2014 and November 2015, many of the activists and artists from the stories in this book gathered together with the editorial and design team to celebrate our movements, reflect on the challenges we all are facing, and contribute to the collective wisdom reflected in the epilogue and throughout these pages and social media platforms.. Though I do not speak for them, most of the activists interviewed in this book read early drafts of the chapter in which their work is featured, adding to and updating the story and sharpening our analysis.

This powerful collaborative process contributes to the "we" in *When We Fight, We Win!* Working together has been an exciting, critical, and creative process, resulting in a beloved learning community of activists, artists, and authors.

It's an ongoing collaboration—all the struggles in this book continue.

WHEN WE FIGHT, WE WIN!

The book's title comes directly out of the experiences of AgitArte, whose members heard the phrase while working on a Boston anti-eviction fight. *When We Fight, We Win!* drives home the overarching points of the book: winning requires a "we," a community, a group, an organization. And transformative change, in the face of powerful forces, requires a fight.

Action, reflection, art, and storytelling keep the fight alive through generations.

When we fight, we often move ourselves out of our comfort zones to face forces and people that view the world differently and may not be ready to change. When we fight—building an organization, joining a community of activists—we win not only communal victories but also our own personal transformation, enabling us to discover common root causes to problems that had seemed unconnected before. Understanding root causes can ally us with others—across issues, cultures, identities. This aggregates individual fights into broad movement struggles, and by working in solidarity together we can realize far-reaching, systemic change. Winning lies not in a single victory, but in many victories and the lifelong struggle to change injustice and create a future based on a bold, transformative vision. Claiming our humanity and right to fight, by standing up for justice and building a community of activists, is a win in itself.

When we fight, we participate in creating the future. We become part of the inspiring history of movements. We learn from history and we are creating it.

Each story and piece of art shared here is a small taste of the massive number of organizations and people in this global struggle to create a just world. Author and activist Paul Hawken calls it the "blessed unrest"—the ongoing work that has to be constantly regenerated and reinvented.

WHAT IS TRANSFORMATIVE ORGANIZING?

Many have contributed brilliant perspectives on the essential ingredients of movement organizing and transformation. Excellent work has been done by Grace Lee Boggs, Antonia Darder, Robert Gass, Adria Goodson, Taj James, Eric Mann, Judith Nies, Manuel Pastor, Rinku Sen, Ella Baker, Howard Zinn, Paulo Freire, AgitArte, the Zapatistas, the black power movements, and so many others. They inform this moment in history and this book.

I chose seven attributes of transformative organizers that emerged from the interviews and structured stories and a chapter around each. Transformative organizers:

- Build organizations that are grounded in the most impacted communities
- Create transformative visions
- Tell powerful stories
- Go to the root cause of problems
- Reclaim the intersection of our struggles and identities
- Disrupt power, changing who has it and what to do with it once reclaimed
- Build solidarity and stand together

Each chapter, and the epilogue, show these attributes in action. Transformative organizers share these seven attributes and many more. These contemporary activists organize with a core group of people, develop an alternative vision of the future, interrupt cultural narratives, enroll allies, and develop global perspectives and broad networks. Transformative organizing transforms activists from bystanders or victims into drivers of change. It involves many levels of transformation: personal and spiritual, organizational and communal, cultural, and political.

Transformative organizing focuses on systemic change that addresses root causes, not just reforms that allow the same systems to reproduce themselves. Transformative organizers link systems of oppression together for all to see. Many may have started their activism by focusing on a single personal grievance; over time they saw the interconnection of their issues with others. Thus, transformative organizing builds solidarity. While they may pursue incremental improvements and reforms, transformative organizers place their work within a much larger vision and strategy.

As he helped me with the interviews, the veteran author David Goodman often called these transformative organizers and artists "transformers." These transformers build the infrastructure of social movements.

These are their stories.

Chapter 1, Reclaiming Wholeness: The LGBTQ*** **Movement.** Paulina Helm-Hernández at Southerners on New Ground and Rea Carey at the National LGBTQ Taskforce show us the cutting edge of a movement in which new conversations and definitions about sexuality, gender, and identity are emerging. Marriage equality is one step in a larger liberation movement that is thinking beyond the traditional fragmented male/female, gay/straight either/or binary. Conversations with these transformers reveal something equally profound: their identities go beyond sexuality into race and class as well. As they celebrate their love, they help us all reclaim a sense of wholeness.

---

* LGBTQ refers to people who identify as lesbian, gay, bisexual, transgender, and/or queer/questioning.

Chapter 2, Grounded in Community: The Fight for the Soul of Public Education. In Chicago, teachers, students, parents, and community leaders are creating a social and economic movement, energized by a community-based teachers union, to defend public education. The power of their alliance illustrates the importance of being grounded in community and underscores that transformative movements are led by those most impacted. Up against a powerful mayor and would-be "reformers" seeking to privatize public education and close schools in the most vulnerable neighborhoods, Chicago's organizing has become a nationally visible, exciting beacon of hope.

Chapter 3, Transforming Visions: Ending Mass Incarceration. The United States has more people in prison than any other country on the planet. The prison-justice movement is achieving incremental and important victories, as their transformative visions challenge us to understand the racist and capitalist underpinnings of the prison industrial complex and to imagine a world without jails. Patrisse Cullors-Brignac (one of the founders of #BlackLivesMatter), Angela Davis, Michelle Alexander, and Walidah Imarisha powerfully illustrate incarceration's relationship to social control, and their words, stories, art, visions, and actions inspire us to imagine what seemed impossible.

Chapter 4, The Power of Stories: The DREAMers and Immigrant Rights. A youth-led immigrant group marched from Florida to the White House, building on decades of organizing that had come before them; they were cheered on along their journey, carrying the hopes of parents for their immigrant children. Inspiring thousands of immigrants to come out of the shadows, shatter the silence, and tell their own stories, the DREAMers are no longer afraid or ashamed of being undocumented. The Trail of DREAMs is one of their stories. They energized and brought attention to a national effort to make it possible for immigrant youth to remain in the United States and go to college. Their organizing is succeeding. Their stories are helping transform a broken immigration system and restore dignity to millions of undocumented Americans.

Chapter 5, "When We Fight, We Win!": The Struggle for Economic Power. The organizing of Occupy Wall Street, anti-eviction activists, and restaurant workers are three stories that inspire increasing activism. The modern economic justice movement dramatically escalates the public discourse around inequality. Thanks to their bold organizing and the larger movement, the notion of the 99%, the need to democratize who holds economic power, and alternatives that put people before profits are now part of the public narrative. These economic justice organizers are fighting to disrupt and change the inequitable status quo.

Chapter 6, Environmental Warriors: Going to the Root of the Problem. A global networked environmental movement is on the rise. Indigenous activist Clayton Thomas-Müller, the LA Bus Riders Union, and 350.org are three of their stories that delve into how transformative organizing goes to the root causes of problems, as opposed to focusing only on short-term solutions. Bill McKibben speaks of "the perverse logic of capitalism: the fact that it's extremely profitable to pollute. . . . There can be no real answer to our climate woes that doesn't address the insane inequalities and concentrations of power that are helping to drive us toward this disaster."

Epilogue: Solidarity—A Gathering.

> First they came for the socialists, and I did not
>   speak out—
>   because I was not a socialist.
> Then they came for the trade unionists, and I
>   did not speak out—
>   because I was not a trade unionist.
> Then they came for the Jews, and I did not
>   speak out—
>   because I was not a Jew.
> Then they came for me—and there was no
>   one left to speak for me.[1]

This famous quote from Martin Niemöller, a German pastor and survivor of the Nazi concentration camps, dramatizes the necessity of movements that speak up, in solidarity, to injustice. Twenty of the transformative organizers and artists from these pages all converged for two days and stood side by side in their struggles. The epilogue is the story of that gathering and some key takeaways that show these transformers' unity and wisdom.

Though each of the modern-day visionaries in this book are in different stages of the struggle, and speak up on different issues, they are participants in one global movement for social justice. Their tales show many of the complex and driving forces behind transformation in a way that demonstrates how you can join in. There are no shortcuts to becoming an organizer or to building organizations and movements. Effective organizing requires action, followed by training, more action, critical reflection with others, more action, more reflection. This is called praxis. These transformative organizers analyze past actions and history, and this inspires and shapes their practice, creativity, and strategy.

THE ART OF
TRANSFORMATIVE MOVEMENTS

Art is a critical element, an integral part of social movements and storytelling. The art throughout the book includes examples from struggles that use iconic images and performance art to engage and inspire, to enrage and move people to action. Each chapter concludes with an artist interview. Art allows those of us seeking change to step outside the current landscape of injustice to imagine a different world.

"Artists are here to disturb the peace," writes author James Baldwin. Art helps us render things visible that we might not have been able to express. It gives us audacity. Art can develop a culture of solidarity, celebration, and liberation.

WHO THIS BOOK IS FOR

When We Fight, We Win! is for all those who yearn for big changes, or have taken some action, or have tried

to make some societal change, whether you have succeeded or failed.

It is for those who wrestle with authority, who question why our country's vast resources and opportunities are so inequitably shared, who seek more potential in their actions. It is for those who often get discouraged but who also sense the possibility of achieving major, enduring social, environmental, and economic change and a fairer, healthier world for all of us.

This book is also for my kids and their friends, all in their teens and early twenties. Like many young people around the country, they want to make the world a better place. Gaggles of them pass through our home, many asking me for the next chapter of this book before it was done, hungrily gobbling up the stories and images and helping me edit.

Sometimes a fight takes you five steps forward, and then you get pushed ten steps back. Losses require us to engage even more. Occupy Wall Street, #BlackLivesMatter and the prison justice movement, the DREAMers and the immigration movement, the environmental justice movement, the LGBTQ movement, and the increasingly powerful parent, student, and teacher networks all grew out of eras of many losses—and only by continuing to fight, do our movements gain strength. In dark times, we all need to add our presence.

Here is mine.

Add your voice, your passion, your story—join the fight.

Organizing for transformation is within reach of everyone. We can be inspired by these experienced leaders to stand up, join in at this historic moment, and make a difference.

■ **DECOLONIZE WALL STREET.**
Ernesto Yerena, Oakland, California, 2011.
Decolonize Wall Street evokes the history of the Dutch colonization of native peoples. After Manhattan Island was "purchased" by the Dutch in 1626 from the Canarsie People, the settlers built a wall to protect themselves from the First Nation People. The path, named Wall Street, became a busy commercial zone, and later was home to the New York Stock Exchange. Ernesto Yerena uses cultural icons, rebels, and everyday people to express his stance against colonization and oppression.

DECOLONIZE WALLSTREET

**WALL ST. IS
ON OCCUPIED
ALGONQUIN LAND**

**DEFEND
MOTHER EARTH**

DECOLONIZE THE 99%

1

RECLAIMING WHOLE-NESS: THE LGBTQ MOVEMENT

■ **REINA. Trans Day of Action, New York City, 2012 (Photo by Sabelo Narasimhan)**
In the photograph, Reina Gossett, a trans activist and artist who works at the Sylvia Rivera Law Project, courageously carries a sign proclaiming, "This is Our Life, This is Our Time," affirming that bodies in all their differentiation can exist outside of society's norms. Critiquing the policing and criminalization of trans bodies and communities is central to Reina's activism. Violence is ever-present in her life and the lives of all those who must struggle against patriarchal and heteronormative structures. Our bodies are asked to perform and navigate through oppressive social conditions of class, race, gender, and sex. Sabelo Narasimhan is a queer trans organizer and photographer.

■ **UNTITLED. Pride Festival, San Francisco, 2013. Banner from original poster art,** *Don't Stop at Marriage! Queers Are Getting Deported!,* **by Julio Salgado (Photo by Jesús Iñiguez)**

More than 1.8 million people celebrated the approval of same-sex marriage in the state of California in 2013. In the photograph, marchers during the San Francisco Pride Festival hold a banner emphasizing that marriage equality does not address all problems. LGBTQ immigrants are at risk when applying for marriage visas, since the visa process includes an investigation by federal immigration officers into the validity of a marriage. This process can be invasive and risky to individuals who may not be out within their immediate community, and most detention centers are not equipped to protect the safety of LGBTQ immigrants. By June 2015, the Supreme Court made marriage equality the law of the land.

*O*ne of the most culturally transformative movements of the twenty-first century is about the freedom to love and build family.

Fifty years ago, gay sex was a crime in every state in the United States. The federal government would not hire openly gay people. Even the American Civil Liberties Union (ACLU) did not consider these discriminatory practices a problem.

Forty years ago, homosexuality was considered a mental illness.

Thirty years ago, President Ronald Reagan's communications director, Pat Buchanan, argued that AIDS was "nature's revenge on gay men."

In 1996, 68 percent of Americans opposed gay marriage[1] and the federal Defense of Marriage Act (DOMA) was passed, explicitly defining marriage in federal law as a union of one man and one woman.

In 2000, no U.S. state allowed same-sex couples to marry, and forty states had constitutional or legislative prohibitions to "defend" traditional marriage.

Acceptance of gays and lesbians—let alone transgender and bisexual people, or marriage equality—seemed more aspirational than achievable.

LGBTQ* activism in the last half-century has forged ahead despite setbacks, winning crucial victories:

- In 1970 and 1971, gay and lesbian activists converged on the annual meetings of the American Psychiatric Association (APA) to protest the classification of homosexuality as a mental illness. In 1973, the APA removed homosexuality from its Diagnostic and Statistical Manual of Mental Disorders (DSM), ending the official designation of homosexuality as a mental illness.
- In 1986, the U.S. Supreme Court declared in Bowers v. Hardwick that anti-sodomy laws were legal. In 2003, following a multiyear grassroots campaign to raise awareness that included the work of a range of legal organizations and the National Gay and Lesbian Task Force, the U.S. Supreme Court reversed itself in Lawrence v. Texas and declared anti-sodomy laws to be unconstitutional.

In this century, attitudes toward LGBTQ people have continued to transform with remarkable speed:

- In 2011, the U.S. State Department announced passport application changes. Gone were questions about an applicant's mother or father. Instead, applicants only list "parent 1" and "parent 2." The State Department reported that this was done "to provide a gender neutral description of a child's parents and in recognition of different types of families."
- In 2013, the U.S. Supreme Court ruled that DOMA was unconstitutional.
- As of 2014, more than half of people in the United States—and 78 percent of people ages eighteen to twenty-nine—support marriage equality, according to a Gallup poll.
- By early 2015, well over half the states plus the District of Columbia had legalized same-sex marriage.
- By June 2015, the Supreme Court made marriage equality the law of the land.

How did LGBTQ rights and same-sex marriage go from being radioactive to mainstream? What underlies the change in attitudes toward the rights of people who are lesbian, gay, bisexual, transgender, and/or queer/ques-

---

* LGBTQ refers to people who identify as lesbian, gay, bisexual, transgender, and/or queer/questioning. Throughout this chapter, speakers often use LGBT as shorthand. Sexuality and gender identity are fluid, and so is the acronym. LGBTQIA is also used by some, with *I* denoting "intersex" (someone whose anatomy is not exclusively male or female) and *A* for "ally" or "asexual." *Queer* is often used as an umbrella term, though by no means always. We honor and celebrate all of these identities, as well as new ones yet to come.

QUEERS DEMAND

A WORLD WITHOUT PRISONS

We reject hate crimes legislation, "gender-responsive" prisons, and all other measures that use gay rights rhetoric to expand the systems that murder and imprison us. We stand against a prison industrial complex that targets people of color, immigrants, queer and trans people, sex workers, and poor people. We believe in queer imagination and transformative justice to build a new world based on liberation and interdependence.

QUEERS DEMAND

We say no to drone strikes, no to wars for empire, no to coerced recruitment of poor and working class youth, no to secret prisons, no to occupation. We reject the fight for gay inclusion in a sexist, homophobic, racist, and imperialist military. We reject the pinkwashing of state violence. Wars have never liberated queers; we will liberate ourselves.

STOP PINKWASHING ISRAELI APARTHEID

AN END TO MILITARISM

QUEERS DEMAND

We recognize gender policing as a tool of state violence, and demand an end to gender as a legal category. We recognize that gender justice is inextricably linked to racial and economic justice, disability justice, and anti-colonialism. We demand an end to the criminalization of our bodies, the right to determine our own genders, and queer and trans liberation on our own terms.

GENDER SELF-DETERMINATION

STONEWALL

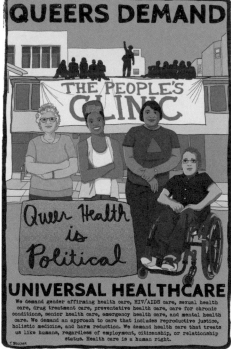

QUEERS DEMAND

THE PEOPLE'S CLINIC

Queer Health is Political

UNIVERSAL HEALTHCARE

We demand gender affirming health care, HIV/AIDS care, sexual health care, drug treatment care, preventative health care, care for chronic conditions, senior health care, emergency health care, and mental health care. We demand an approach to care that includes reproductive justice, holistic medicine, and harm reduction. We demand health care that treats us like humans, regardless of employment, citizenship, or relationship status. Health care is a human right.

■ **QUEERS DEMAND SERIES. Roan Boucher, Philadelphia, 2013**

The Queers Demand series is celebratory artwork of some of the issues that radical queers push in the class struggle: abolition of prisons, an end to militarism, gender self-determination, and universal health care. Queers, particularly queers of color, trans people, and gender-nonconforming people, are hit particularly hard by capitalism, which devalues the lives of working-class people and their mass movements for collective liberation. Roan Boucher is a self-taught printmaker whose work is inspired by queer resilience, social justice movements, and community building.

tioning? What can other movement organizers learn from this change? Is same-sex marriage transformative? What lies ahead for queer liberation?

The answers from organizers and leaders held many surprises. In the news, the struggles of white gays and lesbians for same-sex marriage were often portrayed as a single-issue fight, separate from other movements. The transformative activists and artists interviewed in this chapter viewed their work in a larger context. They see police violence as an LGBTQ issue. They see economic policies that make it harder for LGBTQ folks to make ends meet, immigrant deportations, incarceration, and public education funding cuts as LGBTQ issues. They know that when queer people are in prison or deported they will be treated even worse than others in the same situation. And when that person is poor or black or brown, the problems cascade. These transformers reveal how to unify twenty-first-century social movements.

This chapter tells the story of two organizations, the National LGBTQ Task Force and Southerners on New Ground, which work at the intersections of heterosexism, racism, sexism, and economic inequality. They see overlapping oppressions in the experiences of black, brown, and poor white lesbians, gay men, and transgender people who are suffering multiple forms of injustice. They are demonstrating how to reclaim the wholeness of each life—and of all lives that have been diminished, segmented, socialized, and sorted into distinct and separate markets and human-constructed categories of race, gender, and class. Their organizing, along with that of many others, is transforming that reality.

Evann Orleck-Jetter, a twelve-year-old girl from Thetford Center, Vermont, strode confidently up to the microphone in the Vermont State House. It was 2009, and Evann didn't recall when she had last been there, but her mother did: she had brought Evann in 2000 when her daughter was just three years old to persuade lawmakers to make Vermont the first state to legalize civil unions, a form of legal recognition for gay and lesbian couples.

Now Evann was back, this time to testify to a joint House-Senate committee to urge them to become the first state legislature to legalize same-sex marriage. Evann Orleck-Jetter was a striking sight: a child ad-

dressing her elders. When Evann began speaking in the packed House chamber, it was she who did the teaching:

> I have a wonderful family. I live with my little brother, my grandma and two moms who are with me all the time and support me in whatever I do. I love them very much, and I wish that having to stand up here right now in front of this committee wasn't

an issue anymore. We should be past this. . . .

I have been studying the civil rights movement in school, and I've learned all about the countless acts of bravery that blacks performed to get their rights. But we still haven't reached the Promised Land that Martin Luther King wanted us to reach. . . . We still don't accept that two people of the same gender can be together, married with kids of their own. We need to reach the Promised Land. . . .

If my parents could just have the right to get married, this would make such a difference. It hurts me sometimes when I feel invisible, because few people understand my feelings about my family, and few people want to ask about families with two moms. It's time to ask, it's time to understand, and it's time to accept and honor families like mine.[2]

A few weeks later, the Vermont legislature overrode a gubernatorial veto and legalized same-sex marriage. Several legislators noted that the stories and statements of Evann and other children swayed them.

"Today, love won," declared Jason Lorber, a Vermont state representative who is gay.[3]

LGBTQ people have given moving personal testimonies in state after state in an effort to tear down the closets and make their love undeniable. They have made history.

"It hurts me sometimes when I feel invisible, because few people understand my feelings about my family . . . It's time to ask, it's time to understand, and it's time to accept and honor families like mine."

But before anyone could offer impassioned testimony or any lawmakers could vote to legalize same-sex marriage, organizers had spent decades preparing the ground. Traveling the road toward liberty and equality has demanded hard work, networks and alliances, sacrifice, civil disobedience, thousands of political campaigns, careful strategy, and the courage to share personal stories of love.

ROOTS IN AN UPRISING

Rea Carey, executive director of the National LGBTQ Task Force, traces the modern marriage equality movement to the Stonewall Riots. In the early morning hours of June 28, 1969, New York City police raided the Stonewall Inn, a well-known gay bar in Greenwich Village. Crowds of people swarmed the streets outside the bar and attacked the police. Sporadic fighting between police and members of the LGBTQ community continued for days.

"With the cops holed up inside Stonewall, the crowd was now in control of the street, and it bellowed in triumph and pent-up rage," recounted historian Martin Duberman in a history of the Stonewall riots.[4]

"People were mad, they were fed up, and that launched what most describe as the modern era of the LGBTQ movement out of anger and out of the discrimination and the violence that was happening," Carey says.

It wasn't just that LGBTQ people fought back at Stonewall. It was also *who* fought back. "At the bar that night were not privileged people, by and large. There were a lot of drag queens, a lot of people of color, a lot of young people, and they launched this movement,"

It wasn't just that LGBTQ people fought back at Stonewall. It was also who fought back. "At the bar that night were not privileged people, by and large. There were a lot of drag queens, a lot of people of color, a lot of young people, and they launched this movement."

Carey explains. People experiencing multiple oppressions, like in all transformative movements, led the way.

"In the early years, so much of the movement was focused on the violence we were experiencing, the discrimination that was going on, the lack of access to basic human needs for the LGBT community, and the fact that at that time it was still on the books that homosexuality was a mental illness."

CRISIS AND OPPORTUNITY: AIDS AND MARRIAGE ORGANIZING

The modern marriage equality movement was energized by unlikely circumstances. "We wouldn't have moved as quickly on marriage progress if it weren't for HIV/AIDS," reflects Rea Carey.

"There were a lot of men—including men in urban areas who had some level of class or race privilege—who were being denied access to their partners as they were dying in hospitals because they weren't 'family.' This experience resulted in a broader understanding of the impact of not being able to be legally married. AIDS provided a very tangible experience for thousands of gay men that they too could experience severe discrimination."

Acquired Immune Deficiency Syndrome (AIDS) was first recognized as a disease in the United States in 1981. Gay men, among others, were suddenly dying at alarming rates. The disease was poorly understood at first and was erroneously stigmatized as the "gay men's cancer" and "gay-related immune deficiency" until it later became known that heterosexuals were contracting the disease too. Fear and anti-gay discrimination were hallmarks of the early era of AIDS. A 1985 *Los Angeles Times* poll revealed that about half of adults favored a quarantine of AIDS patients and identity cards for those who tested positive for the human immunodeficiency virus (HIV), while 15 percent favored tattooing people with AIDS.[5] These were draconian measures reminiscent of fascist eras of the past.

Organizers used a variety of tactics to get needed medical care and bring attention to the crisis. Rea Carey talked about how some of the organizers would lobby on AIDS in the morning, then change out of their suits and participate in actions with ACT UP (AIDS

NO PRIDE for SOME of US without LIBERATION for ALL of US.

MARSHA
"Pay It No
Mind" JoHnSon
was a mother of the
TRanS + QueeR LiBeRaTion
movement. She dedicated
her life to helping tRanS
youth, sex woRKeRS and pooR
and incaRCeRaTed Queers.

We
HoNoR
her LeGACY
by supporting TRanS
WoMeN of COLoR to
LIVE + LEAD.

MICAH BAZANT

■ **NO PRIDE FOR SOME OF US. Micah Bazant, San Francisco, 2013**
When Marsha P. Johnson and Sylvia Ray Rivera—homeless black and Latina trans women and self-proclaimed "street queens"—ignited the Stonewall Riots in 1969, they changed LGBTQ politics forever. In the early 1970s, Marsha and Sylvia founded Street Transvestite Action Revolutionaries (S.T.A.R.). The activist organization had a house on the Lower East Side of New York City that provided food, shelter, and clothing to support young drag queens and trans women. Micah Bazant's illustration, *No Pride for Some of Us*, honors Marsha Johnson and the dream of an anti-racist, transgender, and queer liberation movement.

Coalition to Unleash Power), which launched "die-ins" and blocked streets, spilled fake blood while interrupting TV shows, wore the pink triangle (the badge that homosexuals were forced to wear in Nazi concentration camps), and echoed a phrase that would become emblematic of this era: Silence = Death. On the streets they pasted posters of a bloody handprint over the words "The government has blood on its hands—one AIDS death every hour." It was a powerful moment that gave a sense of urgency to the nascent LGBTQ movement.

Like immigrant-rights activists today who defiantly declare themselves undocumented, ACT UP boldly reclaimed its identity from what had been symbols of shame and oppression. Its members stood up, fought back, and were willing to be hated for it in order to draw attention to the AIDS crisis. Their direct actions and shaming were meant to create a moral predicament for the government and for mainstream America about the humanity of gays.

LGBTQ people were also fighting for their humanity by challenging sodomy laws. Prior to 1962, sodomy was a felony in every state.[6] In 1986, the U.S. Supreme Court upheld the legality of anti-sodomy laws in *Bowers v. Hardwick*.

The Supreme Court's anti-gay ruling galvanized the LGBTQ movement. The National Gay and Lesbian Task Force launched the Privacy Project to challenge anti-sodomy laws in every state. As scholar Elizabeth Sheyn observed:

> From 1986–1991, the Privacy Project did not successfully persuade any state legislatures to repeal existing sodomy laws. However, it was able to establish and expand the reach of statewide LGBT organizations, bring together gay and lesbian individuals, educate the public about gay rights issues, and put a human face on the gay rights movement. These achievements, when combined with the work of litigators, historians, and other LGBT organizations, and with the passage of time, ultimately set the stage not only for the subsequent repeal of a majority of state sodomy laws, but also for the total invalidation of *Bowers* by the Supreme Court's decision in *Lawrence v. Texas*.[7]

DIVERSE LEADERSHIP, BROADER GAINS

One glaring deficiency of many of the large national LGBTQ equality organizations can be seen in their overwhelmingly white male leadership. "The leadership reflected who the donors were comfortable with," says Rashad Robinson, director of Color of Change, who formerly worked for GLAAD (the Gay and Lesbian Alliance Against Defamation), the LGBT media advocacy organization (for more on Color of Change see Chapter 3, "Transforming Visions"). "That has continued to play and have a real damaging effect in terms of the fact that none of the big national organizations has ever had a black leader.

"The racial piece is really challenging," he says. "As marriage equality gets passed in states, the question is, what is the fight for the LGBT rights space?" He notes that in Connecticut, "the statewide LGBT advocacy organization closed down after marriage equality was passed. They said their work was done. . . . But marriage equality passing in Connecticut—how does that change life for a black gay boy or girl growing up in Bridgeport?"

Andy Lane, executive director of the Johnson Family Foundation and a longtime LGBTQ funder, agrees. "There had been some efforts over time to try to diversify the movement, but it has proven to be very challenging . . . and slow. I will say from a funding perspective the vast majority of the largest institutional donors to this movement are gay white men, or are foundations controlled by gay white men or staffed by gay white men, myself included. . . . We have a disproportionate role in helping set policy and strategy.

"We are advancing aggressively on multiple fronts, one of which is around law and policy. So that's: Don't Ask, Don't Tell repeal [at the federal level], that's mar-

"The government has blood on its hands—one AIDS death every hour." It was a powerful moment that gave a sense of urgency to the nascent LGBTQ movement.

MARRIAGE EQUALITY:
A PRIMER

Evan Wolfson is a pioneer in the marriage equality movement and the founder and president of Freedom to Marry, which is dedicated to winning marriage equality nationwide. He asserts that "gay people have always fought for the freedom to marry."

Wolfson explains that by 1971, two years after Stonewall, "there were three major cases brought by couples in court systems in different states, all challenging the denial of the freedom to marry. This country just wasn't ready for it. The conversation had not been had. All those cases were denied.

"Then a second wave of marriage litigation began in the very late 1980s and early 1990s. This wave went on to launch an ongoing global movement that has made it possible for gay people to share in the freedom to marry in most of the United States and eighteen countries on five continents.

"Why did the first wave fail, and why did the second wave launch this extraordinary success and momentum? The answer is because of what happened between those two waves. That was AIDS. AIDS broke the silence about gay people's lives and really prompted non-gay people to think about gay people in a different way. It prompted gay people to embrace this language of inclusion, most preeminently marriage. That, in turn, accelerated our inclusion in society and the change in attitudes.

"AIDS changed our movement from a movement fighting just to be let alone—don't harass us, don't attack us, don't beat us up, don't blackmail us—into a movement not just to be let alone but being let in. Let us into the protections and safety net of marriage, of family. That really set the stage for the robust, rich marriage conversation that we've been pursuing. It prompted gay people to understand how vulnerable we are when our lovers are not considered our family, are not treated as who they are to us under the law."

There were also other drivers of the push for same-sex marriage. Historian George Chauncey argues that a "lesbian baby boom [in the 1980s], as much as AIDS, led growing numbers of lesbians and gay men to start thinking the unthinkable: that lesbians and gay men needed and deserved the rights and protections of marriage."[8]

Wolfson has written that while the fight for marriage equality may look linear and strategic, "much has been a response to history and other forces, and the undeniable reality that the work of social justice and inclusion is never done." There have been many challenges, defeats, and imperfections along the way, and Wolfson lists several lessons. "If you can't say what winning is, you're not going to be able to get there as effectively as you need to, because (1) you may not be going in the right direction, and (2) you won't be able to inspire and encourage others to come in and join you. [Winning the freedom to marry made space for] a transformative language that . . . would make everything we seek more attainable. . . . Our fight to win it would be an engine of change. . . . It needed to be multi-year, multi-state, and multi-partner." And, he writes, "the strategy needed to operate multi-methodologically," a phrase he took from Dr. Martin Luther King Jr. "We needed to combine litigation and legislation and direct action and public education and personal persuasion and storytelling and engagement. And we needed to roll those out in synergy."[9]

Wolfson says that opposition within the LGBTQ community to focusing on marriage falls into two camps. "One camp embraced the argument that we shouldn't be fighting for the freedom to marry because we should be pursuing a much more diverse, bigger, much more expansive idea of what family is altogether. Marriage and participation within marriage were just too limiting. We should be fighting to redefine the family. We should be fighting for everything, for everybody, instead of any one particular institutional embodiment of family structure.

"The other ideological camp of resistance was more anti-marriage. They had the idea that marriage is a patriarchal institution, a hierarchical institution, an excluding institution. It's one that's been oppressive to women and reflects privilege."

Scot Nakagawa, a former organizer at the National Gay and Lesbian Task Force who blogs at racefiles.com, elaborates on this important point: "The freedom-to-marry fight is a legacy of the ideological frame that drove the American revolution: a fight for independence that preserved slavery. . . . It's how we frame the notion of liberty and equality that keeps all within an idea of governance that is more about free markets than free people."

Wolfson adds that marriage "is the central social and legal institution of this and virtually every other society . . . That's precisely why most gay people, like most non-gay people, want to participate. It's precisely what's so wrong about excluding gay people from such a central and mainstream institution. . . . We're not fighting for mandatory marriage. We're fighting for the freedom to marry.

"Fundamentally this is about preventing the government from discriminating and denying gay people the same freedom of choice . . . to participate in such an important institution as anyone else."

Wolfson says that the LGBTQ struggle continues to evolve. "You always have to be vigilant. You always have to keep educating. You always have to keep fighting for the next piece and the next person, who may not have yet been fully brought into the gains you've won. I think that is one of the clear lessons of history. It's never really over."

 In June, 2015, Freedom to Marry and other organizing efforts contributed to the Supreme Court ruling that mandated marriage equality. Wolfson says, "I do believe that it's about getting people to take a stand and speak up and think anew, in Lincoln's words, and engage with others and move things. That's what we've been able to do and I believe that is the story of every movement. You have to get up and speak out and work and trust that you can get people to rise to fairness. Then you have to do the work of helping them get there."

riage in [many] states plus D.C. But we are also really in the midst of a cultural revolution in the way LGB people, principally, are portrayed in the media . . . That helps create an environment in which law and policy change are possible."

Lane adds, "I was very intentional in saying LGB because . . . the reality is that transgender persons have very different life experiences, very different paths, and face different obstacles. So the law and policy that we need to change related to gender identity is somewhat different than the law and policy that we need to change related to sexual orientation. We also understand that transgender representations in media and popular culture are way, way, way, way behind LGB representations."

Rea Carey and the National LGBTQ Task Force that she leads have clear views on changing the movement leadership and representations. "Leadership for me is tied to this question of vision . . . and a desire for wholeness. . . . We can't ask someone to be an undocumented immigrant one day, a lesbian the next, and a mom the third day. . . . Our vision is about . . . transforming society so that she can be all of those things every single day and that there would be a connectedness among social justice workers and among the organizations, and agendas, if you will, to make her life whole."

Carey is determined that the LGBTQ movement should expand its efforts beyond marriage equality. "We are not a single-issue movement," she says. "The challenge for us as a movement is to refocus people's attention on the baseline needs of our communities," she continues, noting that health care, racial and economic justice, and immigration reform are also critical. "I . . . see the connectedness between our work in prison justice, in immigration, public education, and activism on Occupy. The vision for me personally does start with this inner connectedness of our lives and the wholeness of who we should be able to be as humans.

"We and other progressive organizations in our brother and sister movements have had to work very hard to connect the dots both for our own constituencies, and also sometimes for the funders of our movements."

Carey says that working across different issues "is challenging to do in the United States with the econom-

ic structure that we have. But I think there has been a lot of hope over the last couple of years with some of the successes around the labor movement, the voices that Occupy put forth. . . . In this next era, the opportunity of it has to be around connecting across movements . . . where we can work cross-issue to address the systemic oppression and injustices that very specifically have to do with economic well-being."

She notes that of the eleven million undocumented immigrants in the United States, hundreds of thousands are lesbian, gay, bisexual, and/or transgender. When LGBTQ folks are locked in detention centers, the abuse they suffer is often worse than what other detained individuals encounter. Immigrants "need a real pathway to citizenship and the American dream now – not the nightmare of gridlock."

To underscore her message, Rea Carey has put her body on the line. In September 2013, Carey was arrested in Washington, D.C., with more than a hundred other women demanding immigration reform.

Carey says, "We are seeing a real palpable hunger in LGBTQ people's hearts not just to be out, but to bring their entire selves. . . . And there is a deep desire for more change, to look beyond marriage equality, with millions of us still facing formidable barriers in every aspect of our lives: at school, in housing, employment, in health care, in our faith congregations, in retirement, and in basic human rights."

This represents an evolution in the movement. There have been some in the LGBTQ community who have not always embraced cross-issue organizing. Carey recalls that in 2011 the National Gay and Lesbian Task Force sent out a press release lamenting the failure of the student immigrants' DREAM Act to pass in Congress. "Sadly, at that time we got emails and posts on Facebook from LGBT people saying, 'Why in the world are you working for those people?'—meaning immigrants."

Carey says the pushback represented "a lack of understanding that we too are immigrants as LGBT peo-

"We can't ask someone to be an undocumented immigrant one day, a lesbian the next, and a mom the third day."

FIGHT PATRIAR-CHY. Favianna Rodríguez, Oakland, California, 2010

Patriarchy and its structures of gender oppression are entrenched in our culture and society. They are based on a system of hierarchical and unequal power relations, where men control women's production, reproduction, and sexuality. Favianna Rodríguez developed this print to expose the many ways in which women, mostly women of color, are affected by the political decisions made by men, mostly white, in power. The National Women's Law Center's Analysis of 2013 Census Poverty Data insists that poverty is a women's issue. Nearly six in ten poor adults are women, and nearly six in ten poor children live in families headed by women. Poverty rates are especially high for single mothers, women of color, and elderly women living alone.

WOMEN PAY THE PRICE

OF THE 50 MILLION DISPLACED FROM THEIR HOMELANDS, 80% ARE WOMEN & CHILDREN
OF THE 1.3 BILLION OF PEOPLE LIVING ON LESS THAN $1 PER DAY, 70% ARE WOMEN

FOR THE DECISIONS MADE BY MEN

SEX TRAFFICKING IS ONE OF THE HIGHEST GROSSING INDUSTRIES WORLD WIDE
AMONG THE HUNGRIEST PEOPLE OF THE WORLD, 60% ARE WOMEN

FIGHT PATRIARCHY

ple, and our parents are immigrants as LGBT people. . . . We've had to . . . educate a broader set of people that immigration is an LGBT issue."

The Task Force is also working to change the face and the public image of the LGBTQ movement. The organization ensures that leadership training is available to those who are historically most excluded—"people of color, transgender people, women, and other groups of people who tend to be underrepresented in the movement"—and trains thousands of people every year to make sure "that there really is a diversity of people who are good in the skills that they need to be able to run organizations, run campaigns."

Carey asserts, "I am certainly not among those people that believe, 'Oh, people are born leaders and it's inevitable.' . . . Some of us happen to have access to more privilege or more influence or more platforms to express leadership, but I truly believe that everyone has the capacity to express leadership."

Carey says it's a strategy grounded in their holistic principles of sexual identity, racial justice, and economic justice.

WHAT DOES AN INTERNATIONAL TRADE AGREEMENT HAVE TO DO WITH LGBTQ LIBERATION?

The LGBTQ movement has succeeded in recent decades in turning losses into victories. This is being put to a new test in the South, as organizers tackle a range of progressive issues.

Paulina Helm-Hernández is a queer immigrant and executive director of Southerners on New Ground (SONG). She and her family moved from Mexico to the United States when she was twelve, after the North American Free Trade Agreement (NAFTA) was passed in 1994. (For more on the effects of NAFTA, see Chapter 4.)

What does an international trade agreement have to do with LGBTQ liberation? North American companies that were subsidized by the U.S. government began aggressively exporting to Mexico and were able to undersell Mexican-owned companies. As a result of NAFTA, her parents' business, like many other small businesses and farms, just collapsed. Her father came to the United States in search of work. Helm-Hernández

learned English quickly, and she began helping her mother, who had started an adult literacy group for Latinos.

Helm-Hernández's mother became associated with the Highlander Research and Education Center, the legendary school for organizers in Tennessee that Rosa Parks, Martin Luther King Jr., and generations of labor, civil rights, and environmental activists attended. At nineteen, Helm-Hernández got a job as a youth organizer and trainer at Highlander.

Not long after she began organizing, a number of southern states began passing voter referendums banning same-sex marriage. This was happening just as she herself was coming out as queer. For Helm-Hernández, coming out meant coming together with other people and issues. "By being around a lot of other gay, lesbian, and trans folks, [I saw] how a lot of them actually were not coming out of LGBT organizing or only just gay stuff, but they were coming out of [organizing around] school-to-prison pipeline [and] immigrant rights."

The involvement of LGBTQ activists in other issues has resulted in a "cross-section between what it means to do anti-oppression LGBT organizing and also connects to a lot of the historical struggles in the South and a lot of the historical freedom struggles here. . . . Our mission [at SONG] has been . . . helping to support other LGBT people to have a political home where they feel like a lot of the intersectional approaches and shared understanding help push our community to have some external wins, and to actually be able to name some things that in the South we think are possible."

At SONG, Helm-Hernández is "trying to bring this

The involvement of LGBTQ activists in other issues has resulted in a "cross-section between what it means to do anti-oppression LGBT organizing and also connects to a lot of the historical struggles in the South and a lot of the historical freedom struggles here."

intersection around immigrant rights work and southern LGBT organizing and thinking about how those two movements are connected, and how some of the re-emergence and rebirth and reimagination of what's happening around immigrant rights work in the South right now is also pretty entrenched and connected to a lot of the southern LGBT stuff that's been happening as well. There's a watershed moment around both movements because there's already so much shared leadership."

Helm-Hernández argues that LGBTQ "quality of life" issues should not be separate from "life or death" issues. She says there is a need for a deeper "connection of the LGBTQ movement to broader anticriminalization struggles . . . around race, the targeting of gender nonconforming folks, mass incarceration, and the detention and deportation crisis. I see these as key to the roots of sexual liberation. Stonewall itself was an anti-police riot."

Helm-Hernández and SONG are finding ways to make progress even when they lose. SONG was involved in organizing in North Carolina against Amendment 1, a 2012 ballot measure to enact a constitutional amendment banning same-sex marriage and civil unions. The anti-gay measure passed with 61 percent of the vote. Helm-Hernández and her colleagues knew that there was little chance of defeating Amendment 1. But they showed up and did the hard work, focusing on "building a progressive infrastructure" in North Carolina.

"We had an internal goal of having one million conversations throughout the state," she says. "Our work was measured not just by a ballot win, but by building political alignment and unity."

Helm-Hernández sees LGBTQ organizers as having an important impact in North Carolina. "Committing to actually have a million conversations with North Carolinians about the future of our state, and about the divisive tactics of the Right, and about the reality of how integrated LGBT communities in North Carolina actually are to immigrant communities, to other communities of color—it really just became a huge opportunity for us, and I would say a success in terms of helping not just amplify the grassroots organizing that makes moments like that possible, but to say it does matter.

"Part of our role has been to push back on this notion that the Right has inevitable control in the South and we're in a trajectory that can't be broken. [We] try to interrupt that narrative, to structurally help create powerful political spaces where people do get to test their own power, to get to see that there is momentum, to . . . learn from people that are doing things that are working well in small towns and rural communities."

SONG is testing that power by organizing to expand the rights of immigrants, workers, and LGBTQ people. One show of the strength of this emerging intersectional alliance came in organizing against HB87, an anti-immigrant law passed in Georgia in 2011 that was based on a similar law in Arizona. HB87 authorizes police to demand papers demonstrating citizenship or immigration status during traffic stops and criminalizes Georgians who interact with undocumented people.

Helm-Hernández explains, "We were able to organize the LGBTQ community in a pretty strong way to come out both in opposition of HB87, but also in support of the mass mobilizations in a way that at least in my experience has really transformed the way that we see what's possible here in Georgia."

Helm-Hernández believes that organizing can help people to change the sense of the possible. She challenges the assumption "that because we work in a hostile region, then it's just inherently hostile at every single turn—it's not. There are so many people that want to move and are willing to move and just need that extra push or need to see other people take brave moves before they're able to make some brave moves themselves." In doing this kind of organizing, "training is crucial . . . in order to take that level of risk together."

Helm-Hernández is critical of mainstream LGBTQ organizations that focus exclusively on marriage equality campaigns and fail to link with other progressive issues. "I'm gay married, not in a state that actually validates it, but I don't think my marriage is going to liberate anybody. I don't think my marriage is going to pull anybody

> *"[We] try to interrupt that narrative, to structurally help create powerful political spaces where people do get to test their own power."*

STOP C.R.A.C.K.

STOP STERILIZATION ABUSE

FREEDOM for all women!

WE DEMAND REPRODUCTIVE FREEDOM for all women!

CRACK (Also known as project prevention or positive prevention) is a national organization that funds women who have a substance abuse problem to be sterilized. Instead of providing treatment services to the women, they encourage them to cash in their reproductive rights for $200. They blame women of color for social problems rather than government and corporate policies that have led to increased poverty in communities of color. Substance abuse is the result of the devastation in communities of color caused by these destructive policies. Reproductive Freedom includes: Free and low cost drug treatment for pregnant and parenting women that offer neo-natal care, pre-natal care, and childcare. Freedom to seek health care services without the fear of being reported to the police, welfare officials, child protections services (CPS), or immigration law enforcement. Harm reductions strategies that reduce the rise of babies being born drug exposed. Resources to address the root causes (rape, poverty, trauma, oppression) for which pregnant women use drugs. The truth about the risks of choosing long term birth control methods like Norplant and Depo-prevera. Supportive community environments where women can make healthy non-coercive reproductive choices.

Info on Poster adopted from material created by the Racism Reproductive Rights Task Force. The Racism and Reproductive Rights Task Force Includes Incite! Women of Color against Violence; Communities Against Rape and Abuse (CARA); Committee on Women, Population, and Environment (CWPE); the Third Eave Foundation; and Asian and Pacific Islanders for Reproductive Health.
For more information, contact incite_national@yahoo.com, or see www.incite-national.org
Poster by Cristy C. Road. For more Art visit http://www.croadcore.org

■ **STOP C.R.A.C.K. Cristy C. Road, Brooklyn, New York, 2011**
This poster features art by Cristy C. Road and was produced by INCITE! Reproductive Justice Task Force. INCITE! is fighting against what is ironically named C.R.A.C.K. (Children Requiring a Caring Kommunity), a national organization that encourages the sterilization of women who suffer from substance abuse. INCITE! Women of Color Against Violence is a national organization of radical feminists of color who are advancing a movement to end violence against women of color and their communities through direct action, critical dialogue, and grassroots organizing.

■ I AM UNDOCUQUEER.
Julio Salgado, Oakland, California, 2012
The marginalization of undocumented LGBTQ people is manifested through social discrimination and systemic disparities caused by anti-immigrant policies. The series portrays many of the activists working with these issues. Each portrait is set up against a solid, bright backdrop to highlight a personal quote that reflects the interlocking identities that constitute LGBTQ undocumented immigrants, or "undocuqueers." This community has played a prominent role in the immigration rights movement. Julio Salgado designed the art project to promote alliance building, in conjunction with the Undocumented Queer Youth Collective and the Queer Undocumented Immigrant Project.

out of poverty. I don't think my marriage is going to stop anybody from getting killed on the streets."

Power lies in linking issues, she says. "If we're going to be out here trying to fight this [anti–equal marriage] amendment, let's actually also help amplify our community's ability to tell their stories and talk about what else is going on in our community . . . that's bigger than same-sex marriage." (We interviewed Helm-Hernandez before the June 2015 Supreme Court ruling that mandated marriage equality in all states.)

Helm-Hernández works in North Carolina with white, Latino, and African American communities. The black-brown divide troubles her. "Poor people [are] being pitted against each other," she observes. "As new immigrant people, we were very much being asked to assimilate." Prejudice quickly surfaced, and she recalls people in her community saying, "'At least we're not black, or at least we're light-skinned.' That just became a huge turning point in terms of how I understood the world and the South and what it meant to want to change things both around racial justice, but also around economic justice. A lot of other young people my age were also being politicized through hip-hop, and really understanding the connection between what new immigrants were experiencing and what poor white people have been experiencing in the past, and then what black folks had been experiencing in this country."

For Helm-Hernández, capitalism is personal. "The kind of people that capitalism has always considered disposable, cheap labor are hardworking migrant folks. You don't have to pay for their health care. You don't have to do anything. All you have to do is use them until they're broken and then you can throw them away. Those are my parents and that's my family and that's me."

Like Rea Carey, she asserts that the movement needs to focus on the economy's systemic problems. She likens the billionaires of today, who drive the media and political campaigns, to darker ages. "Capitalism is a child of slavery. It's a child of colonialism. And it's a child of feudalism. This idea that some feudal lords can have whatever they want at the expense of the rest of us . . . I do think we have to dismantle capitalism if we really want to see true economic justice in this country and in this continent and probably in the world."

Winning LGBTQ and immigrant rights and racial and economic justice in the South is a consuming passion for Helm-Hernández. She recognizes the historical work that organizers have done to get the movement to where it is today and how the ongoing work has to be constantly regenerated and reinvented. "To organize is a huge spiritual calling," she says. "It's about fulfilling your destiny. It's about being accountable to your ancestors for their suffering, for their sacrifice.

"How do we as organizers take that really seriously? . . . When people are taking risks, they know that we have their backs. And they know that there's an entire movement behind them to actually help further those wins."

> "The kind of people that capitalism has always considered disposable, cheap labor are hardworking migrant folks. You don't have to pay for their health care. You don't have to do anything. All you have to do is use them until they're broken and then you can throw them away."

■ **GENDER SUBVERSION. CrimethInc. Ex-Workers' Collective (CWC), Salem, Oregon, year unknown**
Part poster, part zine, part coloring book, the Gender Subversion Kit is an educational tool for undermining patriarchal institutions. Inside pages feature illustrations for both children and adults that experiment with stepping outside the constraints of gender normativity. The art is inspired by and adapted from the *Boys Will Be Girls Will Be Boys* coloring book by Jacinta Bunnell and Irit Reinheimer, which deconstructs traditional gender roles in a funny, provocative way. CrimethInc is "a decentralized anarchist collective composed of many cells which act independently in pursuit of a freer and more joyous world."

For every girl who is tired of acting weak when she is strong, there is a boy tired of appearing strong when he feels vulnerable.

For every boy who is burdened with the constant expectation of knowing everything, there is a girl tired of people not trusting her intelligence.

For every girl who is tired of being called over-sensitive, there is a boy who fears to be gentle, to weep.

For every boy for whom competition is the only way to prove his masculinity, there is a girl who is called unfeminine when she competes.

For every girl who throws out her e-z-bake oven, there is a boy who wishes to find one.

For every boy struggling not to let advertising dictate his desires, there is a girl facing the ad industry's attacks on her self-esteem.

For every girl who takes a step toward her liberation, there is a boy who finds the way to freedom a little easier.

Adapted from a poem by Nancy R. Smith. Copies of this poster are available, as well as a smaller version with a genderrific coloring book on the back side which can be had in bulk quantities, from CrimethInc. Genders Anonymous / PO Box 13998 / Salem OR 97309 or go to www.crimethinc.com.

"WE STAND BEFORE THIS MIRROR WHOLE"

The LGBTQ movement continues to reinvent it-self and gather new energy, as all successful move-ments must do. Today many activists question the rigid images and identities that our culture pre-scribes. They are offering new ones.

When we interviewed Che Gossett, a transgen-der activist of color, for the prison chapter, Gossett asked to be referred to as "they/them"—rejecting the binary language of man and woman and in-stead embracing an identity not based on gender. In this and other ways, Gossett is part of a move-ment that is blazing a path and creating space for transgender people and any of us who may not want to be forced into a biologically defined cate-gory. Language frames thinking. Changing how we speak and write enables us to imagine the future in new ways.

Urvashi Vaid, a professor at Columbia Law School who has held leadership positions at the National Gay and Lesbian Task Force and the Arcus Foundation, emphasizes that the LGBTQ movement has already spawned a post-marriage generation that views sexual preference and gender identity on an evolving spectrum. "What I think is really dynam-ic and amazing about the time we live in right now and the idea of twenty-first-century movements is that all these struggles . . . have produced a younger generation that does not . . . think about identity in the same way. . . . They're very fluid in their iden-tity construct. The idea of 'queer' speaks to them more for that reason, because a straight person can be queer. It's a stance towards the mainstream. It's a relationship to hetero normal activity that is articulated through the use of the word *queer*. It's not just a sexual or gender identity, and I find that encouraging.

"I also feel that the kind of rejection of main-stream politics that happens periodically among progressive, younger activists usually cycles into an engagement," Vaid continues. "I think we are engaged in a power struggle against right-wing forces. And the objective of every progressive per-son, whether they're queer or straight, has to be the defeat of the right-wing cultural war."

Vaid sees hope in a more unified fight against the right-wing attacks on workers and affirmative action, and against the patriarchal teachings of con-servative churches. She reflects on how the move-ments of the 1970s left out so many allies and made the mistake of not joining economic issues with is-sues of racism and gender politics. "Those who were so concerned about economic rights, the tradition-al Left, failed abysmally because [they] rejected women's liberation. [They] ran away from gay and lesbian liberation. Identity organizes and moves people. Identity means something to people."

Vaid sees hope for a more united progressive movement that embraces shared values as well as identity and LGBTQ issues. "You can see it within the character of the immigrant rights movement: [it's] young, it's pro-gay, has tons of women leaders, [and] it's not a bunch of lawyers sitting in Washing-ton." She says that the same character is true in the reproductive justice movement and the prison ab-olition movement.

Like others in the visionary LGBTQ liberation movement, Vaid sees the importance of the con-nectedness among social justice agendas that go beyond equality to reclaim the wholeness of a broader movement.

Michael Bronski, professor of practice in Media and Activism in Studies of Women, Gender and Sex-uality at Harvard University, says, "Liberation and equality are really quite different things.

"The Gay Liberation Front back in 1969 . . . comes out of the anti-war movement, the sexual liberation movement, feminism, and comes out of, to some degree, the more radical race-based movements," explains Bronski. "Gay liberation really has very little to do, sexually and also politically, with what we now think of as the LGBT movement, particularly if it's around marriage equality or anti-discrimination laws, or any number of other legislative or judicial approaches."

Bronski says gay liberation activists would have rejected marriage equality. They "would be shocked that anybody would actually want a campaign that would have the state involved in putting the okay upon your own personal life decisions and your sex life. The gay liberation movement agenda would . . . not be fighting for equal rights, but fighting for what I would call social justice. Fighting for a wider range of things than simply making LGBTQ people equal in the eyes of the law as it now stands. So much of an equality movement is simply about equality under the law as it now stands, not to mention that the law as it now stands may not be a very good one."

Scot Nakagawa thinks that the LGBTQ struggle suggests possibilities for broader movement successes. "Our future needs to be global. We need to think beyond our borders and we need to question the validity of our borders and we need to think about how the economy has transformed the world and how best to respond to it." He is concerned that LGBTQ gains in the United States are in stark contrast to the erosion of rights internationally. "[As conservatives] see the sun setting on the issue of same sex marriage for their side in the United States, they are moving their fight globally, to places like Russia and Uganda and Brazil, and are hoping to build a base there that they can use to turn around and attack us from."

For Nakagawa, the future of the LGBTQ struggle lies in tending to some unfinished business. He says that our "identities were either imposed upon us for the purpose of exploitation, or chosen by us

in order to define us as something other than simply exploitable categories. We have been busting out of the oppressive boxes that were created for us ever since they were first created, even without conscious effort. After all, we never fit in them to begin with."

Nakagawa says LGBTQ people benefit from—and can help expand—the embrace of pluralism in U.S. culture:

One of the reasons that LGBT people have been as successful as we have is that we are able to actually live with difference in a way that many people throughout the world cannot. I think that's not to be underestimated as a really important value in this country and one that we should be building upon.

Colonialism and capitalism, industry and empire put a shattered mirror before us in which we saw and internalized a picture of ourselves as mere fragments of what it means to be whole in our humanity; an image in which our connections were but jagged edges best kept separate. But that's just an illusion. We stand before this mirror whole. To see that, we need to be compelled to look away, and that will require us to be prophets, not just critics.

The transformative organizers in the LGBTQ movement and throughout the other movements in this book create unity across issues of racial, economic, and gender justice. They are showing that when we fight together as a single movement, we win. Together, they are linking issues and reclaiming our wholeness.

JULIO
SALGADO

UNDOCUMENTED AND UNAFRAID, JU-
LIO SALGADO IS A QUEER "ARTIVIST" AND
CO-FOUNDER OF DREAMERS ADRIFT.
JULIO'S UNDOCU-LOVE AND UNDO-
CU-QUEER ARTWORK IS A STAPLE FOR
DREAMERS NATIONALLY. HIS MOST RE-
CENT COLLABORATION WITH WRITER
TINA VÁSQUEZ IS THE COMIC STRIP *LIBER-
TY FOR ALL*, PUBLISHED WEEKLY ONLINE
ON *CULTURESTRIKE*.

Photo by Jesús Iñiguez

I work with a lot of organizations on posters, both independently and as part of an organization called *CultureStrike*, directed by Favianna Rodriguez. I'm also part of a media group called Dreamers Adrift that does a lot of video work and uses humor, art, music, and everything to do commentary on what's going on in immigration.

For the month of June 2014, Dreamers Adrift released a weekly video series titled *Secrets and Borders: Our Stories Are All We Have*. We collaborated with undocumented and queer writers. For me personally, just speaking out on anything can be a little hard to do. So I have to create something. The way I speak up is through art.

Right now, I'm working on a weekly comic strip called *Liberty for All* that is published on the *CultureStrike* website about an undocumented queer writer who graduates from college and is trying to figure out her life. I brought my friend Tina Vásquez in because I really love her writing. She has helped me develop a lot of the characters, a lot of the writing of the actual comic strip. We've taken *Liberty* to another level. We really wanted to do this because a lot of times when the mainstream media talks about queer issues, they only talk about either gay marriage or gays in the military. I feel that as queer people of color, we also care about poverty and a lot of us get deported, and so art allows us to tell different stories that may not be out there or not being told or heard by "mainstream" or gay media.

The beauty about *Liberty for All* is that we also get to collaborate with folks from other communities. There's a black female character whose story we cannot write since that's not our experience. Tina invited her friend Erica Huffnagle to develop and write the character's story lines. With *Liberty,* we want to refrain from doing the thing we criticize: to speak for others.

How do you see the role of art and cultural works and their transformative power in the movements of the twenty-first century?

One of the reasons I started doing art in the first place was because I felt, in 2010 when there were a lot of sit-ins and all the things that undocumented students were doing, that the media covering it were saying, "Illegal immigrants are trying to get rights." Or, "They're trying to get themselves arrested. How dare they?" As somebody who creates culture and art and who has studied journalism, I felt this story needs to be told from our perspective.

For me, the role of art is about how can I be used both as a tool and a collaborator to help tell other people's stories in a really creative way. Through our personal stories, we're going to call attention to whatever is going on. Aside from the important work of organizers, I feel that that's where art becomes a useful tool to change culture.

As immigrants, we are complex human beings. It's important to put those stories out there because when we do that, we are allowing ourselves to be vulnerable and show our complexity. But it is also that we can change the way that we are seen. Because a lot of people get their ideas of who undocumented people are, who queer people are, through the media.

I like to create art that gives a full picture of what's going on. Sometimes it's easy to do, sometimes it's not. We are really lucky to be able to use creativity because not everyone can. I know I can't be an amazing organizer but I can do this. I am a creative person. I get messages from folks who are dealing with these issues and they tell me, "Yo, thank you so much for making me think about this" or "for putting my experiences out there, that I can now use and share with somebody else and be able to tell a story a different way."

I CREATE BECAUSE I EXIST!

Art by Julio Salgado in collaboration with Yosimar Reyes, Oakland, California, 2012

2

GROUNDED IN COMMUNITY: THE FIGHT FOR THE SOUL OF PUBLIC EDUCATION

■ **CHICAGO TEACHERS UNION STRIKE.**
Chicago, 2012 (Photo by Jeff Haynes/Reuters)
The 2012 strike by the Chicago Teachers Union (CTU) focused on issues at the heart of debates over educational policies: school closings, excessive testing, increased class size, protection of benefits, teacher professional development, job security, and increased evaluation. In the photograph, Chicago teachers hold placards as they walk the picket line outside the headquarters of Chicago Public Schools. In a district of 675 schools and more than 400,000 students, the CTU strike has shown that broad attacks on public schooling by corporate-inspired privatization reformers will confront the rising power of workers.

■ **MAESTRA COMBATIVA (Combative Teacher). Papel Machete, San Juan, Puerto Rico, 2008 (Photo by Isamar Abreu)**
The Combative Teacher was originally created by the street theater collective Papel Machete to support Puerto Rico's teachers during their strike in 2008. The puppet joins teachers at schools, marches, and other activities of the Puerto Rico Teachers Federation (FMPR). The Combative Teacher celebrates the struggle of thousands of teachers, mostly women, who have been the face of this and many other resistance movements. This photo was taken at a teachers' demonstration on October 17, 2011, when Arne Duncan made the first official visit by a U.S. secretary of education to Puerto Rico in eighteen years. FMPR protested plans to privatize education by installing charter schools on the island.

When Karen Lewis became president of the Chicago Teachers Union in 2010, the city's public schools faced an unprecedented crisis. Neighborhood public schools were starved of resources and dozens were being closed; students were regularly being shuffled to new schools. Privately run charter schools were proliferating and making money off widespread student dislocation. Teachers were demoralized. Student performance lagged.

Chicago is but one example—or victim—of a nationwide corporate takeover of public schools that masquerades as "reform." High-stakes tests, charter schools, and school closures are hallmarks of the conquest, which has been championed by corporate kingpins such as Bill Gates of Microsoft and the Walton family, founders of Walmart.

For all the upheaval and displacement of students, there has been no improvement in the quality of education with charters and privately run schools. In Chicago, for example, according to Chicago scholar-activists Pauline Lipman and Rico Gutstein, "only 18 percent of the replacement schools were rated high performing, and nearly 40 percent are at Chicago public schools' lowest rating."[1] As a 2014 Nation magazine editorial on charter schools summed up: "Charter school advocates and others who claim the mantle of education reform have now seen their ideas put into practice in a number of areas—from high-stakes testing to digital learning to the takeover of struggling public schools. . . . The results are in. How are they doing? Suffice it to say, if this were a high-stakes test, they'd fall."

A national grassroots movement has risen up to challenge corporate school reform. From Los Angeles to Philadelphia, teachers, unions, parents, and students are working together to fight high-stakes testing and to reclaim their schools and demand that schools be responsive to local concerns.

This is the story of how Chicago teachers, their union, parents, students, and their besieged communities have fought side by side to defend not just teachers' jobs but also public education itself. Reflecting an important dimension of transformative organizing, these activists are grounded deeply in their community. They have transformed their consciousness beyond the individual heroism of the dominant U.S. culture. They show how successful transformation comes communally from the ground up.

It was May 2013 and Chicago mayor Rahm Emanuel had just announced plans to close fifty Chicago public schools, the largest number ever in a single school district. Almost all the schools closed were in African American and Latino neighborhoods, and people of color bore the brunt of the impact: 87 percent of students affected by school closings since 2001 were African American.[2]

The mayor expected some pushback. He just didn't anticipate who would be leading the charge against him.

"Rahm Emanuel thinks that we all are toys. He thinks he can just come into our schools and move all our kids all over gang lines and just say, 'Oh, we can build a building right here. Let's just take this school out. We don't care about these kids.'"

The high-pitched voice rang out in Chicago's Daley Square, ricocheting off the sparkling high rises of Chicago's financial center. The speaker was not a battle-hardened veteran of Chicago's labor wars. He was a new breed of activist: a pint-sized nine-year-old firebrand by the name of Asean Johnson. He was a third grader from Marcus Garvey Elementary School, which the mayor's hand-picked school board had declared should be closed.

Dressed in cherry red basketball shorts and a red T-shirt—the color of the Chicago Teachers Union, whose members surrounded him—the impassioned young African American orator sporting a buzz cut stood on a folding chair and leaned toward the mic.

■ SCHOOL TO JAIL TRACK. Youth Justice Coalition, Inglewood, California, 2009. Original artwork, *Prison vs. College* by Khalil Bendib

Mass incarceration and youth criminalization are primary forms of racial oppression and control in the United States. Instead of allocating dollars for improving schools, policy makers spend public dollars on excessive security procedures, overuse of suspensions, expulsion for minor infractions, and police intervention and other "disciplinary" policies that push youth into juvenile corrections and adult prisons. These zero-tolerance policies disproportionately target youth of color and feed the school-to-prison pipeline. The Youth Justice Coalition uses direct action organizing, political education, advocacy, transformative justice, and artivism to bring about change inside and outside the prison system.

His neck veins bulged as he whipped the crowd into a chanting, coordinated protest machine. He directed his comments at Mayor Emanuel.

"You should be *investing* in these schools, not *closing* them. You should be *supporting* these schools, not *closing* them. . . . This is racism right here."

"Uh-huh. That's right," the crowd responded, in an age-old pattern of call and response.

"We shall not be moved today!" Asean continued. "We are going to City Hall. . . . We are not toys!" His mother nodded approvingly by his side.

"We are not going, not without a fight!" he said, his soprano voice rising in intensity.

The crowd followed his lead. "Education is a right! That is why we have to fight! Education is a right! That is why we have to fight! Education is a right! That is why we have to fight!"

Within hours, videos of Asean Johnson's forceful challenge to the mayor went viral.[3] He appeared as a guest on CNN. He addressed the Chicago Board of Education. He later spoke at the fiftieth anniversary of the March on Washington.

"You are slashing our education. You're pulling me down. You're taking our educational opportunities away," Johnson told the board, tears streaming down his cheeks. "You need to go tell the mayor to just quit his job."

On May 22, 2013, hours before a final vote by the Board of Education, the head of the Chicago Public Schools announced that Marcus Garvey Elementary School would be spared.

Asean Johnson, and a movement, had stood up to America's relentless "education reform" machine.

THE PUSH TO PRIVATIZE

This protest against school closures was another round in a struggle over the soul of public education in the United States. The epicenter of this battle is Chicago, a city that has served as a laboratory for a model of school reform that touts charter schools as a cure for what ails many local public schools. Charter schools receive public funding but they are independently run, and instead of answering to local school boards, many are operated by for-profit private companies or private boards. When they were first introduced in the early 1990s, charters were touted as incubators to test new local ideas with an eye toward improving public education. But they have quickly morphed into lucrative markets for a corporate takeover of public education. As of 2013, there were about six thousand charter schools in the United States serving 2.3 million students—an 80 percent increase in the number of students served since 2009.[4]

As of 2014, Mayor Rahm Emanuel had closed, converted, or phased out more than 150 public schools, almost all of them in low-income neighborhoods of color. In their place, he had sanctioned the opening of more than a hundred charter schools.

Charter schools have a dubious record: compared to public schools, they do not have better educational results on average, despite the fact that they suspend and expel a much higher percentage of students and have fewer special education and English-language learners.[5] Charter schools typically emphasize high-stakes tests, and many push out low-performing students, as well as high-needs students and those with disabilities.[6] Charter school teachers generally cannot join a teachers' union. As public schools are converted to charters, schools have gone from being public trusts to profit centers for private corporations, with little accountability and often evidence of mismanagement.[7]

Community organizations in Chicago have a long and strong history but had been waging an uphill fight to stop the wave of public school closures. Despite community opposition, one school after another in the poorest neighborhoods were being targeted for closure. The community groups could rally besieged parents and students, but they lacked a broad coalition aligned with teachers that had the clout to force a powerful mayor to listen and negotiate—and, they hoped, collaborate—instead of dictate. As neighborhood groups struggled, public education was choked.

> "You should be investing in these schools, not closing them. You should be supporting these schools, not closing them. . . . This is racism right here."

Enter a team of about twenty classroom teachers who had been working in the communities most affected by the cuts. Among them was Karen Lewis, who went on to be elected president of the thirty-thousand-member Chicago Teachers Union (CTU) in 2010. In a break with her union predecessors, Lewis and the CTU have not limited themselves to just defending teachers' jobs. The new CTU leadership has mobilized the union and joined forces with parents and other community activists in a reinvigorated coalition of community and educator organizations. The result was a grassroots, community-driven movement to resist corporate-driven reforms and revitalize neighborhood schools that would serve the needs of all of Chicago's families.

When the mayor pushed back, the CTU led Chicago's first teachers' strike in a quarter-century. Parents and community leaders stood arm in arm with Chicago's teachers and fought the mayor and his corporate school reformers.

Chicago's battle for the future of public education had become a fair fight.

A MOVEMENT STARTS WITHIN

Karen Lewis has been blazing trails since her student days. She grew up in Chicago and attended Dartmouth College in New Hampshire, where she was the only African American woman to graduate in the class of 1974. She vividly remembers when she was a child going to piano lessons by way of the unemployment office, where she patiently stood in line with her father who had been laid off from a manufacturing job. By the time she was ten, her parents had both become teachers. Lewis attended medical school, but in the late 1980s, at age thirty-seven, she changed course and became a high school chemistry teacher.

CORE was initially composed of teachers who advocated reforming the CTU and making it more responsive to classroom educators and community, rather than having the union decisions be driven from the top down, by union bosses.

Teaching high school "gave me a lot of experience in thinking about things from a variety of different ways," says Lewis. Her first school taught a program of reading great books and conducting Socratic dialogue, in which small groups of students discuss and debate questions and ideas. "The kids flourished," she says, and the teachers were very engaged with the students and one another. It was a style of collaborative teaching and leading that she would continue to use.

Lewis served as a delegate in the CTU in the 1990s, but her involvement in union affairs was limited. That changed in 2009, when she joined what began as a study group that soon morphed into the Caucus of Rank and File Educators (CORE). CORE was initially composed of teachers who advocated reforming the CTU and making it more responsive to classroom (aka rank-and-file) educators and community, rather than having the union decisions be driven from the top down by union bosses. CORE advanced the idea of linking teachers' demands to a broader movement and creating "union members in the CTU who saw the struggle as one for what CTU president Karen Lewis calls 'the soul of public education.'"[8]

In 2010, the CORE caucus—just two years old—challenged the union's leadership, which had ruled for some forty years. CORE won the CTU election and took the union in a new direction. The days of focusing on narrow business issues were over. CTU joined forces with community groups, other unions, students, and parents in an effort to empower both communities and educators to have a voice in improving education. A local educational justice movement was blossoming.

In 2012, the CTU linked contract demands to the growing chorus of outrage over school closings and underresourced schools. It was a decision aimed at aligning the union with larger issues of social and racial justice and allying with the organizations most affected by school closings, especially in communities of color. The reenergized CTU posed a direct challenge to Mayor Rahm Emanuel and the billionaire school reformers who were directing the drastic makeover of Chicago's schools.

Karen Lewis does not suffer fools, no matter how wealthy or powerful they may be. She tells us, "These business guys have this notion that teachers should just be compliant and . . . do what they're told and then that will be the end of the problems."

A NEOLIBERAL MODEL OF EDUCATION

The Chicago model of education reform, involving replacing public schools with charters and penalizing schools based on high-stakes testing, has become a national blueprint for transforming America's schools.

The seeds of the Chicago model were planted in 1995, when Mayor Richard Daley successfully persuaded the Illinois legislature to place the city's public schools under mayoral control. The mayor appointed the school board, and he replaced the post of superintendent with that of a CEO who had free rein to impose an agenda. Daley appointed his budget manager and close ally, Paul Vallas, the first CEO. Vallas has been described in *Education Next* as a "charismatic bully [who] . . . does what he wants—sometimes rashly—and bristles at any whiff of opposition."[9] Vallas set about converting a number of struggling inner-city schools into military academies, and began a process of high-stakes testing, copying what was being done in Texas under Governor George W. Bush. This became the basis for what became President Bush's signature education policy, known as No Child Left Behind. These testing policies were also championed by Presidents Bill Clinton and Barack Obama.

Pauline Lipman, a leader of the Chicago chapter of Teachers for Social Justice and professor of educational policy studies at the University of Illinois–Chicago, has been deeply active in the Chicago community for years. Lipman explains, "Chicago and Texas became the two models for No Child Left Behind (NCLB)—the whole top-down accountability, punishing schools, teachers, principals, and students for so-called failures and holding everyone to these very simplistic measures of achievement."

In 2005, assistant secretary of education Diane Ravitch championed NCLB. Four years later, she renounced the law. Ravitch wrote: "The basic strategy [of NCLB] is measuring and punishing. And it turns out as a result of putting so much emphasis on the test scores, there's a lot of cheating going on, there's a lot of gaming the system. Instead of raising standards it's actually lowered standards because many states have 'dumbed down' their tests or changed the scoring of their tests to say that more kids are passing than actually are." She lamented, "I came to realize that the sanctions embedded in NCLB were, in fact, not only ineffective but certain to contribute to the privatization of large chunks of public education."

The Chicago model was part of the wave of education reforms that swept the country in the 2000s under President George W. Bush. A 2004 program under Mayor Richard Daley called Renaissance 2010 provided a playbook for solidifying and proliferating the Chicago model. Renaissance 2010 was based on recommendations from the Commercial Club of Chicago, a powerful organization of influential CEOs and business leaders of some of Chicago's biggest and oldest corporations. This corporate-driven reform was a thinly veiled plan to reap a private windfall from a treasured public asset.

"This was a clearly articulated market model, neoliberal model for education in Chicago," says Lipman.

Neoliberalism is an economic model whose advocates support privatizing public institutions, deregulating business, promoting free trade, eliminating labor unions, cutting social services, and generally freeing private enterprises from any public oversight. Lipman explains:

Neoliberalism came as . . . the response of big business to the successful labor, women's and civil rights movements of the 1920s–1960s that had advanced working-class rights. The goal of neoliberal capitalism is to remove all holds and regulations restricting banks, busi-

"*Chicago and Texas became the two models for No Child Left Behind—the whole top-down accountability, punishing schools, teachers, principals, and students for so-called failures and holding everyone to these very simplistic measures of achievement.*"

ness, and big media so that wealthy investors can invest wherever they want. These investors and large corporations can use whatever business practices they wish and can find new ways to make money by turning over public assets to businesses in order to create a profitable new market.

In education, charter schools are exactly that privatization—public assets turned over to private operators.

What's the problem with this? Private companies are designed to meet the needs of their owners and investors. But public services, like public schools, are designed to serve a common good, not a private one. Privatization, in the case of charters, means that public dollars intended to meet student instructional needs are diverted to make profits for private investors, often with little oversight. In the Chicago model, this has led to many problems including corruption: in 2014, the biggest charter network in the state, United Neighborhood Organization, and the largest charter network in the world, Concept Charter, were investigated for fraudulent activity.

CLOSING SCHOOLS, OPENING PROBLEMS

The United States now focuses on the wrong drivers, using test results to reward or punish individual teachers or schools, technology innovations, and charter schools. We have become the world leader in prisons now, instead of schools.

Public school teacher, scholar, and activist Rico Gutstein and scholar and activist Pauline Lipman described the impact of the Chicago Model and the school closures:

In many cases schools are anchors in neighborhoods stressed by poverty, racism, dismantling of public housing, foreclosures, and social exclusion. Schools are often . . . "the heart of the community." School closings also contribute

to the disproportionate loss of experienced black teachers who know the community and families well. Overall, the percentage of black teachers in CPS [Chicago Public Schools] declined from 40 percent in 2002 to 27 percent in 2012.

School closings and privatization are also part of . . . development policies centered on real estate . . . corporate subsidies, and privatization that has restructured the city for capital accumulation and has pushed out low-income communities of color. In neighborhoods slated for gentrification, closing schools contributes to pushing out the people who live there. The schools are then refurbished and rebranded for a middle-class clientele.[10]

Despite its lack of results, the privatization model of school reform was given an even higher profile in 2009 when Arne Duncan, then CEO of Chicago Public Schools, was named by President Obama to be U.S. secretary of education. It was a sign that neoliberal school reform had become all-American school reform.

Up until the 1970s, the United States was a world leader in graduating students. The opportunity and achievement gaps were steadily closing as schools were integrated and badly needed resources were targeted to programs like Head Start, Title I, and other successful systemic anti-poverty strategies. The United States was focusing on effective educational "drivers": steadily building capacity of the teaching profession, fostering "intrinsic motivation of teachers and students," and engaging "educators and students in continuous improvement of instruction and learning and inspiring collective team work."[11]

Today, with the corporate takeover of education, the United States now focuses on the wrong drivers, using test results to reward or punish individual teachers or schools, technology innovations, and charter schools. We have become the world leader in prisons now, instead of schools.

John H. Jackson, president of the Schott Foundation for Public Education, says the test mania in the United States is the wrong driver for real reform. He cap-

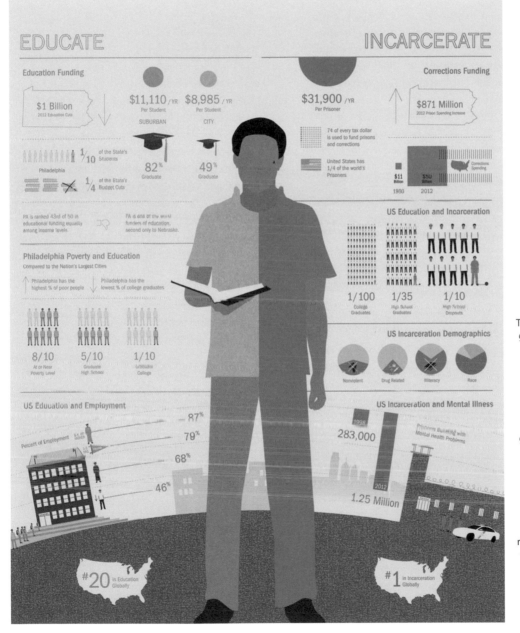

EDUCATE

Education Funding

$1 Billion
2012 Education Cuts

$11,110 /YR
Per Student
SUBURBAN

$8,985 /YR
Per Student
CITY

1/10 of the State's Students
Philadelphia

1/4 of the State's Budget Cuts

82% Graduate

49% Graduate

PA is ranked 43rd of 50 in educational funding equally among income levels.

PA is one of the worst funders of education, second only to Nebraska.

Philadelphia Poverty and Education

Compared to the Nation's Largest Cities

Philadelphia has the highest % of poor people

Philadelphia has the lowest % of college graduates

8/10
At or Near Poverty Level

5/10
Graduate High School

1/10
Graduate College

US Education and Employment

Percent of Employment

87%
79%
68%
46%

#20 in Education Globally

INCARCERATE

Corrections Funding

$31,900 /YR
Per Prisoner

$871 Million
2012 Prison Spending Increase

7¢ of every tax dollar is used to fund prisons and corrections

United States has 1/4 of the world's Prisoners

$11 Billion
1980

$50 Billion
2012

Corrections Spending

US Education and Incarceration

1/100
College Graduates

1/35
High School Graduates

1/10
High School Dropouts

US Incarceration Demographics

Nonviolent

Drug Related

Illiteracy

Race

US Incarceration and Mental Illness

Prisoners Benefit with Mental Health Problems

283,000
1998

1.25 Million
2012

#1 in Incarceration Globally

■ **EDUCATION VS. INCARCERATION. Jason Killinger for Maskar Design, Philadelphia, 2012** The federal, state, and local governments have chosen to expand expenditures for the military, police, and prisons at the cost of quality education, health care, child care, affordable housing, and job training and creation. This infographic compares the cost of education to the cost of incarceration. Studies confirm the benefits of investing in education over incarceration, and of educating the incarcerated. The United States is ranked twentieth in educational attainment globally, but first in incarceration rate. With only 5 percent of the world's population, the U.S. holds 25 percent of the world's prisoners.

tures the absurdity of the current system this way: "In Singapore, Ontario, Finland, and other high-performing countries, if a classroom is cold, they put in a heater. In the United States, they put in another thermometer!" Or they close the school and open a charter.

JOINING TOGETHER ACROSS THE GLOBE

Educational reforms that feature school closings, charter schools, and punishment for struggling schools have appeared across the globe. Wherever the model has traveled, there has been popular resistance, and visionary organizers link these popular struggles into an international whole.

In May 2014, the Chicago Teachers (CTU) Union hosted the eleventh Trinational Conference, bringing together educators from Mexico, Canada, and the United States, including Puerto Rico. Puerto Rico, a U.S. colony, is too often ignored by many U.S. social movements, but has had powerful, successful student and teacher strikes. Right-wing policies of privatization from the U.S. mainland are often field-tested in Puerto Rico. The CTU has a strong alliance with the Puerto Rico teachers union, which has a tradition of activism. The Trinational Coalition to Defend Public Education, which has held biennial conferences since 1993, links people who value public education and "its contributions to democratic society to defend it against privatization." Coalition organizers said they hoped for "coordinated resistance . . . to spread across the continent."

Maria Elena Lara Fontañez, president of the Puerto Rican Teachers Federation, spoke of teachers who had their teaching licenses—and thus their livelihoods—revoked for life by the government in retaliation for organizing against education reform.

> "We would look for the people who were being politicized by that process and try to get them to join this growing movement. These were rank-and-file teachers who were upset about the school closings and the lack of union engagement."

In Mexico, death threats, targeted killings of union leaders, and violent police repression are a chilling reality of the country's political history and its current climate. In 2014 alone, forty-three student activists in Mexico were murdered while en route to a demonstration; Mexican police were implicated in their deaths. Despite the threat of violence, Mexican teachers have continued to organize.

BUILDING A NEW MOVEMENT FROM THE OLD

For Chicago teachers troubled by school closures, high-stakes testing, and corporate takeovers, building a progressive alliance to take on the city's political machine was a methodical process. In the mid-2000s "the union didn't have people who were sympathetic to the fight," recalls Jessie Sharkey, a teacher and early member of the CORE caucus. (Sharkey was a CTU vice president when we interviewed him and is now president.) "We wound up building a healthy, deep relationship with people in black neighborhoods [and] poor neighborhoods who were doing work in their local school council."

Jackson Potter, another former high school teacher and CORE activist who is now a CTU official, told us, "We would look for the people who were being politicized by that process and try to get them to join this growing movement. These were rank-and-file teachers who were upset about the school closings and the lack of union engagement."

As a student at Chicago's Whitney Young High School in 1995, Potter led a walkout to push for equitable funding for schools in Illinois. He later became a teacher at Englewood High School and was the union delegate there when former Chicago Public Schools CEO Arne Duncan said the school had a "culture of failure" and started to phase it out in 2005. Potter and Al Ramirez formed CORE in May 2008 and shortly thereafter joined the Grassroots Education Movement, a coalition of community organizations that were working on defending and strengthening Chicago's public schools.

Because of their long-standing connection, teachers and local communities were natural political allies.

On the South Side of Chicago, the teachers had already been organizing with veteran community organizer Jitu Brown of the Kenwood Oakland Community Organization (KOCO). Brown is now national director of the Journey for Justice Alliance, with offices in KOCO's space, located next door to an abandoned storefront.

The South Side of Chicago has a prominent place in African American culture. "This was one of the two black metropolises of the twentieth century," Brown explains in the bustling KOCO offices, where community members come and go and groups of students spend their after-school hours. "There was Harlem, New York, and Bronzeville," a historically black neighborhood on the South Side. He ticks off a list of African American luminaries who hail from here, including Dr. Daniel Hale Williams, Louis Armstrong, Minnie Riperton, and Muddy Waters. He casually mentions another familiar local, an eloquent young Illinois state senator who once represented this district—Barack Obama.

The decline of the South Side can be seen in the fate of its schools. Jeanette Taylor, a parent and longtime school activist, describes a series of "redevelopment" plans for the area that proposed closing twenty of the twenty-two schools in the neighborhood.

As went the schools, so went the neighborhood.

"How do you kill a community?" says Taylor, her voice rising in indignation. "First you take away the housing. And then you take away the schools."

Taylor is a member of her local school council, akin to an advisory community school board, for Mollison Elementary School. In 2010, Mollison appeared on a list of schools to be closed by Chicago Public Schools. Taylor and her community organized to fight. They teamed up with KOCO, mobilized parents, and turned out almost four hundred students, parents, teachers, grandparents, and community members for a school closure meeting on a frigid winter day in 2010. Shortly after, the community won a victory: Mollison was removed from the closure list.

"It's like you have to go to war with your own school district to have a quality school in your neighborhood," says Brown.

The school closings have been enormously disruptive to students. At times, the dislocation has resulted in violence. Diamond McCoullough, a seven-teen-year-old student at Dyett High School on Chicago's South Side, says that following a wave of school closings in 2003, students from other neighborhoods were abruptly shifted into her high school. With gangs competing for territory, the reshuffling of students "increased the violence. Eventually, someone got killed in [Dyett High] school. In 2008, Dyett had, like, an uprising."

In response, students created a nationally acclaimed restorative justice program in which peers and teachers, victims and offenders—not police—determined appropriate ways to repair the harm they had done, based on the needs of the victims, offenders, and school community. "People were coming from all over the nation to get trained by Dyett students," Diamond says. "We had the largest decrease in student arrests, despite CPS [Chicago Public Schools] not investing in our school. Eventually, the restorative justice program got cut, because it was from a private funder, and CPS didn't want to fund it."

Today, Dyett High School is once again in limbo. It has no school library and no art, gym, or music classes. In a particularly cruel twist, the school competed for and won a 2011 contest sponsored by ESPN to have its gym refurbished. What Dyett's students needed, the school's coach told ESPN, was a chance. ESPN aired a TV special in October 2011 chronicling the four-week makeover of Dyett's athletic facilities.

The euphoria was short-lived. In 2012, CPS announced it was "phasing out" Dyett High School. Shortly after, Dyett's students could no longer access the gleaming new gymnasium. "We don't use the gym," says Diamond, a junior. "It's just there. We don't have a gym teacher."

These glaring inequities spurred KOCO, the Grassroots Education Movement, and other community groups to march on Mayor Rahm Emanuel's house in 2012 to demand an end to school closures and to change the Chicago school board from being appointed by the mayor to being democratically elected. The

> *"How do you kill a community? … First you take away the housing. And then you take away the schools."*

■ DREAM ACT MURAL. Francisco "Enuf" García, Phoenix, Arizona, 2011 (Photo by Ms. Phoenix)

Inspired by the cover art for the March 19, 2009, issue of the *Phoenix New Times,* which ran the feature "Are Your Papers in Order?" by Michael Lacey, Phoenix muralist Francisco "Enuf" García painted the *DREAM Act* mural. A student holding a sign reading "Education Not Deportation" is juxtaposed with the face of Arizona sheriff Joe Arpaio and a Maricopa County deputy in a mask holding a gun. In the background is a deportation van next to the city of Phoenix. The artist's intent was to convey the intimidation and fear of deportation constantly experienced by undocumented immigrants under Arizona's racial profiling law, SB 1070. The mural shows the divided nature of the community, depicting the hopeful face of Cesar Chavez of the United Farm Workers and a group of people marching for immigration reform and the DREAM Act.

community groups reached out to the Chicago Teachers Union to join with them. This labor-community alliance was a turning point.

"We had to do the type of action that we felt would embarrass the mayor and would begin to unify people across community and labor," explains Brown. "Before that action, the CTU was not able to get hundreds of teachers in the street, because they had just come into power and the teachers were demoralized."

The march also highlighted gaping inequities between the city's schools. "When we did the march to the mayor's house, we marched from Lakeview High School to his house," Brown recounts. "To kind of expose the discrimination, we did a cross comparison between Dyett and Lakeview. Lakeview is about two blocks from the mayor's house with . . . [much higher] white enrollment. Lakeview had twelve Advanced Placement courses; Dyett had none. Lakeview has darkroom photography, studio art, advanced chorus, beginning chorus; Dyett students had to take art as an online class."

Brown says CTU leaders were initially reluctant to participate in the march. But when the teachers finally did come, they were transformed by their experience. "You had teachers and students and parents holding hands," recounts Brown. He told the teachers, "This sets the tone for the big fight that we need to have, because you're not going to talk with these beasts with one protest. This is what a movement is: a protracted engagement of people." Following the march, Brown says, CTU leaders told him "it was the best thing they ever did."

STRIKE

Mayor Emanuel joined the national chorus of leaders who blamed educational problems on the teachers' union, not on his campaign of community disinvestment. The mayor's attacks poisoned the waters with teachers.

"The mayor of the city was publicly disrespecting teachers," Karen Lewis recounts at CTU headquarters. "*The teachers got raises,*

"Education is dangerous. Because an educated mind is not a mind that you can easily lull into complacency."

kids got the shaft—that was a front-page headline. The level of hostility and animosity just kept growing and growing and growing to the point that . . . I don't even know if we could have *not* had a strike."

In the summer of 2012, the CTU announced it was going on strike. The teachers linked their demands over working conditions with conditions in the schools. Tens of thousands of community members joined the raucous protests.

President Karen Lewis and the CTU led the teachers into the streets. She offers this tutorial on how to make change. "The whole notion of change is based on a level of discomfort. . . . Pressure isn't from writing op-eds or from just having relationships with a couple of legislators. The pressure is on when two thousand and three thousand—and then five thousand and ten thousand—people show up at your offices and say, 'You're out of control.'

"Part of what we have to do is to empower people to take the next step. And the next step is always about organizing, mobilizing and being there, and truth-telling."

Lewis, a fixture at rallies of teachers and community members, argues that unions need to do more than protect their own economic interests. "We're trying to defend *public education*. You can't do that by just focusing on jobs, because publicly funded public education is about kids and their communities. If we don't draw those kinds of alliances, then we have no real power."

Lewis says that the process of change "is incremental, just like learning is incremental. . . . It takes time. It takes practice. . . . Very few people pick up a violin and are immediately virtuosos. It doesn't work like that. You have to put that time in."

Proof of this movement-building approach came during the teachers' strike. "Teachers' strikes are notoriously unpopular because they inconvenience the heck out of parents," says Lewis. "There has never been a teachers' strike in which the parents overwhelmingly approved of it. It's just unheard of." In a remarkable show of solidarity, two-thirds of parents of schoolchildren supported the strike in Chicago. Some parents joined teachers on picket lines across the city. "That was all foundation work. It was all about having relationships with people in the community so that they supported us."

For Lewis, the fight for quality education is the leading edge of a much larger struggle. Education is "the last bastion of a real democracy in this country," she argues. "Education is dangerous. Because an educated mind is not a mind that you can easily lull into complacency. In order for this system to work, [corporate bosses] need a lot of people who are going to be okay with hovering around the poverty line and being insecure. Because when you're insecure, [big business] figured out that that's a motivator for getting people to do work, especially mind-numbing work or work that's not particularly fulfilling. In order for [big business] to succeed, they need to be able to push education in the direction they want it to be in."

Lewis has a different view of education. "I am concerned that we have conflated education now with vocational training. There's this notion that schools should reflect whatever the global economy is demanding. I don't think that's what education is. I think that what education does is it prepares you to become a citizen of the world, and that means that you participate in your community and you make your community better.

"Our vision is to develop a system that has equity, [which is] what democracy is: that parents and students have a say in what their schools look like and how they are governed."

In 2014, Karen Lewis was on the verge of making a new direct challenge to the powerful institutions that controlled her city and were blocking democracy: she launched an exploratory campaign, running for mayor against incumbent Rahm Emanuel. But in October 2014, she was diagnosed with a brain tumor. She asked Jesus "Chuy" Garcia to run in her stead. He jumped in, and the community, including many education activists in this chapter and the teachers' union, backed him. Though heavily outspent by the developers and corporations who funded Emanuel, Garcia forced a dramatic runoff election that Emanuel eventually won in April 2015.

The CTU is credited by many union activists nationally with revitalizing the labor movement. "The Chicago Teachers Union and its leader, Karen Lewis, have modeled a new breed of union leadership by responding to privatization aggressively and reimagining public education collaboratively," reported *The Nation*.[12]

Lewis offers this lesson: "Organizing is hard work. It requires people to have one-on-one conversations. . . . It's about point-by-point-by-point planning, sticking to a plan, and if things don't work, coming back around and being able to adjust.

"What I would say to any young or experienced organizer is: take a deep breath before you jump in. Understand what your possible wins and losses are and what real wins look like. A lot of people think that you don't get a win until you get everything you want. Or you don't get a win until poverty is completely gone."

She shakes her head and smiles, recalling the many battles she's lost. She says it's important to savor each victory, no matter how small. "You have to stop and constantly pat yourself on the back for the good work that you have done."

COLLEGES AND UNIVERSITIES

The national and international public education movement is growing stronger every day. At the same time, organizing on college and university campuses throughout the country has escalated powerfully, particularly in response to the unprecedented levels of student debt and dramatic funding cuts to public universities, all part of the same neoliberal wave. In the United States, the 40 million people saddled with over $1 trillion in student debt are demanding change. Some have blocked highways, occupied administration offices protesting tuition hikes, and others have launched debt strikes. Strike Debt (debtstrike.org) is a debt-resistance movement and an offshoot of Occupy. Among its demands are for Congress to provide free public education—including college—for all. (For specifics on the immigrant college student movement see Chapter 4, "The Power of Stories.") In 2011, university students

> *"We're trying to defend public education. You can't do that by just focusing on jobs, because publicly funded public education is about kids and their communities."*

in Puerto Rico, like in other parts of the United States, protested a tuition surcharge. In Puerto Rico, they did so by taking over buildings and closing ten of eleven campuses of the University of Puerto Rico (UPR). The protests built on a 2010 strike that shut all UPR campuses for two months and succeeded in reinstating tuition waivers for athletes and honors students. Administrators attempted to preempt the 2011 strike by banning all student protests and having a police presence on campus for the first time in three decades.

UPR students challenged the prohibition on protests by staging massive marches around campus that grew as students streamed out of class. Police responded with almost daily violence and arrests. The public responded to the repression with outrage and widespread sympathy for the student movement.

The UPR strikes coupled student militancy with educational and artistic activities, featuring theater, puppets, and performance. Students disseminated their messages by creating their own media, including pirate radio stations, websites, and a student press center. Many participants of the 2010–11 protests cite the political learning process itself, within a broader long-term struggle against neoliberalism, as their main achievement.

"They fear us because we aren't afraid" (*Nos tienen miedo porque no tenemos miedo*) was a rallying cry of the protests. The UPR president resigned during the 2011 protests and police crackdown. In 2013, following continued student pressure, a new governor of Puerto Rico delivered on a campaign promise to repeal the tuition surcharge.

■TEACHER SOLIDARITY. Overpass Light Brigade, United States (nationwide), 2012 (Internet Campaign, Overpass Light Brigade FB Page)
On September 11, 2012, the Chicago Teachers Union went on strike after Mayor Rahm Emanuel failed to reach agreement with the teachers on a new contract. The fight for educational justice received widespread public support as a necessary action despite what Emanuel characterized as "a strike of choice." The protest shut down the nation's third-largest school district for more than a week. The Overpass Light Brigade, one of forty affiliates of the nationwide Light Brigade Network, took its creative efforts to the streets, expressing solidarity with teachers, students, and parents who were fighting the dismantling of the public school system. Its explicit political messages shed light on issues often ignored by the corporate media.

THE MISSING INGREDIENT: LOVE

When the Chicago Teachers Union struck back, it helped further a vision of a different future. The teachers, parents, students, and community were dreaming—and acting—big. The fight in Chicago was led from the beginning by African American and Latino parents, students, and community organizations, in alliance with educator groups.

Together they have forged a new Chicago model—of resistance. "Neoliberal hegemony rests in part on the conviction that there is no alternative to the market, and there is no other way to imagine society," Lipman and Gutstein have written. "What is emerging in Chicago is a reaffirmation of public education with values of fairness, justice, democracy, interdependency, and the common good."[13]

Lipman describes witnessing parents, students, and teachers in the streets during the 2012 Chicago teachers' strike holding homemade signs expressing their demands and dreams:

> We need more art, more music, more gym.
>
> We need air conditioning.
>
> Stop the testing.
>
> Schools are not businesses.
>
> Our children are not products.
>
> Parents have had enough. Students have had enough. Teachers have had enough.
>
> We're standing up. We're saying no. Enough.

Lipman says that the teachers' strike in Chicago "ignited people across the country. . . . It gave an example nationally of what a social movement teachers union could look like and it provided a national example that you could actually organize to fight these things. Just as importantly, it has really sparked the beginnings of very similar campaigns in a number of cities around the country."

Jackson Potter of the CTU itemizes some highlights of the current public education movement: "new militant teacher union leadership just elected in L.A. and Massachusetts, open bargaining with parents in St. Paul, takeovers of the Board of Education in New York City and Chicago, Pittsburgh rejecting charter expansion," to name a few.

Student unions have joined teachers' unions on the front lines. In 2014, the Philadelphia Student Union (PSU) led thousands of students in a walkout of classes to protest teacher firings, school closings, and the slashing of extracurricular programs. University of Pennsylvania researchers Jerusha Conner and Sonia Rosen chronicle that the PSU is pioneering a new style of youth activism:

> PSU members work hard to "flip the script" by altering how young people are portrayed in the media and viewed by the general public. . . . Framing youth as empowered agents of change fundamentally contradicts the discourse of neoliberal education reform. Neoliberal ideologies view these mostly low-income, mostly Black and Brown urban youth as undeserving beneficiaries of a wasteful system. . . . In this model, young people are positioned as both the cause of the problem and the objects of reform. They become spectators in a show that repeats itself with each new crisis.
>
> Youth organizing, on the other hand, disrupts this pattern of spectatorship. Instead of remaining the objects of reform efforts, PSU members, who view themselves as organizers and leaders, force their way onto the reform stage in order to play central roles in determining what changes are made in schools and across the district.[14]

Adourthus MacDowell, an activist with Chicago's KOCO and a school parent, expresses the alternative vision of grassroots activists. "We're not addressing the corporate agenda. We are addressing the neighborhood agenda," he insists. "We need a new urban educational agenda for the twenty-first century, and we're not talking about charter schools. . . . We will not rest until every neighborhood grade school and high school has a world-class, state-of-the-art facility, as well as becomes a community institution so that [students of] the community learn their history, as well as what they need to be college-ready and beyond in the twenty-first century."

John H. Jackson, president and CEO of the Schott Foundation for Public Education, which works to support equity in education, notes the significance of labor's reemergence in Chicago as an agent of radical change. "There was a time over the last five to ten years that there was a belief that labor couldn't and wouldn't push back, or that labor and community couldn't work together to push back. I think [Chicago] represents the reemergence of an impactful partnership where labor, civil rights, and community come together to try to create a better reality. We don't see that happening enough, but it represents what's possible when it does happen."

Jackson says that the CTU has had a significant impact, helping highlight big questions around resources and providing all kids the opportunities to succeed.

"If we keep schools open, how are we going to make them better? If we don't suspend our young people and we keep them in the schools, what are the additional supports? How do we get those? And how do we keep their communities safe? . . . Chicago still has serious challenges [and] policy makers are not presenting the types of policy proposals needed to resolve them."

The CTU is not only a fighting union, it offers a vision of what education in Chicago could look like. *The Schools Chicago Students Deserve* is CTU's blueprint for school reform. "Every student in Chicago Public Schools deserves to have the same quality education as the children of the wealthy," begins the report, which goes on to highlight "research-based education that is fully-funded and staffed in an equitable fashion throughout the city."

Community and youth activists view the CTU as a welcome new ally in a larger struggle for justice. Raul Botello, associate director of Communities United, a grassroots group in a largely Latino neighborhood of Chicago, says that CTU is "playing a really critical role in not just public education, but in defining and recalibrating the scope of what public service is. . . . Their message about equity and incorporating class and race into their rhetoric is something . . . a lot of community organizations have been [saying] before."

Many point to the CTU as the cutting edge of a broader working-class struggle and fight-back against the war on the middle class. When a major labor union trumpets the message of community activists, "it's a big elephant in the room," says Botello. "The establishment has to respond to them. In some ways, they've catapulted a lot of the work that a lot of the movements in the past have been attempting to do or were doing already."

Botello offers an example. "We're trying to reform the school discipline code to be more than just suspensions and arrests in our schools, and [we were raising the issue of] the school-to-prison pipeline. Previous union administrations would never touch that . . . because the teachers are in the classroom and in some ways, they're the biggest initiators of that discipline. But [teachers'] hands are tied—these are just bad policies."

When Karen Lewis and her team took the reins of CTU, says Botello, "we didn't even have to convince them. This was something that inherently they believe: that black and brown men and boys are being disproportionately kicked out of our public schools." (See the box about the school-to-prison pipeline on page 63.)

Education secretary Arne Duncan and attorney general Eric Holder announced in January 2014 a federal initiative on discipline to address the school-to-prison pipeline. Noting that schools now suspend or expel two million students per year, Holder declared, "Too often, so-called zero-tolerance policies, however well-intentioned they might be, make students feel unwelcome in their own schools; they disrupt the learning process and they can have significant and lasting negative effects on the long-term well-being of our young people, increasing their likelihood of future contact with the juvenile and criminal justice systems."[15]

Botello notes that CTU has made crucial links between issues. "What CTU has brought in is a much more explicit analysis of race and class into policies that impact public education—but equally important is just their impact on the city as a whole."

Lipman explains the connection: "We have to challenge racism in order to fight neoliberalism and capitalism . . . and defend public education in Chicago. We have to find ways for white parents to see that their concerns about schools are very much tied to what's happening to black and Latino students, and that even when they are not facing [school closures, racism, and privatization] themselves, they have to stand up against that. Those things are intimately connected." Lipman notes that during the teachers' strike, parents and students from some predominantly white schools joined protests against funding cuts, large class sizes, and testing.

One lesson from the Chicago struggle, Botello observes, is that there must be "more cross-collaboration of movements, because I think it's taken a while. I think it took too long for the LGBT movement and the immigrant rights movement to come together, or the education folks working with civil rights groups. It's always good to start from your base and where you're at, but there could be a much more intentional, aggressive way to collaborate. There's so much richness to be learned from each other. That will only help everyone."

"Parents don't just want high test scores," argues Lipman. "They want their children treated with respect. They want to be treated with respect when they come to the school. They want the school to be a center of community. . . . They want their school to have the full resources.

"We need a system of mutual accountability," she adds. "While we are holding teachers accountable and schools accountable and parents accountable . . . we have never held the policy makers accountable, the corporations accountable that deindustrialized whole areas of the city, moved elsewhere for cheap labor, and left a huge unemployed population, produced poverty, and affected the schools. The kind of accountability that we need is a collective community accountability in which the communities and the schools set standards for what they want their children to have."

Movements start from within the most affected communities and take the time to build on local leadership. The antidote to the corporatization of our society is this type of organizing, grounded in community.

On the South Side of Chicago, where the education wars have raged hottest, "the future that we are working for is one that's rooted in self-determination," says Jitu Brown. "I think that communities have to have the right to control the institutions that are in their neighborhoods. . . . If we don't have [educated young] people in our community, who becomes the dependable elected officials? Who becomes the teachers, the principals in our community?"

Brown reflects, "A missing ingredient that nobody talks about in all this is love. I know that when you are working with someone or a group of people that you love, you're going to work harder. You're going to pour in every resource, because you care about them. You recognize that your future is linked to theirs." Living this truth about transformative organizing, in September 2015, Jitu Brown and Bronzeville parents went on to lead a hunger strike, putting in every resource they had and succeeded in saving Dyett High School.

A MULTIGENERATIONAL MOVEMENT

Nine-year-old Asean Johnson marched alongside Jitu Brown as they demanded a strong community role in education decisions. Asean has taken his message from the streets of Chicago to a national stage.

"Every child deserves a great education. Every school deserves equal funding and resources," Johnson told a large crowd in Washington, D.C., at the fiftieth-anniversary March on Washington. He said he was participating in the march "for education, justice, and freedom."

Echoing Jitu Brown's call for local leaders, Karen Lewis has already endorsed Asean Johnson for mayor of Chicago—in 2025, when he turns twenty-one. In the struggle for the soul of public education, the next generation is already leading the fight.

Image text (within the print):

MULTI-LINGUAL TEACHING

TEACHING METHODS THAT VALUE ALL CULTURES

CELEBRATING LEADERSHIP AND HISTORY OF PEOPLE OF COLOR

...RACIAL EQUALITY IN SCHOOLS QUALITY OF FACILITIES AND HIRING OF TEACHERS

ORAL STORY TELLING TRADITION VALUED

FIGHT FOR A JUST EDUCATION SYSTEM

■ **EDUCATION IS A RIGHT.**
Meredith Stern, 2009
This print by Meredith Stern combines images, narrative, and liberatory educational practices. The print portrays two young students in a classroom working together to envision a just education system. In the artist's words: "I wanted to make a print that addressed the systemic, institutionalized racism that exists in the American school system and present a print that celebrated a better value system for improving the quality of education that we should be giving to every single child in our society."

ESTUDIANTE MILITANTE (Militant Student), Papel Machete, San Juan, Puerto Rico, 2010 (Photo by Isamar Abreu)

January 11, 2011, marked the return of the student strike in Puerto Rico after the winter break. With a massive crowd of supporters including professors, alumni, and supporters of public education, the students wore masks and held shields to defend themselves from persecution by university administrators and police violence. They commemorated the anniversary of the birth of Eugenio María de Hostos, a towering figure of the late nineteenth-century Caribbean independence struggles. The activity was followed by a vigorous march to protest the rise of tuition fees at the University of Puerto Rico. *Estudiante Militante*, the fourteen-foot puppet in this image, is a symbol of the student movement. The puppet was created by Papel Machete in collaboration with the students, as a gesture of solidarity during the student strike of April–June 2010. *Estudiante Militante* traveled across the eleven campuses of the university accompanied by the Working People's Band.

JOSÉ JORGE
DÍAZ ORTIZ

AGITATOR, CULTURAL WORKER, COMMU-
NITY ORGANIZER, DJ, AND PUPPETEER
JOSÉ JORGE DÍAZ ORTIZ IS ARTISTIC DI-
RECTOR AND A FOUNDING MEMBER OF
AGITARTE AND PAPEL MACHETE. AGI-
TARTE CREATES PROJECTS AND PRAC-
TICES OF CULTURAL SOLIDARITY WITH
GRASSROOTS STRUGGLES FOR SOCIAL
AND ECONOMIC JUSTICE. PAPEL MA-
CHETE'S CULTURAL WORK IS COMMIT-
TED TO CREATING COUNTERPROJECTS TO
HEGEMONY.

Photo by Leonardo March

I am the co-director of Papel Machete and artistic director of AgitArte. I am a cultural worker, an artist, and a puppeteer. And I'm also a community organizer. Papel Machete is a radical puppet, mask, and music collective of workers
based in Santurce, Puerto Rico. That's our laboratory where we experiment in the context of theater for and by the
working class and produce puppetry, masks, and objects for communities, the theater, and the streets. We started
performing on May 1, 2006, during a government shutdown that the government used to justify the imposition of a
regressive sales and service tax on the island.

**How do you see the role of art and cultural work and its transformative power in twenty-first-century political
movements?**

My main goal is to create an effective counterproject to hegemony. Hegemony refers to the institutions parallel to
the state, like schools, civic organizations, and the media, that support the ideology and culture of the ruling class.
We battle those institutions by breaking from the content and forms that shape the way we think and view the world
and what we believe is true and possible in our lives and society.

Our art works against this hegemony. In a broader sense, we strive for a culture that comes from radical perspectives
and practices of liberation from the capitalist, imperialist, white-supremacist patriarchy that is destroying our lives
and community. The transformations that we are interested in are revolutionary.

**How does your political work relate to the collective, and how is it similar to or different from your individual
work?**

The way that I started identifying myself as an artist was through the work of organizing collectives that take on the
kind of art and the kind of productions that we want to see in the streets. We see the production of art as a collective,
and the methods that we use and the processes that we engage as fundamental to the artistic work that we do. There
would be no artistic proposal if it wasn't a collective proposal.

Alienation is a main problem in our daily lives. There are many advantages [to] and beauty in being able to work together and create together to combat alienation and get ourselves back to being creators as human beings, and creating together to figure out how we're going to solve the problems that directly affect our lives. That's something that is totally against this system and considered dangerous.

How do you measure success in your cultural work, and how does it relate to the expectations of organizations or the movement?

A lot of times we focus on the subjective experience or the experience of the people at the moment, which sometimes goes against the "measurables" and the product-oriented mentality that we have because of the society that we live in. People are used to seeing a product.

What I am particularly interested in is success being tied to how we as artists of color of the working class, artists of liberatory movements, are going to create long-term institutions and long-term possibilities so that we can really talk about our success in the future, really talk about success at another level in our lives. Now is the time for us.

¡CON PAPEL Y CON MACHETE ARMAREMOS EL FUTURO!

FREE OSCAR LOPEZ RIVERA. Papel Machete, San Juan, Puerto Rico, 2013. Photo by Javier Maldonado O'Farrill

3

TRANSFORMING VISIONS: ENDING MASS INCAR- CERATION

■ Die In for Mike Brown, #DREAM4JUSTICE March, New York City, 2015. Banner art by Athena Suules (Photo by Erik McGregor)

White supremacy in the United States is starkly revealed in the verdicts in cases of black or brown bodies awaiting justice. The decision of the grand jury not to issue an indictment after Michael Brown's killing by the police on August 9, 2014, in Ferguson, Missouri, has renewed a nationwide dialogue about issues of police accountability and racism in cases of police brutality. This four-and-a-half-minute die-in for Mike Brown corresponds to the four and a half hours that the young, unarmed black man lay in the street after his murder by white officer Darren Wilson. On the national holiday commemorating Dr. Martin Luther King Jr., #DREAM4JUSTICE marched "honoring Dr. King's legacy and reclaiming the stolen dreams of our Brothers and Sisters whose lives were taken by the police. We were reminded that our power lies in our community and we are the ones we have been waiting for!"

■ WE SEE YOU. #IndictAmerica: Turn Up for Mike Brown!,
Ferguson Solidarity March, Boston, 2014 (Photo by Farhad Ebrahimi)
The criminalization of immigrants is related to the proliferation of detention centers and growth of the prison industrial complex in the United States. In the photograph, thousands of demonstrators gather in front of
South Bay House of Correction to show solidarity with detainees. This county jail houses immigration detainees pursuant to an agreement with Immigration and Customs Enforcement. The action, led by #BlackLivesMat-
terBoston, took over a major highway following a call heeded in dozens of cities around the nation.

*T*he United States today has the world's largest population of imprisoned humans. Some 2.2 million people are incarcerated in state and federal jails and prisons—a 500 percent increase over the past thirty years.

Coming out of the darkest and most traumatized depths of our society, the growing movement to end mass incarceration advances a bold transformative vision, fiercely challenging and attacking the root causes that collectively prop up our "injustice system." The stories in this chapter highlight an emergent movement that is grounded in the most impacted communities, transforming powerlessness into power and building links among activists on many issues around a transformative abolitionist vision. These transformers are raising social consciousness, radically changing how we define problems and solutions, and transforming our ability to envision a new future.

Legal scholar Michelle Alexander makes the powerful case that mass incarceration functions much the way slavery and Jim Crow* laws did in past generations: it is a racialized system of control over people of color. The root causes of the recent escalation go back to deindustrialization and high unemployment in low-income communities, when black and brown workers, who had moved north when needed for World War II factory jobs, were later rendered "disposable" by global capital's move to cheaper labor markets abroad. Policy drivers that fuel the "prison industrial complex"† include the racist and class-biased war on drugs, the school-to-prison pipeline, anti-immigrant crackdowns, stop-and-frisk tactics, "tough on crime" policies such as mandatory sentences, and the prison industry. As Alexander says:

> Communities are poor and have failing schools and broken homes not because of their personal failings, but because we've declared war on them, spent billions building prisons while allowing schools to fail, targeted children in these communities, stopping, searching, frisking them—and the first arrest is typically for some nonviolent minor drug offense, which occurs with equal frequency in middle class white neighborhoods but typically goes ignored. We saddle them with criminal records, jail them, then release them to a parallel universe where they are discriminated against for the rest of their lives, locked into permanent second-class status.[1]

The confluence of these forces has resulted in African American males being six times more likely to be incarcerated during their lives than white males, while African American women are incarcerated at three times the rate of white women.[2] Transgender people and other cultural minorities are also disproportionately incarcerated: 21 percent of all transgender women, and half of African American transgender women, have been incarcerated at some point.[3]

Today a movement to end mass incarceration in some of the most ravaged communities links diverse constituencies, ranging from traditional civil rights groups such

---

* "Jim Crow" refers to racial segregation laws enacted in the U.S. South following the Civil War. These laws mandated racial segregation in all public facilities and disenfranchised blacks. Jim Crow remained in force until 1965, when the federal Civil Rights Act and Voting Rights Act officially outlawed such discrimination.

† "The term 'prison industrial complex' was introduced by activists and scholars to contest prevailing beliefs that increased levels of crime were the root cause of mounting prison populations," explains Angela Davis in her book *Are Prisons Obsolete?* "Instead, they argued, prison construction and the attendant drive to fill these new structures with human bodies have been driven by ideologies of racism and the pursuit of profit. Social historian Mike Davis first used the term in relation to California's penal system, which, he observed, already had begun in the 1990s to rival agribusiness and land development as a major economic and political force." Angela Davis. *Are Prisons Obsolete?* (New York: Seven Stories Press, 2003), 84.

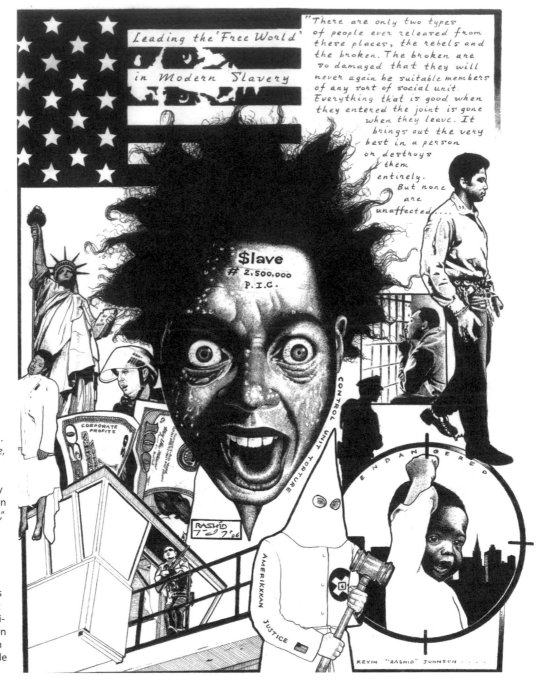

■ CONTROL UNIT TORTURE. Kevin "Rashid" Johnson, California, 2006

The artist, Kevin "Rashid" Johnson, is a prison organizer whose art became the symbol of the California prisoners' hunger strike in 2011. In *Control Unit Torture*, the artist raises his voice against the oppression of solitary confinement. Johnson has been in the "hole," segregated from the general prison population, for eighteen years. He calls for "an end to the psychological warfare that is being waged against humanity by the capitalist regime." Johnson reminds us, "Through solidarity and struggle we will overcome."

as the ACLU and NAACP (National Association for the Advancement of Colored People) to newer groups such as #BlackLivesMatter, the Formerly Incarcerated People's Movement, All of Us or None, Critical Resistance, the Campaign to End the New Jim Crow, several thousand progressive black churches working together in the Samuel DeWitt Proctor Conference, and many organizations featured in this book, from LGBTQ to immigration to education and economic justice groups. This growing movement has had notable achievements:

- New York, New Jersey, and California reduced their prisoner populations by about 25 percent between 1999 and 2012. Notably, violent crime rates in these states fell faster than the national average.
- In 2012, the U.S. Supreme Court ruled in Miller v. Alabama that mandatory life-without-parole sentences for juveniles are unconstitutional.
- From 2002 to 2013, New York City police made more than five million stops, disproportionately targeting young black men, even in low-crime neighborhoods. In 2014, following a years-long campaign by community and civil rights groups, newly elected New York City mayor Bill de Blasio ended the routine racist police practice of stop-and-frisk.
- In 2015, following hunger strikes by tens of thousands of inmates and a landmark court case, California agreed to end its routine use of solitary confinement in prisons.

Behind each of these statistics, and thousands like them across the country, are individual lives that have been devastated, prisoners in jail and their extended families, and entire communities that are impacted for generations.

In their inspiring stories are the seeds of the visionary movement to reclaim our humanity.

Monte Cullors was nineteen when he landed in Los Angeles County Jail. Arrested for joyriding in his mother's car and leading police on a car chase, he was sentenced to thirty-two months in jail. What happened next permanently changed his life. And his family's.

A sheriff's deputy in the L.A. County Jail told Cullors to get in line.

"I am in line," retorted the stocky teenager.

The sheriff pushed him. Cullors instinctively pushed back. Suddenly Cullors was surrounded by deputies. They began beating him with batons. He was shot with Tasers. He recounted how they choked him until he was unconscious.

"When I woke up there was just a pool of blood and I guess they busted that blood vessel and I bled out from my ears and nose," he said. "I just remember there was . . . blood and my head was ringing."

Cullors was the latest victim of sheriff violence in the notorious L.A. County Jail. Los Angeles County has the largest jail system in the world, with an average daily population of 22,000 inmates.

"No jail in the nation matches the level of pervasive, savage, long-standing, and notorious deputy-on-inmate violence of the kind we see in the Los Angeles County Jail system," asserted Margaret Winter, associate director of the ACLU's National Prison Project.

As Monte Cullors was suffering in silence inside the jail, his family was desperately looking for him. "On the outside, we were trying to get hold of the sheriff's department and ask about my brother because my mother had been trying to visit him and they just kept giving us the run around," recounts Patrisse Cullors-Brignac, Monte's sister. "By the time we did see him, he was completely emaciated. They had drugged him on psychotropic drugs . . . and he had never had any history of psychiatric issues previous to his time there." She says that her brother "was starved—they gave him no food and they turned off his water in his cell. He was forced to drink from the toilet.

"If it was another country, we'd call it torture," Cullors-Brignac says. "But because it's the United States, they call it 'excessive force.'"

More than a decade later, Monte Cullors still bears the scars of his incarceration. "My brother battles with mental illness now," his sister notes. "We don't know whether he was prone to it or not, but something deeply shifted for him while he was incarcerated there."

Patrisse Cullors-Brignac is now on a mission to spare others from what happened to her brother. "I'm an or-

> "If it was another country, we'd call it torture," Cullors-Brignac says. "But because it's the United States, they call it 'excessive force.'"

ganizer and activist, so I have been basically on the front lines of his care. Advocating for him is great. But there are larger structural changes that need to happen, and that's what we're in this for."

THE NEW JIM CROW

How did the United States morph into a vast prison colony for blacks and Hispanics?

Michelle Alexander, who worked as an attorney for the ACLU, was initially reluctant to embrace sweeping explanations for why people of color are so much more likely to end up in jail. But the more she examined the data about the war on drugs, launched in the 1980s by the conservative movement and championed by President Ronald Reagan, the less she could turn away from its implications. She writes in her book *The New Jim Crow*:

> The stark and sobering reality is that, for reasons largely unrelated to actual crime trends, the American penal system has emerged as a system of social control unparalleled in world history. . . . Mass incarceration is, metaphorically, the new Jim Crow and . . . all those who care about social justice should fully commit themselves to dismantling this new racial caste system.[4]

Incarceration is dramatically skewed by race. More than 60 percent of those in prison in America are people of color. According to the Sentencing Project, which promotes sentencing reform and alternatives to incarceration, the likelihood that a white man will spend time in prison in his lifetime is one in seventeen; for Latino men, the likelihood is one in six, and for black men, it is one in three.[5]

Keeping human beings behind bars is both a massive industry and a profitable business. And business is very, very good.

Women, who account for 7 percent of prisoners, represent the fastest-growing segment of the prison population. Race is again the distinguishing feature of women's incarceration: Latino women are 69 percent more likely to be incarcerated than white women.[6]

The seemingly inexplicable mad rush to lock up citizens turns out to have a cold logic: keeping human beings behind bars is both a massive industry and a profitable business. And business is very, very good.

The Corrections Corporation of America (CCA) is the biggest operator of private prisons in the country. CCA has had a 500 percent increase in business in the last two decades.[7] Private prison companies have spent millions to lobby state and federal legislators for tougher laws and harsher jail terms to keep the conveyor belt of prisoners humming.

In 2009, CCA worked with the shadowy right-wing American Legislative Exchange Council (ALEC), which is bankrolled by the billionaire Koch brothers and other corporate contributors, to draft model immigration legislation that became the notorious 2010 Arizona anti-immigrant bill SB 1070.[8] This law required local police to determine a person's immigration status during routine stops, thus legalizing racial profiling and resulting in thousands of arrests and deportations. Private and public prisons were ready to receive the surge of new inmates.

In its 2005 annual report, CCA gave its investors a heads-up about developments that could affect its bottom line:

> The demand for our facilities and services could be adversely affected by the relaxation of enforcement efforts, leniency in conviction and sentencing practices or through the decriminalization of certain activities that are currently proscribed by our criminal laws. For instance, any changes with respect to drugs and controlled substances or illegal immigration could affect the number of persons arrested, convicted, and sentenced, thereby potentially reducing demand for correctional facilities to house them.[9]

The text within the artwork reads:

UNTIL THE KILLING OF BLACK MEN

BLACK MOTHER'S SONS BECOMES AS IMPORTANT AS THE REST OF THE COUNTRY THE KILLING OF A WHITE MOTHER'S SON. MOTHERS WHO BELIEVE IN FREEDOM CANNOT REST UNTIL THIS HAPPENS.

ELLA BAKER 1964

RLM

■ **TRAYVON MARTIN
–ELLA BAKER.
Ricardo Levins Morales,
Minneapolis, 2013**
The shooting of Trayvon Martin sparked mass protests across the country among communities of color and their allies. Martin, an unarmed black teen, was killed on his way back to his father's home from a trip to a convenience store on June 26, 2012. His killer, George Zimmerman, a former neighborhood watch captain, would claim that Martin's hoodie made him suspicious. The hoodie became a symbol of solidarity and protest in a case that shone a spotlight on racial injustice and gun control. Ricardo Levins-Morales juxtaposes the face of the young Martin wearing a hoodie with a quote by civil rights leader Ella Baker on the value of a black mother's son.

CCA is always exploring new ways to boost incarceration and generate business. In 2012, the company sent letters to forty-eight governors proposing to take over their state-owned prisons. But there was a catch: the states had to guarantee that the jails would be 90 percent full, or taxpayers would be forced to pay for the unused beds. The prison industry has ensured it will cash in whether crime rates rise or fall.

Activists are now taking aim at the financial underpinnings of the prison industrial complex. In April 2014, ColorofChange.org announced that it had convinced three large investment companies to divest from CCA and the GEO Group, the two largest private prison companies. ColorofChange.org, which has grown to 850,000 members and describes itself as "the nation's largest online civil rights organization," reported that it had "urged company executives to reconsider the financial, moral, and political implications of private prisons and divest." The investment companies—asset management group Scopia Capital, Amica Mutual Insurance, and the DSM Netherlands pension fund—announced they were divesting $60 million from CCA and GEO.

"CCA and the GEO Group, Inc. push hard for criminal justice policy and lucrative contracts that allow them to turn a profit while harming our communities and further corrupting our criminal justice system. We've had enough," said Rashad Robinson, executive director of ColorofChange.org. "With more and more frequency, the business community, the public, and politicians are taking action to dissociate from the industry and protect our society from its devastating model."

The prison divestment campaign is a tactic directly aimed at the companies that profit from mass incarceration. Anti-apartheid activists successfully used this tool to raise awareness and end support for South Africa's white supremacist government in the critical years before apartheid toppled. Climate change activists are leading similar divestment campaigns. Prison justice activists continue this strategy of disrupting the powerful status quo. Their hope is to cleave a fissure into the once seemingly impenetrable edifice of white supremacy: the prison industrial complex.

> "There is a current and ever-present epidemic of violence in this country. . . . How many of us know about this? How many of us care about this?"

STOP THE VIOLENCE

Patrisse Cullors-Brignac was determined to stop the violence. She decided that the most immediate way to spare others what her brother went through was to go after the abusers: the sheriffs who run the jails in Los Angeles. Cullors-Brignac is the co-founder of Dignity and Power Now, a grassroots organization based in Los Angeles that "fights for the dignity and power of incarcerated people, their families, and communities." In 2012, Dignity and Power Now launched the Coalition to End Sheriff Violence in the L.A. Jails. The very police force that was dividing and destroying her community became the focal point for uniting them.

Cullors-Brignac may be best known for being one of three women who created the hashtag #BlackLivesMatter in 2013 in response to the acquittal of George Zimmerman in the murder of unarmed African American teen Trayvon Martin in Sanford, Florida. (The other two were Alicia Garza of the National Domestic Workers Alliance and Opal Tometi of Black Alliance for Just Immigration.) #BlackLivesMatter has since gained worldwide attention when it became the rallying cry of the anti-police-brutality movement in the wake of the killing of Michael Brown in Ferguson, Missouri, in 2014. Cullors-Brignac was named one of "14 Women of Color Who Rocked 2014" by *Colorlines*.

"State violence silences people," says Cullors-Brignac. "These issues here in the sheriff's department have been happening for decades and yet there hasn't been a mass movement to stop it. Mostly people get out and are ashamed . . . and they're scared to death because they're afraid that it will happen again. [It's] sort of the cycle of violence that we see in domestic violence, but on the level of state violence."

In 2013, Cullors-Brignac brought attention to the issue of sheriff brutality in L.A. jails through performance art. She produced and performed *Stained: An Intimate Portrayal of State Violence*. The narrative was drawn from a devastating 2011 ACLU report, "Cruel and Usual Punishment: How a Savage Gang of Deputies Controls L.A. County Jails."

"There is a current and ever-present epidemic of violence in this country. In Los Angeles County, in both Downtown L.A. and Santa Clarita, lives the most violent and overcrowded jail system in the world. How many of us know about this? How many of us care about this?" wrote Cullors-Brignac. "Folks who have been incarcerated and are currently incarcerated are seen as a disposable group of human beings deserving of civil and human rights violations. I want to challenge our community to remind ourselves that what violates one person's civil/human rights violates all people's civil/human rights."[10]

Stained toured around Los Angeles for much of 2013. Cullors-Brignac's performances helped launch the Coalition to End Sheriff Violence in L.A. Jails. The coalition is led by family members of prisoners, survivors of deputy-on-inmate abuse, clergy, attorneys, and concerned community members. The coalition is demanding civilian oversight over the L.A. Sheriff's Department.

Cullors-Brignac is rallying a traumatized community to transform powerlessness into power. "The resilience piece for us is the building of an organization that understands the impacts of trauma, and then pushes the conversation to build our capacity to change both the policy [and] the cultural narrative around the people who have been most impacted. I would say we have empowered and built power in the community and changed our relationship to the sheriff's department."

THE POWER OF A DANDELION

Cullors-Brignac, who previously worked as an organizer for the Labor/Community Strategy Center in Los Angeles (see Chapter 6), uses art to move and organize people. Her artists' collective, Freedom Harvest, uses the image of the dandelion to tell a story. "The dandelion is this weed and nuisance in people's gardens and people pick it out," she says. But the dandelion is also used as medicine. "So we used the dandelion as the imagery of the people who are on the margin and being picked out like weeds."

In March 2013, the Coalition to End Sheriff Violence in L.A. Jails solicited people from around the country to send images of dandelions. The images were assembled in an art installation, and performers brought the story to life. "About 90 percent of the people who performed and contributed to the art have been impacted by the prison industrial complex on some level," says Cullors-Brignac.

"The community here in Los Angeles has been very inspired by this," she adds. "I just actually sat with a group of older black civil rights leaders yesterday and they were like, '*Finally* this is happening. We've been dealing with the sheriff's department for decades and finally a group is taking it on.'"

In spring 2014, the coalition sponsored two debates between candidates for sheriff. Cullors-Brignac explains, "Historically, there have only been three sheriffs [in L.A.] since 1955. The sheriff here has no term limits and you just sort of get who you get. So it's been very significant for the sheriff to see who the community is and who this sheriff is going to be accountable to, and also hold the sheriff's feet to the fire." Seven candidates attended the debate; all but one endorsed the coalition's call for civilian oversight.

How did that happen?

"I don't let folks say no to me," Cullors-Brignac says with a modest laugh. "I also let every candidate know this is super important and you need to be there. . . . It became really high-profile when a few candidates said yes, and then all of them basically had to say yes." Persistence is a key attribute of transformers. Because Cullors-Brignac built a strong organization grounded in her community's powerful stories, she made it difficult for those in power to say no.

Coalition supporters also protested in Los Angeles in a show of support for the 2013 California prison hunger strikes. These hunger strikes involved more than thirty thousand prisoners who were protesting the use

"*The dandelion is this weed and nuisance in people's gardens and people pick it out,*" she says. But the dandelion is also used as medicine.

1 OUT OF EVERY 109 WOMEN IN AMERICA IS INCARCERATED, ON PAROLE OR PROBATION

150,000 women are in jail or in prison

MOST WOMEN ENTERING PRISON HAVE BEEN CONVICTED OF NON-VIOLENT CRIMES

½ OF ALL WOMEN IN PRISON ARE INCARCERATED MORE THAN 100 MILES FROM THEIR FAMILIES

INCARCERATED WOMEN ARE AMONG THE POOREST PEOPLE IN AMERICA. 2/3 HAVE LESS THAN A HIGH SCHOOL EDUCATION. ONE IN FIVE HOMELESS

ALMOST ½ OF THE WOMEN ENTERING PRISON IN 2000 WERE SERVING TIME FOR DRUG OFFENCES

SEVEN MILLION CHILDREN HAVE A PARENT IN PRISON, ON PROBATION OR ON PAROLE

AFRICAN AMERICANS ARE 18% OF N.Y. STATE'S POPULATION

HISPANICS ARE 15.1% OF N.Y. STATE'S POPULATION

79% OF ALL WOMEN IN N.Y. STATE'S PRISONS ARE BLACK OR HISPANIC

OF ALL PEOPLE INCARCERATED IN NEW YORK WITH DRUG OFFENCES:

93% ARE AFRICAN AMERICAN OR HISPANIC

■ **PRISONERS OF A HARD LIFE: WOMEN AND THEIR CHILDREN. Susan Wilmarth, Oakland, California, 2005**
This excerpt from the Real Cost of Prisons Comix series spotlights how the incarceration rate for women is rising at a rate nearly double that of men. This comic book is part of a series of three published in 2005 by The Real Cost of Prison Project after more than ten years of research and popular education projects by anti-prison activists Lois Ahrens and Ellen Miller-Mack. One hundred thirty-five thousand copies were widely distributed among prisoners and by youth educators.

and abuse of solitary confinement in California jails. The strikes, which lasted two months, were a watershed in the prison justice movement. (See more about the hunger strikes at the end of this chapter.)

The Coalition to End Sheriff Violence in L.A. Jails has its roots in the larger prison justice and prison abolition movement, which advocates abolishing the systemic causes that have led the United States to be the largest prison colony on earth. The coalition is a member of Californians United for a Responsible Budget, which is an initiative pushing back against jail construction and jail expansion in the state of California.

Networking is key for movements to take shape. Communities, in this case hollowed out by an epidemic of incarceration, reach out and link arms with other marginalized communities and their broader struggle and visions. A small protest grows into a force that must be reckoned with.

The relentless efforts of these prison activists are paying off in Los Angeles and across the country. In December 2014, following a two-year campaign waged by Dignity and Power Now and the Coalition to End Sheriff Violence in L.A. Jails, the L.A. County Board of Supervisors voted to create a civilian oversight commission to oversee the Sheriff's Department. The newly elected L.A. sheriff endorsed the commission. Oversight is "a major milestone for the troubled law enforcement agency," wrote the *Los Angeles Times*. Oversight makes it possible to shine a light into the dark corners of the system; it is a critical element in the struggles to make police, jails, and prisons accountable to the public and to end their unjust practices.

BEYOND PRISONS

Are prisons obsolete?

So asked Angela Davis in her groundbreaking 2003 book by the same name. Cullors-Brignac and many others cite Davis as an inspiration. Davis, an activist and scholar whose activism dates back to her leadership in the civil rights movement and the Black Panther Party in the 1960s and 1970s, was imprisoned in the early 1970s and later acquitted. She is currently a professor emeritus at the University of California, Santa Cruz. She is a leading proponent of prison abolition, arguing for decarceration and the transformation of our society to end this "new age slavery." Davis sketches what an alternative to prison would look like:

> What, then, would it mean to imagine a system in which punishment is not allowed to become the source of corporate profit? How can we imagine a society in which race and class are not primary determinants of punishment? Or one in which punishment itself is no longer the central concern in the making of justice? An abolitionist approach that seeks to answer questions such as these would require us to imagine a constellation of alternative strategies and institutions, with the ultimate aim of removing the prison from the social and ideological landscapes of our society. In other words, we would not be looking for prisonlike substitutes for the prison, such as house arrest safeguarded by electronic surveillance bracelets. Rather, positing decarceration as our overarching strategy, we would try to envision a continuum of alternatives to imprisonment—demilitarization of schools, revitalization of education at all levels, a health system that provides free physical and mental care to all, and a justice system based on reparation and reconciliation rather than retribution and vengeance. . . . Schools can therefore be seen as the most powerful alternative to jails and prisons.[11]

Davis concludes with a caution:

> Alternatives that fail to address racism, male dominance, homophobia, class bias, and other structures of domination will not, in the final analysis, lead to decarceration and will not advance the goal of abolition.[12]

Imagine: our tax dollars invested in schools instead of jails. Treatment for mentally ill people instead of in-

"Schools can therefore be seen as the most powerful alternative to jails and prisons."

carceration. Poverty reduction instead of warehousing the poor behind bars. Drug decriminalization instead of drug wars. This movement is transforming our visions not just of crime and punishment but of what the structures of a just society would look like. A better future is both imaginable and possible.

A BROTHER-SISTER DUO SPARKING TRANSFORMATIVE ORGANIZING

Walidah Imarisha is an educator, writer, organizer, and spoken-word artist who has taught at Portland State University and Oregon State University and has been a public scholar with the Oregon Humanities Conversation Project. With adrienne maree brown, she has brought twenty organizers and activists together to create an anthology of short stories: *Octavia's Brood: Science Fiction Stories from Social Justice Movements.* She previously lived in Philadelphia, where she worked for the Central Committee for Conscientious Objectors, which supports war resisters, and helped found the Human Rights Coalition, a group of ex-prisoners and their families who are working to change and ultimately abolish the prison system. Two decades ago, she "adopted" a brother, Kakamia Jahad Imarisha—"we adopted each other, actually"—who has been incarcerated in California for twenty-four years. Kakamia is an artist and had advertised his work in a San Francisco newspaper. Walidah, then a high school student, wrote to him to order some art, and "we've been connected ever since. We're family at this point." That act of reaching out to someone behind bars inspires her activism around prisoners.

"I definitely learned a lot of amazing organizing lessons from him just seeing the ways that he has connected with folks on the inside," Imarisha says. "It's been a really important

> *"We absolutely need systems to hold people accountable for harm, but they need to be systems that are focused on restoring wholeness to the individuals in the community, rather than retribution and punishment."*

piece to combat the images we're given around what life is like on the inside. . . . He's helping to create community within the walls . . . [and] build connections and humanity on a daily basis."

Imarisha travels around Oregon speaking to community groups about alternatives to incarceration. She frequently visits prison towns. "I've had guards, wardens, [and] the former head of the department of corrections in my presentations. I'm just getting folks to think. A lot of folks are at a point where, for whatever their motivation, they recognize that prison systems are not protecting us, [are] not rehabilitating . . . but they have no idea that there's anything possible other than prisons."

Imarisha offers people a different way of seeing. "We absolutely need systems to hold people accountable for harm, but they need to be systems that are focused on restoring wholeness to the individuals in the community, rather than retribution and punishment." She stresses the need for transformative justice systems that are focused on changing root causes. "That's more useful than restorative justice, which is restoring back to the way things were before the harm occurred. In communities of color, this is not enough, because those communities are dealing with the systemic violence of poverty, police violence, and the school-to-prison pipeline. As we know, the best way to stop harm from being done is for people to have their needs met—quality education, living wage, health care, housing—and to feel connected to and empowered through their communities. So just restoring the situation to before the harm occurred doesn't address the systemic oppression that is part of the reason the harm occurred. The idea of transformative justice is that we're engaging in a process that will ultimately transform the individuals and the community into something new."

"Transformative justice," writes the community justice organization Philly Stands Up, "recognizes that oppression is at the root of all forms of harm, abuse and assault. As a practice it therefore aims to address and confront those oppressions on all levels and treats this concept as an integral part of accountability and healing."[13]

Imarisha advocates abolishing prison, but that does not preclude notions of prison justice and reform. "We

HARD TIME OUT:
THE SCHOOL-TO-PRISON PIPELINE David Goodman[14]

In March 2007, the eighth-grade class at the Dyker Heights School in Brooklyn, New York, got a substitute teacher. Predictably, the kids got rambunctious. Thirteen-year-old Chelsea Fraser steered clear of the rowdier action, including the boys plastering the walls with Post-its. Instead she doodled on a desk with a marker, penning in block letters: "OKAY."

Two days later, Chelsea called her mom, Diana Silva, from school. She was panicked. "Mom," she said, "I think I'm gonna get arrested."

"For writing on a desk?" Silva laughed, suspecting teenage drama. "Did you write a bad word?"

"No," said Chelsea, a cheerful girl with a flip of black hair over one eye. "I wrote 'okay.'"

"Baby, tell them what you did," counseled Silva, a freelance graphic artist. "You'll probably go to the principal. They might suspend you, and they will probably make you scrub the desk." Silva doubted it would even go that far: Chelsea was president of her class and captain of the volleyball team, and had never even been to the principal's office.

Ten minutes later, the phone rang again. This time it was a school dean saying Silva had better come in. "The children are being arrested," said the dean, telling Silva that the boys who had been stickering the walls were also headed to the police station.

Silva raced to school, and four police officers soon arrived. They handcuffed Chelsea and the boys and marched them out to a police van. As she walked, Chelsea looked up to see her classmates pressed against the windows. Her teacher was crying.

Silva tried to reason with the officers, who told her that writing on furniture was a crime. "Is it a crime to be a kid?" she shot back.

At the precinct, Chelsea was handcuffed to a pole over her head for three hours. While she was interrogated, her mother had to wait in another room. "I was scared, I was sad, and I was embarrassed," Chelsea told me. "I just wanted it to be over."

Chelsea Fraser's case is not isolated. In schools across the nation, disciplinary infractions are increasingly being turned over to police and prosecutors. Denver public schools, for example, saw a 71 percent rise in the number of students referred to law enforcement between 2000 and 2004, most for behavior such as bullying and using obscenities. In Florida during the 2005–6 school year, more than one-quarter of some 25,000 school-related referrals to the Department of Juvenile Justice were for disorderly conduct and trespassing.

In Chicago's public schools, more than eight thousand students were arrested in 2003, almost half for simple assaults or batteries that involved no serious injuries or weapons. A full 77 percent of the arrests were of black students, although they make up just half of Chicago's student body.

School violence is a real concern, but in many places, this fear has motivated rigid zero-tolerance policies that severely punish even minor infractions and treat them as gateway offenses to major crimes. These policies disproportionately affect students of color: black students are three times more likely to be suspended or expelled than their white peers.

In 2006, Shaquanda Cotton, a fourteen-year-old African American girl from Paris, Texas, was sentenced to seven years in prison for shoving a teacher's aide. The aide, who was not hurt, was preventing Cotton from entering the building before the beginning of the school day. Cotton had no criminal record; she ended up serving a full year. Critics noted that the judge who sentenced her had previously let a fourteen-year-old white girl charged with setting fire to her parents' house go with probation only.

One reason why students are increasingly ending up in jail is that police now patrol the halls in many schools. In New York City, the police department took control of school safety in 1998 under the Giuliani administration; by the 2005–6 school year, according to the New York Civil Liberties Union, the city employed 4,625 school safety agents and at least two hundred armed officers, making the NYPD School Safety Division the tenth-biggest police force in the country—larger than those of Washington, D.C., Detroit, Boston, or Las Vegas. "We are treating the kids like potential criminals," says Donna Lieberman of the NYCLU. In January 2008, a five-year-old named Denis Rivera was handcuffed behind his back by an NYPD school safety officer for throwing a tantrum in his kindergarten class in Queens.

Chelsea Fraser, for her part, missed three school days going to court, served another two days of in-school suspension, and had to pay $45 in restitution for the desk. She agreed to talk because "I want to help everybody else who is getting in trouble."

can't only focus on abolition and say, 'Well, we're not going to engage in reformist politics.' Because there are people on the inside every day who need to survive." Imarisha says reforms are useful, but only if they are in the context of a larger strategy and vision that advances the end goal of abolishing prisons.

The Black Panther Party, she notes, had more than a hundred programs to meet basic needs within the community, including a free breakfast program and health care clinics that were part of the party's Survival Pending Revolution Program, which she says is "really a useful framing of things. These are programs that in and of themselves [are] not going to fundamentally change the system. But if you're doing it within a radical framework that is building folks' consciousness and building the community's capacity to address its own issues, then those are moving towards revolution while still making sure that people are alive and healthy enough to be able to engage in creating that radical change on a long-term basis."

Imarisha is a keen thinker about the system she is trying to change. She cites the scholarship of Michelle Alexander, Angela Davis, Mumia Abu-Jamal, Ruth Gilmore, and other grassroots intellectuals, including many who are incarcerated, as having shaped her analysis. That analysis draws a line from slavery to Jim Crow segregation to Third World liberation and black power movements to the explosion of the prison industrial complex. Echoing Michelle Alexander, she says, "We can't understand the prison system and the role that it plays now without understanding the idea of controlling potentially rebellious communities that had shown that they were able to destabilize the existing order and have the potential to completely overthrow it and reenvision something new." To some people with power or privilege, she adds, "that was terrifying."

Imarisha understands that the incarceration boom has its roots in the changing needs of capitalism, and she beautifully encapsulates some of the bold ideas documented by Kimberlé Crenshaw, Angela Davis, and others. "Black folks were recruited from the South during the Great Migration to come and work in [northern] factories when capitalism needed them during World War II." Then, in the 1970s, numerous factories closed as a wave of deindustrialization swept American inner cities, causing 60 to 80 percent unemployment in some communities of color. Imarisha continues, "Capitalism said, 'Oh, it's actually more cost-effective for us to move production overseas and exploit Third World labor.' Suddenly these black bodies that were doing this labor are no longer needed. What do you do with them?

"As Bob Marley said, 'a hungry man is an angry man.' So how do you make sure that that anger doesn't get turned against you? . . . Prisons are about warehousing and controlling populations that capitalism no longer needs."

Highlighting truths well documented by scholars such as Michelle Alexander, Imarisha tells us: "People are not sitting in prison because they were selling drugs or doing drugs. There are people selling drugs across college campuses right now . . . who will never spend a day in prison. They're sitting in prison because they were selling drugs and doing drugs, and because they were poor or brown or women or trans or the intersections of them. It's not just the behavior. It's the behavior plus the identity that's criminalized."

Violence, she argues, is not a by-product of prisons. "Violence is the foundation of prisons/policing. They cannot function without it."

Claude Marks is a prison activist and the director of the Freedom Archives, which maintains audio and video recordings that chronicle the history of U.S. and international progressive movements. He says, "There is a way in which people talk about prisons as institutions that aren't working well. The counterargument is that actually the prisons are performing the functions that they were designed to do *extremely* well. They're not dysfunctional, but highly functional if you place them in the context of carrying out the interest of the colonial power: enforcing slavery."

> "Prisons are about warehousing and controlling populations that capitalism no longer needs."

■ **YOUR LIFE MATTERS.**
LMNOPI, Brooklyn, New York,
2014 (Photo by LMNOPI)
The #BlackLivesMatter social media
campaign was born in response to
the systematic dehumanization of
and state violence against black
lives. Created by Alicia Garza,
Patrisse Cullors-Brignac, and Opal
Tometi, it was launched in 2013 as
an online platform, designed to
connect people through dialogue,
collective action, and protest
against racism. LMNOPI's art is
dedicated to Myles McKever "with
the hope that he and other kids
of his generation will grow up in a
world where they will be free from
fear of being targeted, harassed
& brutalized by the police and
vigilantes because of the color of
their skin." #BlackLivesMatter aims
to keep the racial justice dialogue
alive, strengthening the black
liberation movement in an effort to
bring about fundamental change.

TRANSGENDER PEOPLE, WOMEN, AND PRISON

The criminalization of queer people—especially transgender people—epitomizes how incarceration is a tool of social control and conformity.

Trans people are routinely targeted by police. The Silvia Rivera Law Project, a legal advocate for transgender people, has reported: "As a group, transgender and gender non-conforming people are disproportionately poor, homeless, criminalized, and imprisoned. Discrimination against transgender people in housing, employment, healthcare, education, public benefits, and social services is pervasive, pushing transgender people to the margins of the formal economy. With few other options, many low-income and poor transgender people engage in criminalized means of making a living, such as sex work. Transgender people also encounter pervasive violence and physical brutality at the hands of family members, community members, and police because of entrenched social stigma and prejudice."[15]

Che Gossett (see Chapter 1), an activist who organizes around prison and LGBTQ issues and who self-identifies as a "black trans/gender queer femme," says, "There's a lot of ways in which criminalization and the prison system have always been a site of queer struggle and trans struggle."

Gossett talks about the ways that many LGBTQ people face an inexorable slide into the prison system. "As a young queer person growing up, I knew so many people who were kicked out of their homes as high school students. When you get kicked out of your home or you're living on the streets, you're more subject to criminalization and policing." Homelessness has been increasingly criminalized, so people must find a shelter to go to.

Gossett adds that transgender people also face the criminalization of "walking while trans." Police often assume they are sex workers. When Gossett lived in Washington, D.C., "the police in D.C. set up what are called 'prostitution-free zones' in gentrifying areas. That meant that trans women of color and/or poor women who were walking in these areas would get harassed by the cops. It's the same logic as the drug-free zones, which is, you see a group of brown and black men in a drug free zone, they get targeted too."

Gossett says that linking issues is vital to advance justice on a broad front. "I'm really inspired by voices or organizations really centering . . . queer issues on prison justice issues."

Moving toward decarceration—reducing or eliminating imprisonment—requires that we normalize transgender identities. As transgender actress Laverne Cox, perhaps best known for her role on *Orange Is the New Black*, said on *Democracy Now!*, "I think the bigger picture is, how do we begin to create spaces in our culture where we don't stigmatize trans identity, where we really create spaces of gender self-determination? It is so often acceptable to make fun of trans people, to ridicule trans people . . . Look at the epidemic of violence against trans folk. . . . But how do we begin to create spaces where we accept trans people on our own terms, and really listen and let trans people lead the discussions in terms of who we are and what the discussion about our lives should be?"[16]

WOMEN FIGHTING BACK

Walidah Imarisha is one of many women who are actively working to end mass incarceration. When she was organizing in Philadelphia with the Human Rights Coalition, the membership was predominantly former prisoners and their families: "The vast majority of our leadership were . . . working-class mothers whose children had gone to prison. Some of them were raising their grandchildren. These are the folks who are bearing the brunt at home of the prison system." Like many transformative movements, the passionate leadership comes from those most impacted. She continues, "When one out of three young black men have disappeared [into prison] and an ever-growing number of young black women and young black trans folks, who takes care of the children? Who is filling that hole in the community?"

Imarisha tells another movement truth: "It's really important that we recognize that prisons disproportionately affect many more people than just who is sitting in a prison cell." And those most affected are building a powerful movement that is redefining the problems of our society and helping us imagine a transformed future.

> *"There's a lot of ways in which criminalization and the prison system have always been a site of queer struggle and trans struggle."*

RISE OF THE DANDELIONS

■ **DANDELIONS RISING! Drawing by Gonji Lee of Freedom Harvest and graphic by Andrés "RHIPS" Rivera from Street Inc Media, Los Angeles, 2013** The dandelion is a wildflower known for its medicinal properties and high resiliency. The Coalition to End Sheriff Violence in L.A. Jails hosts the artists' coalition Freedom Harvest: Rise of the Dandelions. They use the flower as a symbol for their movement of organizers, activists, and artists working to transform the ways in which state violence destroys communities of color. In their own words, "The dandelion, like our people, can operate as a tool for healing. We see the seeds of the dandelion spreading and pollinating the messages of abolition."

I DON'T WATCH MY NEIGHBORS.
I SEE THEM.
WE MAKE OUR COMMUNITY SAFER TOGETHER.

Art by Micah Bazant

Justice for Families
Night Out for Safety and Democracy

 **WE MAKE OUR COMMUNITIES SAFER TOGETHER. Micah Bazant, San Francisco, 2013**
This poster was commissioned by the organization Justice for Families to promote Night Out for Safety and Democracy. This community action was a response to National Night Out, sponsored by police and neighborhood watch organizations. The poster and campaign are intended to humanize communities of color and counter the us-vs.-them mentality of the neighborhood watch movement. It counters mass-media images that promote the view of poor and working-class communities of color as criminal.

AN ABOLITION MOVEMENT GAINS GROUND

Rashad Robinson, executive director of ColorofChange .org, says, "As a campaign organization, we've been thinking a lot about what are the points of intervention that could be systemic in terms of decreasing the power of the entities that are making money off of [incarceration]—through shame, through organizing, through all the things that we're successful at."

Robinson has a model: GLAAD (formerly the Gay and Lesbian Alliance Against Defamation), which focuses on changing the image of LGBTQ people in popular culture. Before moving to ColorofChange.org, Robinson worked at GLAAD as the senior director of media programs. "So much of what happens in public policy follows culture," he explains. "In terms of social movements and social change, winning people's hearts and minds is critical."

ColorofChange.org is using GLAAD's model of pressuring Hollywood to change the negative depiction of people of color in popular media, especially in the wildly popular police and courtroom TV shows. In 2013, ColorofChange.org succeeded in getting Fox Broadcasting to stop airing *Cops*, a reality TV show that had run for twenty-five years. "Black people will no longer tolerate dangerous and dehumanizing stereotypes," Robinson declares.

Robinson observes that reality often mimics fiction. "The perception—the way in which black men and boys in particular, and Latino men and boys, are viewed—impacts public policy decisions around prisons. Around how people can and should be treated, and who's of value. It impacts policing in our country."

Stressing what has worked in other movement victories, Robinson adds, "Being able to have a north star—something to fight for, not just against—is critical to building a movement. Having an aspirational undercurrent is incredibly important."

If a movement knows where it is going, no matter how far it may be thrown off course, as long as it has a north star, it is never lost. The north star of this movement is a bold transformative vision: abolishing all the causes of imprisonment, from racial profiling to underfunded schools, state-sponsored violence, and the very underpinnings of white supremacy that undergird our immigration, education, and economic policies.

There are now signs of progress on many fronts in the movement to end mass incarceration:

Closing the school-to-prison pipeline. After mounting protests over skyrocketing rates of out-of-school suspensions and criminalization of school infractions, the Obama administration released new guidelines in January 2014 to end the use of harsh punishment in schools. U.S. attorney general Eric Holder declared, "A routine school disciplinary infraction should land a student in the principal's office, not in a police precinct." The National Opportunity to Learn Campaign declared this effort a "huge win for students." (See more on education in Chapter 2.)

Community-based alternatives to policing and prison. In response to soaring incarceration rates and costs, a national effort is growing to provide alternatives. Some models of community-based alternatives include Safe OUTside the System (alp.org/community /sos), a New York City–based anti-violence program led by and for LGBTQ people of color that "organizes and educates local businesses and community organizations on how to stop violence without relying on law enforcement," and Creative Interventions (www .creative-interventions.org), which offers a practical community guide to stopping interpersonal violence. In addition, intensive community-based programs are now serving four youths for the same cost as incarcerating one. For example, alternative programs in Alabama reduced the number of youths in state custody by half from 2006 to 2013, and 90 percent of graduates of a program in Massachusetts had no new arrests.[17]

California prison hunger strike. In California, some thousands of prisoners are in long-term solitary confinement, locked in their cells for about twenty-two hours per day. In July 2013 thirty thousand California prisoners began a sixty day hunger strike to protest this practice. This was the biggest hunger strike in the state's history. The prisoners succeeded in getting state lawmakers to hold public hearings on conditions in solitary and to consider legislation to sharply limit the use of isolation. "There's still much to be done," the hunger strikers said in a statement. "Our resistance will continue to build and grow until we have won our human rights."[18] Two years later, they won an end to "indeterminate solitary confinement" and a dramatic reduction of people in isolation.

Marijuana legalization. The war on drugs has been a major factor escalating mass incarceration of people of color. The movement to legalize marijuana is one of the most successful efforts to end the drug war. As of early 2015, medical marijuana was legal in some two dozen states. The District of Columbia and four states—Oregon,

Washington, Alaska, and Colorado—had legalized recreational use of marijuana. Many formerly incarcerated people, such as Rob Kampia, executive director and co-founder of the Marijuana Policy Project, are leaders in this movement.

However, as Michelle Alexander observes, even the positive changes underscore the pervasiveness of racism:

This movement to end mass incarceration and the war on drugs is about breaking the habit of forming caste-like systems and creating a new ethic of care and concern for each of us, this idea that each of us has basic human rights. That is the ultimate goal of this movement. The real issue that lies at the core of every caste system ever created is the devaluing of human beings. . . . I'm thrilled that Colorado and Washington have legalized marijuana and DC has decriminalized it—these are critically important steps in shifting from a purely punitive approach. But there are warning flags. I flick on the news, and I see images of people using marijuana and trying to run legitimate businesses, and they're almost all white. When we thought of them as black or brown, we had a purely punitive approach. Also, it seems like its exclusively white men being interviewed as wanting to start marijuana businesses and make a lot of money selling marijuana.

I have to say the image doesn't sit right. Here are white men poised to run big marijuana businesses after 40 years of impoverished black kids getting prison time for doing the same thing. As we talk about legalization, we have to also be willing to talk about reparations for the war on drugs, as in how do we repair the harm caused. . . . We suddenly have a positive attitude about marijuana when the images of users are white. But we had a punitive approach when we thought about users as black and brown."[19]

Ending mandatory sentences. Citizens have taken the initiative to end mandatory sentencing. For example, in 2012, California voters scaled back the state's draconian "three strikes and you're out" law, which was sending some third-time offenders to prison for life because of relatively minor offenses.

Sentence reduction. In 2014, the U.S. Sentencing Commission unanimously voted to retroactively reduce sentences for 46,000 people serving time for federal drug offenses. Also in 2014, Californians voted to reclassify a half

dozen low-level property and drug offenses from felonies to misdemeanors, making ten thousand prisoners eligible for resentencing.

Challenging police brutality: A wave of protest swept the United States in 2014 and 2015 following police killings of unarmed black males, from the shooting of Michael Brown in Ferguson, Missouri, and the shooting of twelve-year-old Tamir Rice in Cleveland to the choking death by police of Eric Garner in New York. "I can't breathe," "Hands up, don't shoot," "This stops here," and "Black lives matter" became the rallying cries of the grassroots movement to demand change. Scenes of local police using military-style weapons against protesters sparked a backlash and calls to end the provision of military hardware to civilian police forces (more than $4 billion in military hardware has flowed from the Pentagon to local police since 2006).[20]

Alexander says that the movement to end mass incarceration must give voice to those who have been silenced. She says she is "especially encouraged by formerly incarcerated people who are finding their voice and organizing to man the restoration of their basic civil and human rights" in organizations such as All of Us or None and Just Leadership USA.[21]

Indeed, the movement to end mass incarceration—and even end prison itself—has generated new groups and promising alliances (a larger listing of groups working on prison justice can be found at our website and at www.newjimcrow.com).

Michelle Alexander concludes:

Our vision is for a grassroots, bottom-up human rights movement that is committed to ending mass incarceration entirely. This means more than a reduction in the rates of incarceration. It means a fundamental shift from a punitive model to a healing and transformative model of justice. . . .

Our movement carries with it a vision of a society in which we value education over incarceration, jobs over jail, and a society that finds better uses for 1 trillion dollars than waging a drug war on its poorest and most vulnerable members. Our movement is one in which the voices of those who have been locked up, locked out and left behind can be heard loud and clear. We are committed to boldly employing nonviolent strategies for large-scale change, inspiring others through deeds, not words.[22]

DUMP THE PRISON STOCK!
INVEST IN HUMANITY!

PRISON INDUSTRY DIVESTMENT CAMPAIGN

ABOLISH PRISONS. FREE ALL IMMIGRANTS IN DETENTION.
NO MORE DEPORTATIONS. STOP THE RAIDS. LEGALIZATION NOW!

FOR MORE INFO: ENLACEINTL.ORG. INFO@ENLACEINTL.ORG. 213-284-3802   DESIGN: MELANIE CERVANTES | DIGNIDADREBELDE.COM

■ **DUMP THE PRISON STOCK!**
Melanie Cervantes
of Dignidad Rebelde,
Oakland, California, 2012
Wall Street counts on "prison stock" as a solid investment, while prisons and jails "rent" or "lease out" prisoners as cheap labor. Melanie Cervantes created this poster for Enlace, a coalition of low-wage-worker centers, unions, and community organizations in Mexico and the United States. The poster is part of a divestment campaign aimed at the two largest private U.S. prison companies, Corrections Corporation of America (CCA) and GEO Group, which have both received billions of taxpayer dollars. *Dump the Prison Stock!* depicts the racist and capitalist nature of anti-immigration and incarceration policies and the corporations and institutions that support it.

KEVIN "RASHID" **JOHNSON**

PRISONER, JOURNALIST, ORGANIZER, ARTIST, AND THE MINISTER OF DEFENSE OF THE NEW AFRIKAN BLACK PANTHER PARTY–PRISON CHAPTER. KEVIN "RASHID" BECAME POLITICIZED WHILE INCARCERAT-ED. HE CONTINUES TO WRITE AND ORGA-NIZE ABOUT CONDITIONS IN PRISON.

I am a prisoner who became politicized while incarcerated. My original state of confinement was Virginia; however, I am presently being held in Texas for Virginia.

In my political work I've produced a substantial amount of art and writing on a range of subjects, all related to struggles for social justice and empowerment and the ongoing fight against this predatory world-dominant system of capitalist imperialism.

One field of focus for me has been reporting on the barbaric conditions prevalent in U.S. prisons, which I often contrast with U.S. officials' constant self-righteous and hypocritical condemnations of human rights violations elsewhere, especially when it's in countries that they dislike, while conditions here and in U.S. prisons in particular are as bad and often much worse.

Through organizations like Prison Radio, the Real Cost of Prisons, and other outlets, including my own website (rashidmod.com), these writings and related art found a broad and attentive audience and many of those who have become actively involved are speaking out in protest against these conditions. I often receive letters of support and encouragement for shining a much-needed light into these dark places.

Of course, the response from prison officials has been quite different—the exact opposite, actually. The reaction typically is retaliation, and discouraging and frustrating this work. Since prison officials top the list of power holders conditioned to absolute impunity, prisons function by design to not just keep captives but also to keep the public out. This plays largely into the openly fascist conditions inside them that are the established norms. So I recognized, as do officials, that our real strength and support lies in public awareness and involvement.

What do you think is the role of art and cultural work in twenty-first-century political movements?

The role of culture and its mediums of transmission—art, literature, et cetera—is a huge one. It is a major front in movement work that I feel is underestimated and underused by many people. In fact, I feel most don't grasp its role.

It is through cultural forms that the establishment trains everyone's values, views, and aspiration from cradle to grave, from toys and video games [and] art to music and theater, from schools to the so-called information media. These are all the sources and forms of transmitting cultural values—they are the means of cultural influence and expression. And it is not by accident that the wealthy ruling class controls the outlets that produce them.

To counter this we must take control of similar mediums and promote through them a mass culture that emphasizes and cultivates the values of unity, diversity, tolerance, community, love, cooperation, mutual support, environmental sustainability, harmony, and protection, and all those many other "people not property"–based values and practices that will break the mental bonds of oppressive programming. We must cast the masses in the role of the real heroes and counter our conditioned awe and emulations of the wealthy and establishment power.

This is what culture has the power to do. It's why Joseph Goebbels, the head of the German Nazi propaganda system, often repeated the words of Hanns Johst, the first official Nazi playwright: "When I hear the word 'culture,' I release the safety catch on my gun.'"

I try to educate using both words and art to reach both irrational and emotional levels of the mind. This allows a dialectical balance of consciousness-raising, reaching many people despite the limitations of my physical conditions and availability of materials. In fact, my art has been copied, circulated, and seen on a vastly larger scale than my writings.

Art makes knowledge accessible across boundaries of status, race, gender, location, and nationality, and properly used can bridge the separations.

Success will come with the overthrow and end of all forms of oppression and exploitation of people by other people. That will come from true mass awakening and mobilization on all fronts, in which culture plays a major role.

DARE TO STRUGGLE, DARE TO WIN! ALL POWER TO THE PEOPLE!

Art by Kevin "Rashid" Johnson in support of California Prison Strikers, Red Onion Prison, Virginia, 2011

4

THE POWER OF STORIES: THE DREAMERS AND IMMIGRANT RIGHTS

■ **UNDOCUBUS No Papers, No Fear: Ride for Justice, Phoenix, Arizona, 2012 (Photographer unknown)**
Deportation programs, controversial laws, Immigration and Customs Enforcement (ICE) harassment, silent raids, and detentions define the recent undocumented immigrant experience. On July 29, 2012, the UndocuBus, of the No Papers, No Fear campaign, embarked on a journey from Phoenix, Arizona, to Charlotte, North Carolina, site of the Democratic National Convention. The two-month bus tour confronted power and raised awareness about anti-immigration policies. The riders were "undocumented and unafraid" people from all over the country, including people going through deportation proceedings.

■ **UNTITLED. No Papers, No Fear: Ride for Justice, Charlotte, North Carolina, 2012. Banner designed by César Maxit (Photo by Kris Krug, via Creative Commons)**
UndocuBus riders took over a street in Charlotte, outside the arena where the Democratic National Convention was being held, to pressure President Obama to stop deportations of all undocumented immigrants. The civil disobedience action resulted in the arrest of the protesters, some of whom faced deportation. Here, activists recognize that being present in the political system often means overcoming fear and putting their own bodies on the line. They demand dignity in the campaign spearheaded by No Papers, No Fear to confront the systemic violence they experience daily as immigrants without papers.

A powerful illustration of the key organizing strate-gy of storytelling is the DREAMers, the young un-documented immigrants who have grown up in the United States and want to attend college, drive, work, and thrive in the United States. Their courageous actions are reclaiming a language of humanity that is reshaping public conscience and sparking change in our nation's policies. Through telling our stories, we learn about our-selves and a contagious "we" is created; the storytellers transform themselves and give courage to others to take action. Through stories we teach each other how to orga-nize for change.

There is much to change in the unconscionable way immigrants are treated in this land—where all but the na-tive peoples are immigrants—and with their stories, the DREAMers are leading the way.

Illegal—that's how more than eleven million people who live, work, and attend school in the United States have been branded.

Deported—that's the fate of more than two million people under the Obama administration, which hunted down, imprisoned, and deported as many undocument-ed citizens in its first five years as were deported from the United States in the entire twentieth century.

Denied—that's what happens to the three million children of undocumented immigrants in the United States when they attempt to attend college. Barred from financial aid or in-state tuition at public universities, a generation of immigrants has had its dreams deferred.

In the years since 9/11, the United States, a nation of immigrants, has targeted this generation of immi-grants—especially people of color—who work and live within its borders and who enrich our culture. Unlike the European immigrants who were fortunate enough to get visas and were welcomed at Ellis Island in New York and elsewhere following World War II, the discourse about immigration today too often is dominated by demands for higher fences, longer jail terms, and harsher penalties for the people called "illegal."

The DREAM (Development, Relief, and Education for Alien Minors) Act has been a beacon of hope for undocu-mented immigrants. First proposed in 2001 as a pathway to citizenship for undocumented youth who had attended high school and lived in the United States for five years, the bill has died multiple deaths in Congress in the years since it was introduced and reintroduced. But the DREAM-ers fought on.

In 2010, four immigrant college students in Florida—each of whom had experienced the despair and fear of be-ing undocumented—undertook a simple, bold, and cre-ative act. It was an act that built upon years of organizing by other immigrants around the country and was deeply rooted in past struggles.

They took a long walk.

On January 1, 2010, Juan Rodriguez, Felipe Matos, Gaby Pacheco, and Carlos Roa, all in their early twenties, set out from their homes in Miami. They declared that they would walk fifteen hundred miles to the White House on a Trail of DREAMs. Their goal, like DREAMers around the country, was to bring undocumented youth out of the shadows, protest their plight as second-class citizens, stop the separation of families and the deportations, and rally support for the DREAM Act.

In Florida, these Trail of DREAMs walkers met fearful migrant workers on farms. In Georgia, they confronted the Ku Klux Klan and dared a racist sheriff to arrest them. In town after town, they were joined by undocument-ed immigrants who "came out" and marched alongside them, revealing the depth and breadth of the immigrant community.

The students marched in T-shirts emblazoned with the slogan "Undocumented and Unafraid," a courageous ral-lying cry of the immigrant rights movement. Everywhere they went, they told their stories, publicly declaring their undocumented status.

At the White House, surrounded by throngs of sup-porters, they challenged President Barack Obama to stop deportations, pushed for passage of the DREAM Act, and gave hope to all the young undocumented people who were hidden in plain sight.

In 2011, Pulitzer Prize–winning journalist Jose Antonio Vargas publicly declared his undocumented status in a cover story for the New York Times Magazine. He cited the Trail of DREAMs walkers: "Their courage has inspired me," he wrote in the Times.[1]

In early June 2012, in the heat of the presidential campaign, undocumented activists occupied President Obama's campaign offices in a dozen cities to demand that he stop deportations and enact the DREAM Act.

The immigration conversation soon abruptly took a leap forward. On June 15, 2012, President Obama announced that authorities would no longer deport certain DREAM Act–eligible undocumented youth. It was an important victory in the larger struggle for immigrant rights. Five months later, Obama won a landslide reelection, winning 71 percent of the Latino vote.

In early 2013, the New York Times pronounced in an editorial that the United States was experiencing an "Immigration Spring"—reminiscent of the Arab Spring pro-democracy movement that had transformed the Middle East in 2011. "It has been amazing this year to watch immigration reform, that perennial train wreck of an issue, keep rolling forward without losing steam or blowing up."[2]

Even the fundamental language of the immigration conversation changed. In April 2013, the Associated Press announced it would no longer use the term "illegal immigrant" in news stories, following a concerted campaign led by Colorlines publisher Rinku Sen and numerous immigrant rights groups to "drop the i-word."

In November 2014, with Congress having failed to enact immigration reform, President Barack Obama announced that he would circumvent Congress and use executive action to protect nearly half of the estimated eleven million undocumented immigrants from deportation and offer them temporary legal status.

Years of organizing by countless individuals and organizations brought the immigrant rights struggle to this turning point. Millions of undocumented immigrants bravely protested in the streets over the past decade. Through this fight, they have declared that there is a limit, an ethos, a social contract. Basta! Enough is enough! Undocumented students attended trainings to tell their sto-

ry and move people to action. Groups such as United We Dream grew from seven chapters in 2008 to sixty chapters four years later. With their bold and risky actions, young DREAMers have harnessed the power of this movement to impel a transformation.

This is the story of one group of DREAMers in this movement fighting to make their dreams a reality. Bravely telling their story, they declare their humanity and enroll others in the fight to win fundamental change.

"THERE IS POWER WITHIN OUR STORY"

Gaby Pacheco has an easy smile that belies a steely resolve. The self-assured young woman strides to the microphone to address an audience during the Trail of DREAMs walk.

"I've been in the United States since I was seven years old in 1993, when I emigrated from Ecuador with my family and settled in Miami, Florida. I consider myself to be an all-American girl. I was part of the ROTC program during high school, and after graduation wanted to enlist in the Air Force. Because of my undocumented status, I could not. But I went to college and now hold a bachelor's degree in special education. There are many others like me."

Pacheco is one of the lucky ones. As a top high school student, she qualified to attend a tuition-free program at Miami Dade College. But she watched as her sister and brother were forced to abandon their dreams of getting a college education because of the simple fact that they were not American citizens and could not get financial aid or in-state tuition at local colleges. Pacheco was thrilled to be in college. But every time she went home to her family, she was reminded that this dream was still beyond reach for many other undocumented immigrants.

Undocumented people often live in silence and fear. Pacheco saw unmarked white vans from U.S. Immigration and Customs Enforcement (ICE) cruising the neighborhood. She heard about how they would pull up at a house and whisk away people in the dead of night. She knew that immigrants enjoyed few of the basic rights that American citizens took for granted. Her neighbors were detained in prisons and lacked access to attorneys. Midnight raids, deportation, parents taken from children—are all daily threats for the undocumented.

Pacheco refused to be silent. "In eighth grade I made a decision that I was going to start telling people my status and my situation because I felt that I was not the only one," she recounts. "And if there were other people like me, maybe someday I'll figure it out how to fix their status. So in high school . . . friends came to tell me that they had a secret. They would say, 'I'm just like you,' or 'I don't have papers either.'"

She continues, "In the work that I've done as an activist, being able to reach that point of liberation and not have this fear of the what-ifs—what if immigration comes to get you?—allowed me at a very young age to . . . set an example to the country and other DREAMers that there is power within our story."

When Pacheco enrolled at Miami Dade College, she made a vow to everyone who had confided their immigration status in her. "I put my hand on [my first college] schedule and I made a promise that I was going to fight so that other people [would] have the same opportunity I had been given to go to college."

PUNISHMENT—AND RESISTANCE

Pounding on the door awakened the Pacheco family at 6:00 a.m. on July 26, 2006. It was the moment that every undocumented immigrant family dreads.

Swarms of heavily armed ICE agents were looking for the young woman who had dared to speak out. They found her family instead. ICE agents marched Pacheco's parents and sisters out of the house, put them into a windowless white van, and took them to the local Department of Homeland Security building.

Her sister called her from the booking center. "Gaby, they want me to tell you that we should thank you for what is happening to us," she said through sobs.

Gaby was hysterical. She remembers, "That was just one of the hardest things I had to hear."

Gaby immediately went to the Department of Homeland Security processing center. "What I negotiated was that I was not going to talk to the media anymore and that I was not going to continue to do what I was doing. And under those conditions he let me go."

The agent announced, "I'm going to let your family go, but they're going to still go through the deportation and immigration process."

The ICE officer got what he was really after: silence. Or so he thought.

"That really was what spurred a different type of fight in me—to fight for my family," Pacheco says. That fight would sow the seeds of the Trail of DREAMs.

Pacheco responded to the threat the way she knew best: she organized. She was the student government president at Miami Dade College and founder of a campus group, Students Working for Equal Rights. When the Pacheco family was supposed to report to the offices of the Department of Homeland Security to receive their final deportation decision in 2008, Gaby determined they would not go alone.

With Students Working for Equal Rights, Gaby organized a march from Miami Dade College to the immigration courthouse. Hundreds of undocumented youth and their allies, all wearing black T-shirts emblazoned with the word "Undocumented," protested in front of the courthouse.

Armed ICE agents stood in front of the building in a show of force. The traditionally quiet undocumented youth were shouting: "We're not afraid! We're undocumented! We're standing together to fight for our people!"

Pacheco stood, chanted, and marveled at the sight around her. The authorities wanted her and her family to go quietly. Instead, they aroused a sleeping giant.

"It was just the most beautiful thing," she says. The protest helped buy time for her family, whose deportation was delayed when the judge didn't show up. Several other Miami Dade College students, including Juan Rodriguez and Felipe Matos, were also at that protest.

"That entire experience of being able to put myself out there and stand in front of ICE agents at the Homeland Security building with my 'Undocumented' shirt . . . really transformed me as a leader," Rodriguez recalls. Like Pacheco, Rodriguez went from being soft-spoken to outspoken, from in the shadows to out of the closet.

Midnight raids, deportation, parents taken from children—are all daily threats for the undocumented.

WHY I RIDE (El porqué yo viajo). Julio Salgado, Berkeley, California, 2012
There are many faces and experiences of immigration. Julio Salgado's poster series exposes the many stories behind the lives of those who risk everything to work in the United States and labor under conditions of exploitation. Julio believes undocumented immigrants should be leading and constructing the narratives of their own struggle. *Why I Ride* exposes the reasons for challenging unfair deportations and aims to build migrant political power.

nopapersnofear.org
sinpapelesysinmiedo.org
#undocubus

ng it for my queer and
umented community."

-Gerardo

EL PORQUÉ
YO VIAJO.

nopapersnofear.org
sinpapelesysinmiedo.org
#undocubus

"Lo hago para promover la autodeterminación de las
comunidades, exponer los abusos en centros de detención
de migrantes y traer justicia para nuestras familias."

-Fernando

DOCUBUS:
NO PAPERS, NO FEAR

WHY
I RIDE.

nopapersnofear.org
sinpapelesysinmiedo.org
#undocubus

"I refuse to keep on limiting myself by the unjust laws that refuse to see
my humanity and recognize that undocumented immigrants are as
much a part of the community as everyone else."

-Ireri

UN DOCUBUS:

nopapersnofear.org
sinpapelesysinmiedo.org
#undocubus

WHY
I RIDE.

nopapersnofear.org
sinpapelesysinmiedo.org
#undocubus

EL PORQUÉ
YO VIAJO.

nopapersnofear.org
sinpapelesysinmiedo.org
#undocubus

e tiene que manejar en la
miedo a que los arresten."

-Miguel

UN DOCUBUS:
NO PAPERS, NO FEAR

"I'm doing it because I am tired
of the separation of families."

-Angel

"Yo lo estoy haciendo por las familias que
tienen miedo de no regresar a su casa."

-Nataly

UN DOCUBUS:
NO PAPERS, NO FEAR

Juan Rodriguez remembers the day when his dreams were shattered.

Rodriguez was valedictorian at the start of his senior year at South Broward High School in Hollywood, Florida. He excelled in math and science and planned to become an aerospace engineer. The son of a farm worker, Rodriguez was the embodiment of the American dream—the notion that if you work hard, you get ahead.

There was just one problem: in the eyes of the government, he wasn't American, so he wasn't entitled to dream here.

Juan Rodriguez's family fled violence-torn Colombia in 1995. Colombia was the third-largest recipient of U.S. military aid in the 1990s (after Israel and Egypt). It was a front line in the U.S. drug war, which forced many Colombians to flee their country and come to the United States. Rodriguez's family would become another statistic in that war.

One day, armed gunmen showed up at the home of Rodriguez's family in Colombia. It was a warning. Within twenty-four hours, twelve members of his family boarded planes and flew to Miami, where they settled. Another U.S.-backed war had blown back to our shores: the members of the Rodriguez family were now undocumented immigrants.

During his senior year of high school, Rodriguez visited his guidance counselor. Her office was adorned with posters for colleges from around the country. People told him he was destined to attend a prestigious university. The guidance counselor welcomed him inside and posed a simple question: "What is your immigration status?"

Rodriguez, who prided himself on his ability to solve tough math problems, was stumped. "I had no idea what any of those documents were," he recalls. "I had never heard of them before."

Rodriguez came home

There was just one problem: in the eyes of the government, he wasn't American, so he wasn't entitled to dream here.

and asked his father for the documents so he could show his guidance counselor and continue planning for college.

"You have to go back and tell them that you don't have any of those things," replied his father, who spent long days picking fruit in Florida.

Rodriguez returned to his guidance counselor and reported what his father told him. The counselor replied bluntly, "If you don't have these documents, then it means that you're an illegal and you're not supposed to be in the country. You're probably never going to be able to go to college because these documents are required. You should think about what you want to do when you become an adult so you can go back to your home country and pursue your education there."

Rodriguez was shattered. His grades fell, and to top it off, his father was arrested for driving without a license—a common problem, since most states will not grant a driver's license to undocumented people. The double whammy of losing his college hopes and seeing his father in jail sent the high school senior into an emotional tailspin.

"Finding out that my father wasn't going to be able to attend my graduation just completely destroyed any desire in me to want to even attend," he recounts, the emotion still evident in his voice. Rodriguez ultimately graduated fifth out of a class of five hundred.

Rodriguez learned that his guidance counselor had been wrong: his strong high school performance qualified him to attend the honors program at Miami Dade College at reduced tuition. He became president of the college's student government and led a campus immigrant rights group. But he was especially moved by his experience in 2008, when he protested at the offices of the Department of Homeland Security to stop the imminent deportation of Gaby Pacheco's family.

"That campaign really radicalized me because it was the first time that our organization ordered 'Undocumented' shirts to be able to conquer the fear that we had been living in."

Rodriguez and Pacheco became close friends after the demonstration. They talked about what it would take to change the immigration system so that they and their families were not in constant danger of being arrested and deported. They knew about the tactics

THE GREAT MIGRATION

Why Do Immigrants Leave Home to Settle in the United States?

Gaby Pacheco's parents moved their family from Ecuador to Miami in search of a safer community and better education.

Many workers come to the United States in search of jobs. U.S.-backed wars combined with more recent corporate-friendly U.S. trade policies have fueled migration, particularly in Central and South America. The 1994 North American Free Trade Agreement (NAFTA) and 2004 Central American Free Trade Agreement have resulted in deepening poverty and widespread job loss in Central and South America.

Jose "Chencho" Alas was a former Salvadoran priest who worked for the poor in El Salvador alongside Archbishop Óscar Romero, the Catholic leader who was murdered in 1980 for siding with the poor peasants and denouncing human rights abuses by the Salvadoran government, which was aligned with the fourteen wealthiest Salvadoran families and the U.S. government. Alas said that "free trade" would do more harm to Central America than all the years of U.S. wars there. His warning has proved prophetic.

Take the case of Mexico, where the extreme rural poverty rate was 35 percent before NAFTA but soared to 55 percent in 1996–98, following NAFTA's implementation.[3] NAFTA removed many of the tariffs and import restrictions that protected small farmers in Mexico, allowing large U.S.-based multinational companies, which receive government subsidies, unfettered access to Mexican markets. (See Paulina Helm-Hernández's story in Chapter 1). One result: Mexico went from importing 30,000 tons of pork in 1995 to importing 811,000 tons of pork in 2010, causing a loss of some 120,000 Mexican jobs in that one sector alone.[4] Many of those pig farmers went from supporting themselves and their families in Mexico to being undocumented workers in pork factories in North Carolina.[5]

For immigrants fleeing poverty and starvation, there is almost no alternative. "The globalization of capital . . . has produced its corollary—the globalization of labor," Journalist Juan González writes. "The wealth gap between the developed countries and the Third World has . . . fueled unprecedented mass emigration to the United States and Western Europe, as displaced peasants and impoverished workers seek a share of the torrent of profits flowing to the rich nations. . . . The result has been a dramatic ethnic and racial transformation of the working classes of Europe and the United States."[6]

From One War Zone to Another

How are immigrants received once they arrive in the United States?

Many immigrants from El Salvador, Honduras, Haiti, and Colombia fled U.S.-backed wars at home. Others fled U.S.-imposed economic warfare, only to arrive at the U.S.–Mexico border, another war zone. Heavily armed

THE GREAT MIGRATION (continued)

Border Patrol agents, emboldened with new powers since 9/11, prowl the air and ground in southern Arizona, Texas, and California. The U.S. Border Patrol has more than doubled in size in a decade, from 10,000 agents in 2002 to over 21,000 today.

In addition, numerous policies were implemented in 2006 that target undocumented immigrants and their employers. Among the most notorious programs is the Secure Communities Act. This law authorized local police to enforce immigration laws—previously the domain of federal immigration and customs agents—enabling them to arrest people on the pretext of rounding up "criminal aliens." By 2014, Secure Communities had resulted in 250,000 arrests, but "the program's effect on crime has been zero," reported the *New York Times*.[7] On November 20, 2014, after much pressure, President Obama announced that he was ending the Secure Communities program.

In 2013–14, nearly seventy thousand unaccompanied children, many sent by parents who were desperate to have their kids escape violence and joblessness, crossed the southern border, only to be summarily deported once they were apprehended.

The crusade against undocumented residents peaked under President Barack Obama; deportations reached a record 1.5 million people in his first term alone, averaging more than one thousand deportations per day.[8]

The vast majority of people detained on immigration charges are not criminals, but they are subjected to treatment normally reserved for mass murderers. On any given day, some three hundred immigrants are held in solitary confinement in bathroom-sized windowless cells. The *Times* editorialized that this treatment was "wildly inappropriate" and that immigrants are held in "a ramshackle network of private and public lockups, prone to abuses and lacking legally enforceable standards for how detainees are treated."[9]

A driving force behind the immigration detention business is private companies who profit from it. In 2012, the U.S. government spent more than $1.7 billion on detaining immigrants. About half of immigrants being detained in the United States in 2009 were held in facilities owned by private companies, according to Detention Watch Network.[10] Those companies, such the Corrections Corporation of America and the GEO Group (see more about these companies and the role of the for-profit prison industry in perpetuating mass incarceration in Chapter 3), spend lavishly to keep their prisons full: from 1999 to 2009, the private prison industry spent over $20 million to lobby Congress. Prison industry lobbyists have even drafted model anti-immigrant state legislation that, with the help of the American Legislative Exchange Council, which is funded by corporations and the billionaire Koch brothers, has been introduced in Arizona and around the country.[11]

"For years, private prison firms have played a critical role in shaping public policy around immigration detention, pursuing the bottom line at the expense of basic civil rights and taxpayer dollars," says Emily Tucker, Detention Watch Network's director of policy and advocacy.[12]

STOP JUAN CROW NOW!
LEGALIZED HATE OUT OF MY STATE!

SB 1070: WE WILL NOT COMPLY

■ STOP JUAN CROW. **Favianna Rodríguez, Oakland, California, 2012** Arizona's anti-immigrant bill, SB 1070, signed into law in April 2010, legalized racial profiling in the state. In *Stop Juan Crow*, artist Favianna Rodriguez draws a link between the Jim Crow laws that enforced racial segregation of African Americans after the Civil War (that ended with the civil rights movement) to the racism faced by Latinos today. The international migrant rights campaign We Will Not Comply opposes the oppressive legislation and demands full human rights for all people living in the state.

used by civil rights activists in the 1960s to bring change. How could they connect their struggle with past efforts?

Marshall Ganz was among those who helped DREAMers make the connection. In the 1960s, Ganz was an organizer with Cesar Chavez, the legendary civil rights leader and co-founder of the United Farm Workers, the pioneering Latino-led labor union that has fought for rights for migrant workers and others. In recent years, Ganz has been teaching at Harvard's Kennedy School of Government and advised the 2008 Obama campaign on grassroots organizing strategy. In 2009, Pacheco, Rodriguez, and Felipe Matos attended trainings run by Ganz, Joy Cushman of the New Organizing Institute, and the Center for Community Change, groups that train progressive movement organizers.

Ganz advised the activists that their story could be their most potent tool for social change: "Put telling your story as a central piece of the organizing process." He taught them the critical parts of storytelling: how to transform their personal story into a call to action, moving from "me" to "we" to "now."

"I remember particularly describing how [Chavez and the farm workers] thought up our 1966 march from Delano to Sacramento," Ganz says. The idea of a march, with roots in the farm workers' struggle, resonated with the immigrant youth.

The Center for Community Change trainings helped mobilize networks that were just forming. In December 2008, immigrant student groups from around the country—including the Student Immigrant Movement of Massachusetts, the California DREAM Network, the New York State Youth Leadership Council, and the University Leadership Initiative in Austin, Texas—joined forces to form United We Dream, a national group focused on enabling immigrant youth to pursue higher education.

In October 2009, Juan Rodriguez attended a national leadership conference in New York with DREAMers and other immigrant rights activists. "We started talking about how much hopelessness there was amongst the youth in our movement, because the DREAM Act had been

"Put telling your story as a central piece of the organizing process."

introduced in 2001 and there we were eight years later without a law passed through Congress.

"Depression is a very serious issue in the immigrant youth movement," Rodriguez told the others. "In 2009, there were several cases of [undocumented] students across the country who took their lives just out of their sense of hopelessness. What can we do to keep the youth alive?

"One of the people there started talking about the Underground Railroad . . . [which] gave so much hope to people who were oppressed in the South. [Black people during slavery were] benefiting from the support of a network of allies across the country who guided them along the way to freedom."

"Where is our Underground Railroad in the immigrant rights movement?" asked one of the students.

One of the activists proposed an immigrant journey to freedom, a relay walk across America that would end in Washington, D.C., to call attention to the plight of the undocumented. "Yes, we could totally do this if we really set our minds to it—in about three years," declared another.

Rodriguez left the conference in despair. When he arrived home in Florida, he was greeted with the news that one of the undocumented youths he worked with had just attempted suicide.

"I went straight to the hospital and spent the entire night holding his hand as his stomach was being pumped. It hit me in that moment . . . [that] if change was ever going to happen we needed to just do it, and believe in our communities and believe that enough people in this country care about justice and equality to make it a success regardless of whether or not we have staff or funding or grants or marketing strategies for it."

Rodriguez returned to the home he shared with his boyfriend, Felipe Matos. "I'm putting on my shoes and I'm going to start walking," he told Matos, who tried to talk him out of it.

"Do you have any idea what you're saying? We're talking about a fifteen-hundred-mile walk to D.C. No normal human being ever does that. How do you know you'll even survive?"

"I don't care if I survive or not," shot back Rodriguez. "Our people are disappearing. How many more until we've had enough? If there's any sacrifice I can make to keep from losing any more people, I'll do it."

Matos urged Rodriguez to wait and enlist others in his effort. He counseled his partner to harness his rage and despair into a political act—to make it a movement. Matos proposed that they embark on this political pilgrimage on January 1, 2010. "We can start the new decade on our own terms," Matos proposed.

The two men raised the idea with their fellow student immigration activists at Miami Dade College. Carlos Roa and Gaby Pacheco "immediately jumped up and said, 'Yes, I'll walk with you to D.C.,'" Rodriguez recounts. "They didn't even question it."

BLAZING A TRAIL OF DREAMS

For four months, Juan Rodriguez, Gaby Pacheco, Felipe Matos, and Carlos Roa walked. Sometimes they walked alone. Mostly they drew small crowds, including many undocumented immigrants who openly joined the four students, reveling in "coming out," if only briefly. They were hosted along the way by churches and supporters. They chronicled their pilgrimage through daily updates on blogs, Twitter, and other social media.

As the Trail of DREAMs participants walked day after day through conservative and sometimes hostile country, they wore their T-shirts declaring they were "undocumented and unafraid."

"It was an act of civil disobedience," says Pacheco. "That's what we saw that happened with the lunch counter sit-ins [in the 1960s]. That's what Rosa Parks did. We're not going to hide anymore. We're not going to be in the shadows. We're going to share who we really are."

In the tiny farming community of Mayo, Florida, they met farm workers who lived in daily fear of being arrested. The Trail of DREAMs walkers decided to confront this. "We learned that in [Mayo] and the neighboring community, [immigrants] are so afraid of the police that there [were] crimes happening and nobody would do anything about it," says Pacheco.

The four DREAMers responded to local needs by organizing an impromptu workers' rights workshop in the community. "We learned that there were all these workers' rights violations and people just [felt] like

that was the norm until we stopped in that town to do another rights workshop," says Pacheco.

They also met with the sheriff and the police chief. "What are you doing?" the four DREAMers demanded of the police officials— ignoring the fact that they could be arrested at any moment. "You're hurting your community as a whole because these people fear you so much that [they] are not reporting the crimes that are happening."

"We decided that the act of walking itself wasn't the most important thing, but rather really connecting with the community that we were walking through and trying to empower them," says Pacheco.

In Nahunta, Georgia, the Trail of DREAMs walkers encountered a rally of about fifty Ku Klux Klan members. The hooded white men were protesting the "Latino invasion" and called for undocumented immigrants to be sent "back" to Mexico—despite the fact that none of the DREAMers on the walk were Mexican.

The NAACP organized a counterdemonstration attended by the four Trail of DREAMs walkers and other allies. The Klan encounter forged an important alliance. As Juan Rodriguez reflected on the Trail of DREAMs blog, "Ultimately, the success of today was to be able to stand hand in hand with our friends from the NAACP singing liberation songs together and acknowledging our united struggle for racial justice. We ALL deserve to be treated with dignity and respect. We all deserve to be acknowledged for our humanity."

The Trail of DREAMs linked its struggle to the larger historical movement for justice. "We were following in the footsteps of leaders of the past who had set foundations for this type of work for equality," explains Rodriguez. Stopping at symbolic civil rights locations in the South, he says, they "would talk about how the work for equality is still not over, and we need our communities to stand together in order to pass better laws that don't alienate members of the community just because of their race or ethnicity or language or anything."

> *"We're not going to hide anymore. We're not going to be in the shadows. We're going to share who we really are."*

■ NO HUMAN BEING IS ILLEGAL Y CADA UNO TIENE UN SUEÑO. Pancho Pescador, in collaboration with 67 Sueños and the Community Rejuvenation Project, San Francisco, 2011 (Photo by Pancho Pescador)

67 Sueños project organizer Pablo Paredes led a group of young migrants to clean an empty lot and paint their stories under the guidance of Oakland-based artist Pancho Pescador. Declaring that "no human being is illegal," they demand an end to the labeling of immigrants without documents as "illegal." The mural and the organization raise concerns about the way the DREAM Act and related immigration policy privilege certain people (for example, students), yet exclude the majority (67 percent) of immigrants. The artists painted graves of people who died crossing the border, people suffering from the fear of deportation, and youths, who have historically been left out of the immigration debate.

In Gwinnett County, Georgia, the Trail of DREAMs walkers, still sporting shirts emblazoned "Undocumented," made a surprise visit to Sheriff Butch Conway, who has championed a Georgia law known as 287(g) that permits local police to enforce federal immigration rules. Critics charge that the law sanctions racial profiling and fast-track deportation. Conway declined to meet with the marchers, but the provocative visit, joined by a throng of supporters, garnered widespread media coverage.

All along the way, they told their story. Pacheco reflected on the people they spoke to; in one case, "in two hours, this man went from hating us, wanting to hit us, and blaming us to saying, 'I'm sorry.'" She muses, "We were realizing the power that we had and how we were making a difference. . . . To say, 'You are my brother. You are my sister. You could be in my shoes. Let me tell you my story so that you could really understand me'—our stories are the most powerful tool that we have."

After four months and fifteen hundred miles of walking, the four walkers arrived in Alexandria, Virginia, only a few miles from the nation's capital. "There were two or three blocks full of [immigrant] mothers on both sides of the road," recalls Rodriguez. They had followed the DREAMers' journey. "All of them were crying and checking our legs, our arms, our hands, saying that we were a symbol, a representative of their own kids, of all of the things they ever dreamed of a future for their kids, and all of their hopes were invested in us.

"Of all moments, that was the most overwhelming."

"'You are my brother. You are my sister. You could be in my shoes. Let me tell you my story so that you could really understand me'—our stories are the most powerful tool that we have."

UNDOCUQUEER

A striking feature of the DREAMers has been their embrace of the language of the LGBTQ rights movement. Undocumented youth speak openly of when they "came out" about their immigration status. The choice of words was intentional, says Matos. "When we started using that language . . . that opened up that space to talk about both LGBT issues and immigrant rights issues."

But while the Trail of DREAMs walkers dared undocumented people to come out, they hid the fact that two of their group, Juan Rodriguez and Felipe Matos, were a gay couple. Rodriguez says the group reluctantly decided that "for the sake of our collective safety . . . it would be best if we minimized the risk to the group by Felipe and I not being public about our relationship and not having public displays of affection."

He says that host churches would sometimes request that he and Matos sit separately and "have no contact throughout the course of the event. It would put our entire institution in jeopardy."

The decision still pains the two men. "The Trail was really a pretty horrible experience for both Felipe and me on a personal level because it forced us both back into the closet," says Rodriguez. "Felipe and I definitely needed to have taken more of a bold stand and stand up for ourselves. . . . I just remember us feeling, 'Oh well, we're here fighting for immigrant rights. Let's not make things complicated.' But really, on a personal level, it was affecting us a lot and it hurt us a lot." Juan's acts of bravery continued; in 2012, Juan Rodriguez became Isabel Sousa-Rodriguez. Reflecting on this transition in 2015, Isabel wrote, "Every single day since then has been liberating for me."

In contrast to their initial silence on LGBTQ issues, the group was keenly attuned to the issues of women in their movement. When cameras and reporters appeared at Trail events, Pacheco was often the one to take the microphone. That was intentional.

"We had the understanding that women are never heard," says Matos. "That was our way of honoring her leadership. If you take away women from the movement, the movement will stop to exist," he continues, "because they mobilize, they're leaders, they're respected in their local communities."

NATIONAL RELUCTANCE MEETS GRASSROOTS LOVE

The young DREAMers were impatient with the mainstream immigrant rights groups and wanted to push them to take more dramatic action. The Trail of DREAMs walkers at times felt abandoned or ignored by the more established organizations, which provided little support.

Pacheco recalls that other activists dismissed their

LEARNING FROM OTHER MOVEMENTS

The Trail of DREAMs began in 2010. Like the larger DREAM movement and all successful movements, it has roots in learning from the rich history of freedom walks and immigrant organizing.

"We knew that we were going to use similar tactics that we had seen in the civil rights and farm worker rights movements," explains Gaby Pacheco. "We have seen that it works.

"In March 1965, mostly black and a few white activists marched for five days over fifty-four miles from Selma to Montgomery, defying for a third time violent Alabama state troopers. This third march was led by Revered Martin Luther King Jr. and culminated with 25,000 people descending on the Alabama state capital to demand voting rights and justice for murdered civil rights activists. We learned that there had to be a level of sacrifice and a level of pain that had to be visible for others to realize the inhumane situations that we were going through. Just showing our deep desire by putting our bodies through this physical pain of walking 1,500 miles for four months to D.C., we were going to be able to show that we really just wanted an opportunity, wanted to change the situation that ourselves and our families are in."

On March 17, 1966, Cesar Chavez, then head of the National Farm Workers Association (later co-founder of the United Farm Workers with Dolores Huerta), led a 340-mile march of striking grape pickers from Delano to Sacramento. The march brought the farm workers to national attention and led to the United Farm Workers winning the strike and becoming a force in the movement for economic justice. The United Farm Workers themselves used similar tactics as past movements following, among others, the practices that the leader of the Mexican Revolution, Emiliano Zapata, had used to fight for the rights of native peoples against powerful landowners.

Juan Rodriguez notes that they were also inspired by Otpor! ("resistance" in Serbian), the nonviolent youth movement that helped bring down Yugoslavian dictator Slobodan Milošević in 2000. Otpor! was famous for its creative use of public theater in street demonstrations, boycotts, and occupations. In 2009, Otpor! trainers ran a workshop in nonviolent resistance for DREAMers.

The four Florida activists also built upon the efforts of a broad immigrant rights movement that had laid the foundation for the conversation that they urgently hoped to expand. In 2006, millions of immigrants and their allies took to the streets in more than a hundred U.S. cities to demand a change in immigration policy. In Chicago, 300,000 people marched. A half million marched in Los Angeles and Dallas. On May 1, 2006, millions took part in the Great American Boycott, a one-day walkout from schools and businesses to demonstrate the importance of immigrants throughout the United States and in the economy. This general strike was a show of force by immigrants, who were opposing a wave of anti-immigrant laws that were pending in Congress. Churches, labor unions, and progressive organizations joined forces through Spanish-language radio and TV and through social networks of young Latinos using the Internet. The 2006 immigration protests were a watershed moment in the immigrant rights movement.

effort, some "calling it a suicide mission." Fellow DREAMers doubted the four walkers. United We Dream organizer Carlos Saavedra recalls, "I was like, why are they doing this? Why would you walk? I was just thinking [of lobbying] Congress members." He concedes now, "I was in the wrong fight."

Others have echoed Saavedra. Many of the Washington, D.C.–based immigrant rights organizations thought they had a friend in the White House with Obama and were trying to play the inside power game. They now readily admit they were wrong. It was through direct action, dramatizing the human stories, that the movement got anywhere.

What gave Pacheco and her three friends the strength to go ahead with their effort in the face of opposition?

"I learned from the suffrage movement," Pacheco replies. "Women didn't have the support [and] were killed and put in jail for fighting for their rights. For us the spirit of our ancestors and the people that had fought for us in the past just gave us that push and the fire to continue."

She pauses, then adds, "We have done everything we could and our friends were getting deported, our families were getting detained. . . . We didn't have any more to lose."

For Pacheco, there was one more all-important inspiration to take the first step on her 1,500-mile journey: "At the center of all this was this love that we have for families, for ourselves, but also for this country."

NEVER BACKING DOWN

In June 2010, six weeks after the Trail of DREAMs ended with a rally outside the White House, Juan Rodriguez received a surprise invitation to a meeting inside the White House.

There was a catch: Rodriguez was the only Trail of DREAMs participant who was invited to this meeting with a small group of national advocates. He was told that he could meet the president because he had recently received permanent resident status. The others were undocumented and thus could not attend.

Rodriguez's instinct was to refuse to participate, but his three comrades insisted that he had to meet the president to "represent all of the people who were excluded from the meeting and the families who were separated under Obama's deportation policies and the quotas." Rodriguez, acutely sensitive to the symbolism, saw the chance to bring his protest right into the White House.

On the day of the meeting, Rodriguez and other advocates were ushered into the ornate Roosevelt Room of the White House. President Obama entered and shook each person's hand in friendly greeting. The president extended his hand to Rodriguez.

"I'm sorry, I can't shake your hand," said Rodriguez, standing stiffly. He tried expressing to the president that his presence and demonstration of disappointment represented the families who had been separated by the deportations. But before he could speak, a flash of anger crossed Obama's face. He directed everyone to sit down.

Rodriguez recalls, "It shifted the entire tone of the meeting from [being] a friendly gathering between Obama and his friends who care about immigrants to an accountability session on the president around the policies that he kept supporting, as well as the lack of leadership on . . . immigration reform."

Confrontation and direct action had gotten the DREAMers the attention of the White House. Juan Rodriguez was not going to abandon that approach now.

Obama opened the meeting and was visibly annoyed. "I'm the only one trying to help you and you're always hard on me," Rodriguez recalls him saying. "You even bring Juan Rodriguez and he doesn't shake my hand."

Obama turned to Deepak Bhargava, executive director of the Center for Community Change, and complained that Bhargava had unfairly criticized him in recent blog posts. The president said the activists should focus their criticism and pressure on Republicans.

The activists did not back down. "Mr. President, it's not just Deepak," said Gustavo Torres, head of the Latino rights group CASA of Maryland, as he recounted to the *Washington Post*. "All of us are very disappointed."[13]

"At the center of all this was this love that we have for families, for ourselves, but also for this country."

DEPORTING AND DETAINING PARENTS SHATTERS FAMILIES. Meredith Stern, Providence, Rhode Island, 2013

■ DEPORTING AND DETAIN- ING PARENTS SHATTERS FAM- ILIES. Meredith Stern, Prov- idence, Rhode Island, 2013 According to the Applied Re- search Center study *Shattered Families: The Perilous Intersec- tion of Immigration Enforcement and the Child Welfare System*, in 2011 the United States deport- ed a record 397,000 people and detained nearly that many. This is the first national investigation on threats to families when im- migration enforcement and the child welfare system intersect.

It finds that "in areas of high immigration enforcement, chil- dren of non-citizens are more likely to be separated from their parents and face barriers to re- unification; and immigrant vic- tims of domestic violence and other forms of gender-based violence are at particular risk of losing their children." Meredith Stern's print is a collaboration with *Colorlines* and is part of the Migration Now Portfolio, which seeks to put an end to the prison detention system and the abuse of immigrants.

IF CAPITAL CAN CROSS BORDERS, SO CAN WE!

Nearly 800,000 people migrate across each year in search of work. Mothers and fathers are forced to leave their families behind. Migrants trek through dangerous conditions going to where globalization takes jobs. It's time that international trade agreements be held accountable. UPHOLD THE HUMAN RIGHTS OF MIGRANT WORKERS!

¡SI EL CAPITAL PUEDE CRUZAR LAS FRONTERAS, TAMBIÉN PODEMOS NOSOTROS!

Casi 800,000 personas emigran cada año en busqueda de trabajo. Madres y padres son forzados a dejar atrás a sus familias. Los migrantes atraviezan condiciones peligrosas para llegar a donde la globalización lleva los trabajos. Ya es hora que los acuerdos de comercio internacionales se hagan responsables. ¡DEFIENDAN LOS DERECHOS HUMANOS DE LOS TRABAJADORES MIGRANTES!

물품이나 자본이 국경을 자유로이 넘을수있다면, 사람들도 마찬가지다! 우리의 노동이 세계경제를 이끈다!

IF CAPITAL CAN CROSS BORDERS. Jesús Barraza, Dignidad Rebelde, Berkeley, California, 2008

Jesús Barraza's print calls for a human rights approach to migration that challenges capitalists. Multinational corporations and their "capital" freely cross borders. Through international government agreements, the U.S. government imposes economic policies, trade agreements, and military interventions to enforce these policies. Migration is the result of more than a century of U.S. imperialism in Latin America. If capital can cross borders, so too should people.

The activists itemized their grievances. "There have been record deportations unlike anything that we've ever seen before. There's more collaboration between police and immigration all over the nation than there's ever been," Rodriguez recalls them saying. They demanded that Obama take executive action to stop the deportations and enact comprehensive immigration reform.

"The only way change was accomplished in [Obama's] first term was through outside agitation, including pushing the administration pretty heavily," observes Bhargava. He contrasts the progress made by immigrant rights advocates with "how organized labor or environmentalists did in the first term. They tended to play within the rules of politics as generally run in Washington. . . . They didn't get very much for it."

The Trail of DREAMs was an expression of hope that powerful and time-tested forms of action—personal storytelling, directly confronting power, freedom marches—could move citizens and leaders to change. It was also an expression of outrage that after years of polite lobbying, conditions for undocumented citizens had markedly deteriorated.

In September 2010, the DREAM Act and repeal of the anti-gay military policy "don't ask, don't tell" failed to pass in the U.S. Senate—four votes shy of the sixty needed to break a Republican-led filibuster. More than 250 DREAMers from across the country left the Senate gallery in tears that day. They all went back to a church and recommitted to the movement. Young activists across the country vowed to pursue a new strategy: pressuring Obama to enact key provisions of the act by executive action.

Meanwhile, DREAMers elsewhere were finding success. In 2011, Governor Jerry Brown signed into law the California DREAM Act, giving up to 25,000 undocumented students in California access to private scholarships and financial aid.

The presidential election of 2012 offered a new opportunity to apply pressure. In April 2012, Gaby Pacheco received a surprising invitation. U.S. senator Marco Rubio, a Florida Republican and Tea Party favorite, wanted her help drafting a bill that would offer legal status to some undocumented children.

After meeting with Rubio, Pacheco reached out to the White House. Within hours, Pacheco and other United We Dream activists were on a call with White House aides, who did not want Republicans to score points on the immigration issue at Obama's expense.

Pacheco used her leverage. "We're not married to the Democratic or Republican parties," Pacheco told the *Washington Post*, echoing activists like Dr. Martin Luther King Jr. "We're going to push what's best for the community."[14]

Meanwhile, other DREAMers were ratcheting up their direct-action protests. In June 2012, undocumented students launched a campaign of sit-ins and hunger strikes at Obama campaign offices in more than a dozen cities.

The DREAMers had the president's attention. On June 15, 2012, President Obama ordered his administration to stop deporting undocumented citizens who would be eligible for the DREAM Act. In the first two years of the Deferred Action for Childhood Arrivals (DACA) program, as the initiative was known, 673,000 undocumented people applied, and 553,000 applications were accepted.

With the threat of deportation lifted for two years, DACA beneficiaries took swift advantage: since getting DACA status, nearly 60 percent reported getting a new job and obtaining a driver's license, and nearly half opened a bank account and increased their earnings. Many enrolled in college. The newly "DACAmented" went from living in fear to legally supporting themselves and their families.

When Gaby Pacheco learned of Obama's announcement to stop deportations and start DACA, she realized that she had helped to change the culture. "My first immediate reaction was just a huge sense of pride and accomplishment. I could finally, like, breathe."

In November 2014, President Obama conceded to a key demand of immigration rights activists when he declared that he would use executive action to extend legal status to some five million undocumented immigrants. Included in this is an expansion of the original DACA program, removing the original age limits and making about 1.5 million people eligible for the program.

ACTIONS AND STORIES CREATE
SPACE FOR THE LARGER BATTLES

• •

DREAMers from across the country have profoundly changed the national discourse and influenced organizing tactics around immigration—catapulting an issue forward using particularly well the key strategies of telling their stories and disrupting power. Deepak Bhargava says that the DREAMers have "really reaffirmed the power of personal story and transformation. I think it has to have an impact on public conscience and dialogue and politics. It's affirmed the importance of direct action, which has been very important."

DREAMers have changed the conversation, Bhargava says. "They really focused on this kind of model that I think is part of all movements in a sense, coming out of 'undocumented, unafraid' . . . . It's the kind of individual transformation moving into the public sphere that requires an enormous act of courage. That was a big part of why they broke through."

Storytelling combined with direct action transforms people into activists. Or, as Juan Rodriguez says, it "radicalized me."

The work of the DREAMers continues. The goals of the immigrant rights movement have yet to be realized. For some, the goal is comprehensive immigration reform that offers a path to citizenship for the eleven million undocumented people in the United States. For others, the goal is more transformative: breaking down nationalism, borders, and the idea of citizenship itself. By the power of their actions and their stories, the DREAMers have created space for the larger battles—over immigration and other social and economic struggles—to be waged and won.

"The immigrant rights movement is a lever that will transform the rest of American politics and culture for generations, much like the civil rights movement was a movement that wasn't just about Afri-can Americans, it had deep ramifications for politics and culture and power," argues Bhargava. "Today the immigrant movement has that kind of potential to start a workers' movement to really change politics in the country. The possibility for a real workers'/poverty/economic justice movement—I can see the possibilities and I think the country's ready for it. That makes me hopeful."

Juan González echoes Bhargava's comments: "The beleaguered and crippled American trade union movement must be transformed into the main power center for immigrant workers . . . . Latin American immigrants can play a leading role, because many of them developed a more combative trade union spirit in their home countries, because many are accustomed to multiparty political systems back home, and because many grasp the importance of Spanish-language and other alternative media in spreading news and information to millions of 'forgotten' people. . . . The rise of a radical, democratic, and socialist alternative is indeed possible . . . and those immigrant workers will point the way."[15]

Gaby Pacheco understands this fight is not optional. "We are fighting for the ability to be full-fledged human beings in the only country we have known as home," she declares. "When we fight for the DREAM Act, we are fighting for our lives. And when you're fighting for your life, you don't stop until you win."

DECLARATION OF IMMI-GRATION. Salvador Jiménez, in collaboration with Yollocalli Arts Reach and Radio Arte, Chicago, 2009 (Photographer unknown) Located in the city's largely Latino Pilsen neighborhood, this two-story-high, thirty-foot-wide mural is dedicated to all the activists who have advocated for immigrants' rights. It asserts that America is a nation of immigrants, that no human being is illegal, and that we should tear down all borders. Salvador Jiménez led the youth mural art crew in a special partnership with the National Museum of Mexican Art. In an act that generated much attention, the mural was vandalized with a racist slur before it was completed. After it was repaired, the mural went on to become the backdrop for many important immigration rallies in Chicago since 2010.

FAVIANNA
RODRIGUEZ

Photo by ZS Grant

CULTURAL ORGANIZER, ARTIVIST, PRINT-MAKER, AND THE FOUNDER OF PRESENTE .ORG, FAVIANNA RODRIGUEZ CREATES PRINTS THAT ADDRESS ISSUES RANGING FROM WAR AND GLOBALIZATION TO WOMEN'S RIGHTS. HER CURRENT PROJECT, THE PUSSY POWER IMAGINARY, SEEKS TO REDEFINE THE PUSSY AS A SOURCE OF EMPOWERMENT, DEEPENING THE RELATIONSHIP BETWEEN WOMEN AND THEIR OWN BODIES. FAVIANNA IS ALSO THE DIRECTOR OF CULTURESTRIKE, A GRASSROOTS COLLECTIVE OF ARTISTS.

I've been an artist and an activist since 1999. What I do is I look at the role artists in culture play in transforming our lives, whether it's by presenting visionary stories of what our society can look like or challenging stereotypes or bias, or whether it's making an emotional connection to a viewer and therefore humanizing who we are as people living in the margins. I make art with that purpose.

What is the role of art/cultural work and its transformative power in twenty-first-century political movements?

Art can combat the lack of multidimensional stories and content in culture as a result of racism and sexism, whether it's women portrayed in very narrow, hypersexualized ways, or the fact that you rarely see Latinos on television or in film, and what you do see of young black men or Latinos is extremely inaccurate. That creates something called "unconscious bias." You see it with anti-immigration sentiment. When you begin to perpetuate that, it creates a culture of hate, a culture of bias, and a culture of dehumanization.

Culture is what surrounds us every single day. What you're listening to or you're engaging with in the visual landscape, what you are reading, where you go to eat—all of that is a cultural choice. You're surrounded with messages. If there is not content and messages that humanize us, then the core issue of us being portrayed in inhumane and one-dimensional ways ends up creating bad policy. Because then people don't value the lives of young black men. Or they think it's okay to warehouse immigrants because they see them as second-class people.

So the role of art is to counter this, because art can show multidimensional stories. When you show people in their complex truth, you make them human. Because we live in a culture of white supremacy, those that are seen as whole humans are white folks. You see white characters everywhere you turn. It's no wonder that whiteness is the norm. So art and culture can combat that.

The way you build that compassion is through storytelling. When you have an increasingly privatized infrastructure that's cutting our stories out, plus you have the proliferation of the right wing telling us everything from how to have sex to how we should value the lives of migrants or people of color, you need counter narratives. Not just counter communication strategies, but you actually need to speak to people's hearts. That to me is the most important role of culture—that it creates a space. We humanize the issue in order to have the ability for policy to win.

How do you measure success in your cultural and artistic work, and how does that relate to the expectations of organizations and/or movements?

The way that movements are measuring success needs rethinking: we look at short-term engagement and we look at things like voting and how many people attend a rally, or how many people read an op-ed or whether or not Senator XYZ changes his mind. Instead, the metrics that I look at in terms of culture are outcomes. For example, by me creating a pussy power piece, or a piece about a butterfly, what kinds of conversations am I creating? What kind of ways are people taking this symbolism and adopting it, reusing it, remixing it, and putting it out there?

I don't look at metrics in the quantitative way because culture is very hard to quantify. I more look at: is there a change in the way that people are thinking? Are they reapproaching the problem with a more creative set of solutions? Are they connecting more with the story? Is one cultural output creating more cultural output?

I look at the way people feel. How does this experience transform the audience member? Is there a way that the organization we're working with is also transformed? Do they realize that by working with artists, they're much more effectively reaching their audience?

DECOLONIZE! PUSSY POWER!

FAVIANNA RODRIGUEZ. Photo courtesy of the artist

5

"WHEN WE FIGHT, WE WIN!": THE STRUGGLE FOR ECONOMIC POWER

■ WE SHALL NOT BE MOVED. AgitArte, in collaboration with City Life/Vida Urbana, Boston, 2010 (Photo by Kelly Creedon)

In October 2010, the grassroots tenants' organization City Life/Vida Urbana (CL/VU) held an action in Copley Square, Boston, during the American Bankers Association convention to highlight the role and responsibility of Wall Street and big banks such as Wells Fargo, Bank of America, and JPMorgan Chase in the foreclosure crisis. In the photograph, foreclosed homeowner Marshall Cooper performs in a skit where he fights an eviction, proudly asserting, "I ain't going nowhere." The popular theater skit was created and performed by CL/VU members and led by AgitArte artists. We Shall Not Be Moved is a multimedia project by visual journalist Kelly Creedon that documents families fighting to protect their homes and communities against the devastating impact of foreclosure.

■ **FANNIE AND FREDDIE. AgitArte/Papel Machete, masks by Deborah Hunt,
Honk! Festival, Somerville, Massachusetts, 2013 (Photo by Leonardo March)**
Demanding that the Federal National Mortgage Association (Fannie Mae) and the Federal Home Loan Mortgage Corporation (Freddie Mac) change their practices in regard to predatory lending, housing activists honk in protest. The demonstrators seek an immediate halt to foreclosures and evictions. One in three homeowners nationwide is underwater, meaning they owe more on their mortgages than their home is worth. This is the highest risk factor for foreclosure. Freddie Mac and Fannie Mae are government-sponsored enterprises that own 59 percent of mortgages in the United States, yet refuse to offer relief for the crisis they created. For Somerville's Honk! 2013, AgitArte/Papel Machete paired up with the Rude Mechanical Orchestra, a "thirty-odd-piece New York City radical marching band and dance troupe" to support CLVU in their anti-foreclosure campaign.

*T*oo many people are working hard and sinking deeper into debt. Over the past thirty years, the top 1 percent saw their incomes skyrocket by 275 percent. Meanwhile, many in the middle class have joined the ranks of those struggling to cover basic needs. Today more than one-quarter of the children in the United States live in poverty.[1] Economic recovery has been limited to the rich: Oxfam, an international anti-poverty organization, reports that the wealthiest 1 percent of Americans captured 95 percent of post-financial-crisis growth since 2009, while the bottom 90 percent became poorer.[2]

Warren Buffett is one of the billionaires in the top 1 percent. He makes his money primarily off of his investments. He observed that the share of taxes he pays has fallen while at the same time his secretary's taxes have risen. He said, "There's class warfare, all right, but it's my class, the rich class, that's making war, and we're winning."[3]

This class war stretches around the globe: the world's richest eighty-five people now control more wealth than the bottom half of the world's population.[4] In the United States, the four hundred wealthiest people have more wealth than the bottom 50 percent of households—a level of inequality not seen since 1928, a year before the stock market crash that triggered the Great Depression.

"We have now returned to Gilded Age levels of inequality," says Josh Bivens of the Economic Policy Institute. The Gilded Age (the 1870s to 1920s) was marked by conspicuous wealth for a few industrial tycoons and deep poverty for many. This horrible inequality sparked the rise of labor unions to fight for working people and economic justice. Over the following half-century, workers won the forty-hour workweek, the weekend, the right to organize, Social Security, and Medicare.

Today, a new generation of activists is taking action to demand economic justice for the many. Every story in this book could be seen as part of this larger struggle. This chapter features three stories of twenty-first-century struggles that directly address economic inequality and focus on changing who holds economic power: Occupy Wall Street, the anti-eviction campaign of City Life/Vida Urbana, and the campaign by the Restaurant Opportunity Centers to gain livable wages and dignity at work.

While organizing different constituents and using different tactics, these activists all make deep connections between race, gender, and class, and they call for transforming the economy into one based on people—on the needs of workers and their families—instead of markets, speculation, and profits for the 1 percent. They share a common enemy in the class war. "When we fight, we win!" is the rallying cry of anti-eviction activists. It captures the spirit of the diverse movement to reclaim our economy, and our lives.

OCCUPY WALL STREET

"On September 17, flood into lower Manhattan, set up tents, kitchens, peaceful barricades and occupy Wall Street." So began the blog post on July 13, 2011, by *Adbusters*, a Canadian anti-consumerist magazine. The blog post proposed that twenty thousand people be part of a "leaderless resistance movement."

This action was an attempt to inspire an American version of the iconic Arab Spring demonstrations that toppled rulers throughout the Middle East and North Africa earlier that year. *Adbusters* was not the first to propose this action. Activists from Brooklyn, Egypt, Greece, Spain, Japan, the Bronx, and many more had been meeting in New York City for several months in the spring of 2011 to plan for American demonstrations. Small workgroups considered, and then dismissed, the idea of issuing a single demand, instead opting to allow many voices and ideas.

Several organizations made calls for occupations and proposed action. At around noon on Saturday, September 17, 2011, several hundred people appeared in

Occupying Wall Street? "That's not going to work," she declared flatly. "We are going to be there for ten minutes and then we are going to get chased out by the cops. It's going to be depressing."

Zuccotti Park, a tidy open space of honey locust trees and polished granite benches shoehorned between Wall Street and the World Trade Center site in lower Manhattan. By evening, the group had swelled to nearly a thousand people. They held a general assembly. A few hundred people stayed overnight.

"We are the 99%!" declared numerous signs. The meme stuck, and Occupy Wall Street (OWS) was launched. Within days, Zuccotti Park became the epicenter of a mass protest. Within a month, Occupy demonstrations and occupations of public spaces had occurred on every continent except Antarctica.

Many Occupy encampments became thriving communities. They had libraries where books were donated. They developed communal kitchens and media and health tents. Each had a working group that helped the community function. Occupy tried not to anoint leaders. Its goal was a "horizontal" movement in which decisions were reached by consensus. No one—and everyone—was empowered to speak for the movement.

The grievances and demands of protesters were a broadside against the inequities and injustice of capitalism and were stated on homemade signs, and with puppets and other art:

Banks got bailed out, we got sold out.

Money for jobs and education, not for war and corporations.

Protect the planet.

Let us realize a society based on human needs, not hedge fund profits.

Protect schools, not millionaires.

Fifty-nine days after activists took over Zuccotti Park, police violently evicted the protesters in the middle of the night, posting trucks and troops to prevent reentry. The same happened all across the country. Their libraries full of books were thrown into dumpsters. Tents, sleeping bags, and kitchens were trashed. The occupation was over.

Wherever the fight continues, the movement spark lives on. The Arab Spring, Occupy Wall Street, and many others have help spread a vision of a world not ruled by militaries, dictators, corporate kingpins, or markets, but rather a world of greater equity and democratic participation. "We are the 99%" has become a rallying cry across the globe. Occupy and the 99% have become part of our language.

"I HADN'T EVER SEEN SUCH SPONTANEOUS ORGANIZING"

Manissa McCleave Maharawal's father, an immigrant New Yorker from India, told his twenty-eight-year-old daughter, "You should go to Zuccotti Park." The Occupy Wall Street protest was just a few days old. The man who had long lectured his daughter about injustice was excited by what he heard of the Wall Street protests. He wondered: Could this finally be the revolution?

"No, *you* go," Manissa shot back.

A doctoral student in anthropology at the City University of New York (CUNY) who taught courses on social movements, Manissa McCleave Maharawal was already occupied—taking and teaching classes.

Besides, she was skeptical. In August she had attended a planning meeting for the protest and had participated in trainings around consensus decision making. She walked out. Occupying Wall Street? "That's *not* going to work," she declared flatly. "We are going to be there for ten minutes and then we are going to get chased out by the cops. It's going to be depressing."

Maharawal knew firsthand the power of the police. She had attended LaGuardia High School, a selective magnet school in New York City, but this had not protected her and other students of color from being harassed by cops in their Brooklyn neighborhood. In 1999, when New York City police fired forty-one shots and killed Amadou Diallo, an unarmed twenty-two-year-old black man from Guinea, "it really made a big impact on me, thinking about the police, and thinking about the police state, and thinking about violence and thinking about all these things that I was seeing happening," she recounts. Soon after, she helped to organize a walkout at her high school to protest "cops in schools and police brutality." That was the beginning of her activism.

"When I started at CUNY in 2008, they were just putting through a major round of budget cuts to the CUNY system, connected to the financial crisis . . . and were raising tuition. So I got involved in organizing around that."

Her father's experience was influential. "In India, [my dad] was really frustrated with the caste system," Maharawal explains. "He came to the U.S. with really high hopes . . . that people here didn't believe in stuff like that. . . . He thought those problems were different in the U.S., around social stratification and oppression and poverty. . . . He discovered that India's caste system had stark similarities to the class system in the U.S., where privilege and power is confined to a self-perpetuating elite."

A few days into the Occupy Wall Street protest, friends began reporting back from Zuccotti Park. One told Maharawal breathlessly, "I went and I didn't know anyone there. It's not the same people we are used to seeing."

That piqued Maharawal's curiosity. Then on September 24, New York City police officers were caught on video intentionally pepper-spraying three female protesters who were already caged behind barricades. "If the cops are taking it seriously, that's interesting," she thought.

A week into the occupation, she biked over to Zuccotti Park. People were debating. Talking with visitors. Imagining a better world.

"I hadn't [ever] seen such spontaneous organizing and thinking happening so quickly," she recalls. "Even though it was Sunday morning there were all these people walking by, tourists coming from Ground Zero . . . just milling around, reading the signs and talking to people. I was really impressed by the way that it was communicating something to passersby."

One encounter stuck in her mind. "I met this guy from New Jersey, South Jersey, who had just gotten there the night before with his backpack, a black man, and he started talking to me about how he had lost his job and how mad he was and how something needs to change. He was just going to see what this was about. I think there are a lot of people who came like that. I found talking to him really moving."

A few days later, Maharawal went to a general assembly with some South Asian friends. The assembly was about to pass the Declaration of Occupy Wall Street, a bold statement of principle. As she listened, one line jumped out at her: "As one people, formerly divided by the color of our skin, gender, sexual orientation, religion or lack thereof, political party, and cultural background . . ."

Formerly divided? Maharawal surveyed the overwhelmingly white crowd.

"It totally erased any current racism or classism," she recounts indignantly. "You can't erase entire histories of oppression in two words. It's not possible. It's not okay."

Maharawal turned to her friends with a look of astonishment. She felt like someone had punched her in the gut. Her friend Hena rose to object to the offending line in the declaration. The facilitators tried to defer the issue to a later time. They warned Maharawal and her friends that blocking consensus was "a serious act."

"We knew it was a serious act. And that is why we did it," she wrote later in the book *We Are Many: Reflections on Movement Strategy from Occupation to Liberation*.[5]

Maharawal summoned her courage and addressed the assembly. She insisted that they strike the offending line entirely. The assembly debated it and finally agreed to her demand. She exhaled.

"You did good," her friend Sonny whispered to her as she sat down on the cobblestones. "I wouldn't have been able to stand up in front of two hundred people or so and bring this up unless it was all of us doing it together."

Maharawal felt a jumble of emotion. She wrote lat-

> *"He came to the U.S. with really high hopes. . . . He discovered that India's caste system had stark similarities to the class system in the U.S., where privilege and power is confined to a self-perpetuating elite."*

屋崙華埠的老人正被逼遷！

STOP EVICTIONS
OF OUR ELDERS IN CHINATOWN

CHRISTINE WONG YAP

■ **STOP EVICTIONS OF OUR ELDERS IN CHINA-TOWN. Christine Wong Yap for Causa Justa/Just Cause Oakland. Printed by Jesús Barraza, San Leandro, California, 2003**
In April 2003, more than forty elderly, low-income tenants in Oakland's Chinatown received eviction notices because a developer wanted to sell their affordable housing units as market-rate condos. In response, housing activists and Chinese community groups organized to defeat the evictions and to preserve affordable housing. To "stay in place" is an act of defiance against centuries of displacement. On March 20, 2008, the Stop Chinatown Evictions Coalition (SCEC) celebrated a victory. After nearly five years of legal and political maneuvers, the developer agreed to a settlement that will preserve affordable housing in Oakland's Chinatown. Causa Justa/Just Cause is a multiracial, grassroots organization building community leadership to achieve justice for low-income San Francisco and Oakland residents.

The owner of the Pacific Renaissance Plaza, Lawrence Chan, wants to evict 50 families from their homes at 988 Webster Street. These tenants are our neighbors. They are low-income people, seniors and disabled people from the Asian community.

The tenants of the Pacific Renaissance want to stay in their homes. They want the evictions to stop. They want affordable housing. Help win this victory for the whole community.

STOP CHINATOWN EVICTIONS COMMITTEE
For more info, email stopevictions@justcauseoakland.org or call 510-763-5877 (Just Cause Oakland).

Many organizations from the Asian community and from the tenants' movement have united with the tenants of the Pacific Renaissance to keep them in their homes.

富興中心業主陳文聯正在逼遷五十戶家庭，當中包括低收入人士、老人、及傷殘人士。這些人很多需要華埠的醫療服務、所以他們不能遷出現有居所。請不要強迫這些家庭離開。他們的收入低微，不能應付唐人埠鄰近昂貴的租金。他們需要低收入房屋，請為他們伸出援手。他們憩住在現在的家－富興中心。

華埠停止逼遷協會
如有任何問題及建議，請電：
中文熱線：組合亞裔力量 (PAO) 510-834-8920 內線 300
很多亞裔及住客行動組織以聯合行動幫助這些被逼遷的住客。請支持我們！

108

er, "Let me tell you what it feels like as a woman of color to stand in front of a white man and explain privilege to him: It *hurts*. It makes you tired. Sometimes it makes you want to cry. Sometimes it is exhilarating. Every single time it is hard. Every single time, I get angry that I have to do this; that this is my job, that it shouldn't be my job. Every single time, I am proud of myself that I've been able to say these things because it took hard work to be able to and because some days I just don't want to."[6]

She points out that "so often in movement work . . . where someone says . . . a pretty racist thing . . . [there] is often not space to take that on. That's been hugely frustrating for me. I've left things because of that. So the fact that at OWS there was space—even if it's space that we fought for, or had to fight for and that we made ourselves—it mattered hugely that there was still space for it."

From that moment forward, Maharawal was all in.

"WHEN WHITE PEOPLE HAVE A COLD, BLACK PEOPLE HAVE THE FLU"

When Maharawal joined a group with other women to figure out how to deal with men who were dominating the talking, she was relieved to have room to speak and hear other women speak. That made her all the more aware that another issue remained largely silenced.

"I was surprised when I found out that there wasn't a people of color group . . . because it seemed like this was a place where people were really talking . . . not only about what's wrong with the world and the banks and the financial industry and capitalism, but also interpersonally. . . . Gender had been brought up but race had not been yet. Race is harder a lot of times. . . . I've had an easier time saying, 'As a woman, I feel XYZ way' . . . than saying, 'As a brown person, I feel XYZ way.'" She surmises that in the United States, "we live in such segregated spaces. . . . The tools we have to talk about race are so different than the tools that we have to talk about gender."

A critical shortcoming of OWS in New York City was its failure to implement a strong anti-oppression platform that made it clear that they were against racism,

sexism, homophobia, and oppressive behaviors of all kinds. In other cities, Occupy was quick to take on more explicit proposals. In an essay that went viral a month into the occupation, Arizona activist Joel Olson wrote, "The key obstacle to building the 99% is Left colorblindness, and the key to overcoming it is to put the struggles of communities of color at the center of this movement."[7]

Part of the problem was obvious to anyone who participated in Occupy: eight out of ten protesters were white. Surveys by Occupy Research found that just 5 percent were Latino, 5 percent Asian/Pacific Islander, 4 percent Native American, and 3 percent African American.[8]

Although fighting economic inequality is an important basis for coming together, no movement can afford to ignore the racism prevalent in the everyday lives of people of color— a racism deeply embedded in our economic structures that unwittingly reproduces itself within social movement work.

"We are not going to dismantle capitalism unless we also dismantle racism," Maharawal insists. "Capitalism uses racism to perpetuate itself in all sorts of ways that are worldwide and local and are connected to histories of colonialism and slavery. The ways that wealth and inequality are affecting the white middle class right now are huge, but are very different than the ways that wealth and inequality are affecting poorer working-class people of color.

"When white people have a cold, black people have the flu," says Maharawal, quoting an activist with Occupy the Hood, which organized many people of color in the Occupy movement. The quote highlights how the problems of economic inequality, ranging from unemployment to low wages to school funding, have fallen hardest on people of color.

Maharawal says that some activists "are really scared [that] if you start talking about the ways we are

> "Capitalism uses racism to perpetuate itself in all sorts of ways that are worldwide and local and are connected to histories of colonialism and slavery."

different, then you will divide people and then they won't be able to work together. I actually think the opposite. If you talk about the ways you are different and are really explicit about it, those ways don't come back and divide you later on," she argues. "You can then build a movement or a group that is actually dismantling all the oppressive structures that go along with capitalism, instead of just focusing on whatever one micro thing your group is working on."

In a move that made many activists of color hopeful, on October 21, 2011, a large contingent from Occupy Wall Street joined Occupy Harlem, another of the many Occupy-branded offshoots, led by people of color, to protest the New York Police Department's stop-and-frisk policy, which overwhelmingly targets ethnic minorities. In 2011, nearly two thousand people per day were subject to stop-and-frisk in New York City. Between 2002 and 2011, 90 percent of those stopped were black and Latino.[9] Police targeting and attacking Occupy made many of the white protesters temporarily have something in common with the blacks and Latinos who know police violence daily.

CONVERSATIONS ABOUT CLASS

As summer shifted into autumn, days of protest blended into nights of occupation at Zuccotti Park. A community of solidarity and outrage took shape on the sidewalks of the financial district. Working groups continued to make progress and organized an OWS library with five thousand books, a communal kitchen, a free university, a newspaper (*Occupied Wall Street Journal*), and medical services. Pizzas ordered by generous supporters from around the world were constantly being delivered.

"Talking about class in the U.S. is very hard because of the myth that everyone is upwardly mobile . . . and heading to the American Dream. And there is the myth that we all can become rich. This ignores the class, racial, and education barriers to mobility."

Students visited daily to hear discussions about inequality, capitalism, anarchism, and socialism that were unlike anything they heard in their classes. Plans were under way about how to winterize the camps.

Class struggle was a frequent topic of debate and discussion. Karl Marx had famously written about the subject in great detail in the nineteenth century, but for many participants this concept was new. "Occupy was about class struggle. Wealth inequality is an entry point. Class struggles focus on workers and bosses and property," reflected Maharawal in 2014. Some people learned about class struggle through Occupy.

"Talking about class in the U.S. is very hard because of the myth that everyone is upwardly mobile . . . and heading to the American Dream. And there is the myth that we all can become rich. This ignores the class, racial, and education barriers to mobility. 'The 99%' is a simplified way of talking about class," she says. It highlights how most people are in the same boat, only a few paychecks or one illness away from being on the street. In Marxist terms, the 1 percent is the "capitalist class" that owns the means of production and continues to hold power through inheritance and exploitation of workers and imperialism.

Noted activist and public intellectual Noam Chomsky was one of the most popular authors in the OWS lending library. He wrote:

The business classes are very class-conscious— they're constantly fighting a bitter class war to improve their power and diminish opposition. . . .

In the U.S., organized labor has been repeatedly and extensively crushed, and has endured a very violent history as compared with other countries . . . because it is the base of organization of any popular opposition to the rule of capital, and so it has to be dismantled. There are attacks on labor all the time. . . .

The enormous benefits given to the very wealthy, the privileges for the very wealthy here, are way beyond those of other comparable societies and are part of the ongoing class war. Take a look at CEO salaries. CEOs are no more productive or brilliant here than they are in Europe, but the pay, bonuses, and enormous power they get here

FORECLOSE ON·THE 1%

OCCUPY THE BANKS

WWW.DIGNIDADREBELDE.COM

■ **FORECLOSE ON THE 1%. Jesús Barraza, Dignidad Rebelde, San Leandro, California, 2011**
Banks have systematically attacked communities of color through predatory lending, which has led to huge waves of foreclosures and the devastation of entire neighborhoods. Those who have managed to keep their homes remain trapped by underwater mortgages. At a time when the federal government and banks have failed to provide solutions for homeowners in crisis, organizing is critical. This poster was developed for actions against banks in Oakland led by housing activists and occupiers who were organizing to stop foreclosures and evictions. The demand here was a moratorium on foreclosures and that banks stop their investments in detention centers and dirty energy. Dignidad Rebelde has consistently provided graphics to advance the stories of the 99%.

are out of sight . . . a drain on the economy, and they become even more powerful when they are able to gain control of policy decisions. . . .

It also illustrates the considerable shredding of the whole system of democracy. . . . The bottom 70 percent or so are virtually disenfranchised; they have almost no influence on policy, and as you move up the scale you get more influence. At the very top, you basically run the show. . . .

So you end up with a kind of plutocracy in which the public opinion doesn't matter much. It is not unlike other countries in this respect, but more extreme. All along, it's more extreme. So yes, there is a constant class war going on.[10]

Maharawal recalls that the Labor Working Group played a key role as one of the biggest and most active subgroups of OWS. "Many of the marches would not have happened without this labor connection . . . and pushing unions to reclaim radical unionism and striking."

A goal of some in OWS was to hold a general strike on May 1, 2012—also known as International Workers' Day, or May Day. "This was inspired by past labor struggles," says Maharawal. But the May Day general strike never occurred "because Occupy was destroyed before it could happen and because so many unions are not as radical."

GLOBAL NETWORKS

Occupy, like all struggles, was built on the foundations laid by movements that came before it. Human beings have been grappling with issues of class, power, and democratic control of their work and economy for centuries.

In late 2010 and early 2011, protests spread first throughout Tunisia and then Egypt and other countries, where rulers were forced to resign after years in power. This was the beginning of the Arab Spring—and a worldwide movement for change. On January 25, 2011, some fifty thousand Egyptians occupied Cairo's Tahrir Square to protest the thirty-year rule of Egyptian dictator Hosni Mubarak. Led by students and labor unions, crowds soon swelled to more than a million. Following

a violent crackdown by government loyalists and then a massive popular uprising, Mubarak was forced to resign. Measured by the amount of U.S. aid dollars, he was the biggest of several formerly untouchable U.S.-backed Middle Eastern strongmen to fall in the months that followed.

Worldwide protests spread, notably in Spain, where in May 2011, *indignados*, "the indignant ones," took over public squares and buildings to protest corporate-driven economic policies and austerity measures being imposed throughout the country that cut funding for schools, health care, and jobs. "We drew inspiration from the *indignados* and Spanish unions and workers party," says Maharawal. "Occupy is part of a continuum from Spain where they talk much more explicitly about class . . . about how we are dispossessed from our means of production by elite actors. Occupy did not necessarily go far enough. There was not enough focus on this dispossession and those who are truly very marginalized by the system. There is much more willingness to talk about class and capitalism in Europe than in the U.S. . . . People are proud to be working-class there and look down their noses on the elite."

Occupy and the international movement challenged inequality, economic power, and the unsustainability of global capitalism itself. For the first time in decades, people in the United States began having serious conversations in public circles and the mainstream media about what alternatives to capitalism might look like.

A worldwide movement was on the rise. A future was waiting to be ushered in.

CLASS WARFARE BECOMES ARMED CRACKDOWN

As the fall wore on, violent clashes with the police intensified. A coordinated national crackdown on Occupy encampments was under way. Riot police in Oakland were especially violent, at one point shooting a tear gas canister at point-blank range and fracturing the skull of Marine veteran Scott Olsen, twenty-four, who served two tours in Iraq and was participating in an Occupy demonstration.

On November 15, hundreds of NYPD officers moved

in force to "clean" Zuccotti Park. They destroyed the library, the kitchen, and all signs of the encampment. Police charged wildly into the crowd and beat protesters bloody. Maharawal found herself thrown down by a policeman in full body armor. "I saw people walk away because they were like, 'I don't want to be hit in the head by a cop ever again,'" she says.

A week after the eviction, protesters in Zuccotti Park milled about as armies of helmet-wearing police stood watch and periodically attacked demonstrators. "It felt very much like a police state," Maharawal reflects. "We live in a police state all the time, but at this time the full force of our militarized police system was visible and turned on us."

The police state was, in fact, "more sophisticated than we ever imagined," wrote Naomi Wolf in the *Guardian*. She reported on FBI documents obtained by the Partnership for Civil Justice fund that "show a nationwide meta-plot unfolding in city after city in an Orwellian world: six American universities are sites where campus police funneled information about students involved with OWS to the FBI, with the administrations' knowledge; banks sat down with FBI officials to pool information about OWS protesters harvested by private security; plans to crush Occupy events, planned for a month down the road, were made by the FBI—and offered to the representatives of the same organizations that the protests would target; and even threats of the assassination of OWS leaders by sniper fire —by whom? Where?—now remain redacted and undisclosed to those American citizens in danger."[11]

The armed crackdown against Occupy was reminiscent of even more brutal past state repressions such as COINTELPRO, an FBI program that began in the late 1950s and became stronger in the 1960s and 1970s. It targeted Dr. Martin Luther King Jr., the American Indian Movement, peace activists, the Black Panthers, and even U.S. senators. Anyone who was critical of capitalism or the Vietnam War and was promoting programs of racial justice was a potential target. COINTELPRO tactics included state surveillance, disruption, infiltration, and murder committed by U.S. government agents. The program foreshadowed today's National Security Agency domestic surveillance program and the collaboration between local, state, and federal agencies to infiltrate and undermine movements and organizations that support self-determination, particularly of people of color.

The crackdown would be echoed in Egypt. A year and a half after Egyptian activists and the public took over Tahrir Square, the U.S.-backed Egyptian military forcibly retook the square and overthrew the elected president.

OWS activists "didn't have a chance," Maharawal reflects about the coordinated power of corporations, public and private security services, media, and government. Whenever and wherever the 1 percent's hegemonic control is threatened, they respond. Occupy was challenging this control of economic power and state power and the media's stories about capitalism. A popular movement was on the rise. Maharawal says we can't "underestimate the power the state has to crush movements right now."

OCCUPY-INSPIRED ACTIVISM

Occupiers were brutally evicted from public spaces all around the United States in late 2011. But the spirit of Occupy lives on. The uprising emboldened ordinary citizens to stand up to the banks, corporations, and complicit political leaders who rule their lives and communities. Occupy allowed people to define themselves and imagine a world beyond capitalism.

Occupy appeared in new guises and inspired activism in countless other ways. Occupy Wall Street morphed into Occupy Our Homes (an anti-foreclosure campaign), the Free University, Occupy Student Debt, Occupy the Department of Education (public schools), Occupy Philanthropy, and other activist organizations. Many activists in this book cite Occupy as a source of inspiration for their work.

Since her days in Zuccotti Park, Maharawal organizes around a variety of issues, built on the many networks formed through Occupy. She has focused on anti-displacement and eviction organizing, which is quite

> *"We live in a police state all the time, but at this time the full force of our militarized police system was visible and turned on us."*

■ OCCUPY THE HOOD. Kevin "Rashid" Johnson, Amarillo, Texas, 2011

Occupy the Hood is a nationwide grassroots movement that is an extension of Occupy Wall Street (OWS) and of the Occupy movement in general. It emerged in response to the lack of overall participation of people of color in the Occupy movement and its failure to recognize racism and its connections to white supremacy, patriarchy, imperialism, and capitalism. The artist statement, "At the Bottom of the 99% We got Nothing . . . but chains to lose," is a call to a qualitative leap in the class struggle and the consciousness of people of color by targeting Wall Street and the 1 percent. Occupy the Hood's online call to action was created by Queens resident Malik Rhasaan and Ife Johari Uhuru, an activist from Detroit, Michigan.

114

related to Occupy "even if it doesn't have the name 'occupy' in front of it," Maharawal says. "This is one of the salient lasting effects of Occupy."

On the second anniversary of OWS, founding member Justin Wedes reflected in the *Guardian*: "The crackdown on Occupy began a diaspora that continues to this day: protesters returned to their community deeply affected by the experience. Those who once shared food in the OWS kitchen now feed the hungry of the 99% in their hometowns. When Hurricane Sandy hit New York City in October 2012, Occupy Sandy organized 70,000 volunteers to provide critical aid to survivors, leading the *New York Times* to note that Occupy was 'capable of summoning an army with the posting of a tweet.'"

The rise of the 99% continues and can be seen throughout this book and many other places:

- In Richmond, California, many bold campaigns are under way to seize underwater mortgages from Wall Street firms in an effort to keep residents in their homes and increase democratic control of the local economy. Gayle McLaughlin, a city councillor in Richmond and its former mayor, once marched with Occupy. (For more on Richmond, see Chapter 6.)
- Workers at Walmart and fast-food chains staged their first-ever strikes starting in 2013 to demand a living wage of $15 an hour (which was double the minimum wage that year) and better working conditions.
- Following the police killing of Michael Brown in 2014, demonstrators across the United States held die-ins and protests at malls on Black Friday, the day after Thanksgiving and the biggest shopping day of the year. Declaring, "No justice, no profits," protestors drew a link between police killings of people of color and the political and economic systems that undergird the police state.
- The National Domestic Workers Alliance won passage of the landmark Domestic Workers Bill of Rights in New York State in 2010—the first law in the United States to guarantee overtime pay, paid leave, and legal protections from harassment and discrimination for domestic workers. "We are re-

ally trying to develop a whole new generation of women workers who can provide leadership not only on issues affecting domestic workers, but on . . . what the twenty-first-century economy and democracy need," says alliance director Ai-jen Poo.

- Voters in Seattle approved raising the minimum wage from $9.32 to $15 an hour by 2018, lifting the pay of more than 100,000 people, or one-fourth of the workforce. Similar campaigns to raise the minimum wage have passed in Los Angeles (for hotel workers), in San Francisco, and even in Republican-dominated states such as Alaska, Arkansas, South Dakota, and Nebraska.

Organizing for working-class power has been going on for a long time and predates Occupy. Two of the many cutting-edge economic justice efforts are the anti-foreclosure campaigns and the low-income-worker campaigns. Each of these struggles is made up of many organizations that work with different communities and use different organizing models. They are all battling the same war on workers' rights being waged by corporate elites. All have won important victories since Occupiers took to the streets. We share the stories of two organizations.

SAVING HOMES, SAVING LIVES

Aloysius Nwankwo has lived with his wife, four children, and mother in the Grove Hall section of Boston for two decades. After his small business failed, the family struggled to pay its mortgage. In early 2013, Nwankwo came home to find a notice from Bank of America that the bank would foreclose on his home on April 10, 2013, after which he would be evicted. The Nwankwos were about to become another casualty in the national foreclosure epidemic.

When banks peddling risky loans got into trouble, they received billion-dollar public bailouts. When

> *Organizing for working-class power has been going on for a long time and predates Occupy.*

working-class homeowners got into trouble, they received eviction notices.

The foreclosure crisis devastated individuals and families in the United States. Since 2008, five million homes have been foreclosed nationwide, displacing some ten million people—more than during the Great Depression. By 2012, about one-third of all borrowers in the United States—and half of borrowers under the age of forty—were underwater on their homes (carrying mortgages in excess of the value of their house).[12]

The foreclosure crisis has had a distinct racist tinge. Journalist Laura Gottesdiener, author of *A Dream Foreclosed: Black America and the Fight for a Place to Call Home*, observes, "African American neighborhoods were targeted more aggressively than others for the sort of predatory loans that led to mass evictions after the economic meltdown of 2007–2008. At the height of the rapacious lending boom, nearly 50 percent of all loans given to African American families were deemed 'subprime.' The *New York Times* described these contracts as 'a financial time-bomb.'"[13]

Aloysius Nwankwo refused to go quietly. His home provided shelter for his family, but it was also a source of pride and stability. Bank of America declined to sell the house to him at the current market value or allow him to remain in the house as a tenant. Nwankwo went looking for help. He attended a meeting at City Life/Vida Urbana (clvu.org), a community organization in Boston with a forty-year track record of fighting evictions. City Life is part of Occupy Our Homes (occupyourhomes.org), a national network of anti-foreclosure groups that "stand in solidarity with the Occupy Wall Street movement and with community organizations who help the 99% fight for a place to call home."

Racing against the eviction deadline, City Life began organizing in the Nwankwos' neighborhood. Large "Eviction Free Zone" signs festooned the Nwankwos' home and stretched along the street. City Life/Vida Urbana contacted local politicians and Bank of America to alert them that they would face resistance if they went through with their eviction. The Nwankwos' private nightmare had become a public crusade.

The public image of Bank of America was already tarnished. In 2012, it was one of five banks that paid $25 billion to settle charges that they "robo-signed" foreclosure documents (that is, they signed thousands of foreclosure documents without verifying the information to which they were swearing).[14] In 2013, former Bank of America employees revealed that they lied to customers and deliberately denied loan modifications to eligible homeowners.[15]

Hours before the Nwankwos' eviction was to be carried out, Bank of America backed down. "Move is canceled" was all that the bank wrote in an email to City Life organizers. The eviction blockade turned into a public celebration of people power.

Aloysius Nwankwo addressed dozens of supporters and politicians who had gathered in front of his house. "The banks and investors are chasing black people out one by one. . . . Where is the outrage? We should stop this. . . . We should just take a stand. We have more power than we know."

Dozens of protesters then marched to a nearby Bank of America branch with signs that read "Beat back bank attack!" and "Don't evict—negotiate." The bank locked its customers inside while the marchers rallied outside.

After the eviction blockade, a sympathetic benefactor offered to buy the Nwankwos' home back from the bank and then sell it to Nwankwo when he had the cash.

For City Life/Vida Urbana organizer Steve Meacham, the Nwankwo case was more than an isolated victory. It was the power of turning a personal calamity into a movement. "The fact that . . . the community came out to defend one of their own," Meacham says, "is such an age-old, moral understanding: we are our brothers' and sisters' keepers."

Anti-displacement organizers have succeeded on many fronts. In 2010, following grassroots pressure,

"The banks and investors are chasing black people out one by one. . . . Where is the outrage? We should stop this. . . . We should just take a stand. We have more power than we know."

Massachusetts unanimously passed tenant protections in both legislative houses that prevented banks from pressuring tenants to leave unless they could show "just cause," and in 2014, a lawsuit by the Massachusetts attorney general resulted in the Federal Housing Finance Agency agreeing to start selling back foreclosed properties to their previous owners.

Success confirmed City Life's strategy of having "a practical solution for the person . . . that also challenged the system. It's accomplishing a goal that nobody thinks is possible—and that wouldn't have been possible without public protest and action," says Meacham.

"In order to really do something about someone facing displacement from gentrification or market forces, you have to have an analysis that frees yourself of market ideology," he continues. "That allows you to do very effective grassroots organizing that has an immediate appeal, but it also creates a growing group of radicalized leaders that want to go somewhere else."

Going to the root causes, or radicalization, in this context means that activists begin to question market-driven home ownership and sometimes the concept of private property. They begin to question who deserves the riches, who should benefit from the fruits of their own labor, and who makes the decisions. Meacham says that when effective street protest is "combined with political and economic analysis around class, racial, and gender injustices, then that's a rich array of things that leads people to become all-around social change organizers rather than just foreclosure fighters." He credits the Occupy movement with changing "the nature of the debate almost overnight in terms of pointing at the privilege of the 1 percent."

City Life has been doing economic justice organizing since the 1970s. According to its mission statement, it is a "grassroots community organization committed to fighting for racial, social and economic justice and gender equality by building working class power. We promote individual empowerment, develop community leaders and build collective power to effect systemic change and transform society."

Occupy Boston, like many Occupy sites, struggled with process and the leaderless model of the movement. Meacham insists that the problems of Occupy highlight the need for "trained grassroots leaders . . . [who] can help orient people in these inevitable debates around how to organize a multiclass and multi-

racial movement . . . how to make decisions in a way that's democratic, how to be radical and yet give people the space to develop their own radicalism, how to be bold and not be male chauvinist knuckleheads."

Meacham is critical of Occupy's leaderless movement model. "One of the things that Occupy always said, which was really wrong, was that 'we have no leaders.' . . . That's never true. There are always leaders. The only question is whether they're accountable. We in the United States have to get over our reluctance to plan the Left," he says. "Because if you don't plan it, it comes into existence anyway and you may not like what it looks like." Meacham says that Occupy was more than a momentary awakening. "I think any time you have a viral explosion of something like that where people spontaneously begin to use an idea and self-organize around it, that's a movement to me."

Some veteran activists were nevertheless ambivalent about Occupy Boston. Meacham reflects, "There's a lot of people in City Life saying, 'Well, WTF—I mean, we've been organizing protests like this for years, and we're not getting coverage because we're black.' . . . Partly that's exactly what is happening. On the other hand, can we engage [Occupy] in ways that take this energy that's potentially tremendous and was actually very valuable to our movement and influence it?"

Meacham feels that Occupy, despite its problems, was ultimately helpful. He quotes a Service Employees International Union organizer who was working closely with Occupy and who told him, "You know, we could really carefully construct a beautiful sailing ship, but we can't create the wind. [When Occupy appeared,] the wind just arrived so we better go take advantage of it."

ORGANIZING LOW-WAGE WORKERS

The cutting edge of new labor organizing can be found among the lowest-paid workers. Restaurant and other low-wage workers have long been beyond the

> "The fact that . . . the community came out to defend one of their own," Meacham says, "is such an age-old, moral understanding: we are our brothers' and sisters' keepers."

■ **MARCH FOR RIGHTS, RESPECT, AND FAIR FOOD.**
Mona Caron and David Solnit in collaboration
with the Coalition of Immokalee Workers,
Immokalee, Florida, 2011 (Photo by Mona Caron)
On March 5, 2011, the Coalition of Immokalee Workers (CIW)
called a mass convergence on the supermarket chain Publix in
Tampa, Florida, as the culminating event of the Do the Right
Thing Tour, in which they asked supermarket chains to support
labor reforms in Florida's agriculture industry, as part of their
Campaign for Fair Food. Publix, a major supermarket chain,
refused to sign on to the CIW's Fair Food Program. The protest
included massive street pageants with four 20-foot-tall puppets,
portable murals to be used for storytelling, signs, and other
objects. People testified onstage about the abuses farmworkers
endure and the rights they were demanding. Among the many
events around this campaign, the farmworkers organized and
staged a *mística*, an allegorical theater piece originating from
the Brazilian landless movement, which narrated the story of
CIW's alliances and victories over thirteen years of struggle.

reach or interest of most labor unions. They are often invisible to the outside world, are frequently exploited, and endure long hours, racism, sexism, and low pay. Restaurant Opportunities Centers United (ROC) has pioneered effective and confrontational ways to organize and improve working conditions among the lowest-wage workers who have traditionally lacked collective bargaining rights. They have taken aim at big employers and their lobbyists and scored remarkable successes against powerful adversaries.

Saru Jayaraman is co-founder and co-director of Restaurant Opportunities Centers United (rocunited .org). ROC-NY was founded after the 9/11 attacks as a way to help surviving workers from restaurants located in the World Trade Center, including Windows on the World, where seventy-three employees died. In 2006, ROC opened a cooperatively owned and run restaurant, Colors. ROC workers not only ran the restaurant but also established free training programs for other struggling restaurant workers.

In 2008, ROC expanded into a national organization, ROC-United. ROC-U now has more than thirteen thousand worker members in twenty-six states and has won more than $10 million in financial settlements and improvements in workplace policies.

Jayaraman explains the challenging landscape confronting ROC: "The restaurant industry right now is the second-largest private sector employer in the United States. It's over ten million workers. One in twelve Americans work in the restaurant industry. It's absolutely the fastest-growing sector of the U.S. economy."

> "The NRA has created a situation where restaurants can engage in de facto legal gender pay inequity because 60 percent of all tipped workers in America are women."

While many restaurant chains are reporting record sales, this good fortune has not been shared with the workers. The restaurant industry is "the absolute lowest-paying employer in the United States," says Jayaraman. And restaurant workers typically lack benefits such as paid sick days and adequate health insurance.

Well-connected lobbyists have played a key role in keeping wages low. The National Restaurant Association—"the other NRA," quips Jayaraman—has led the fight against reform in the industry. The trade association, formerly headed by Republican presidential candidate Herman Cain, spent $2.7 million on lobbying and gave $1.3 million in political donations in 2012. The NRA has helped to keep the minimum wage for tipped workers frozen for two decades at $2.13 an hour.

But the very notion of "tipped workers" is a misnomer: many supposedly tipped restaurant workers receive little or no money in tips. According to Jayaraman, they are simply "single moms who are earning $2.13 an hour and living in extreme poverty. They have three times the poverty rate of the rest of the U.S. workforce and use food stamps at double the rate of the rest of the U.S. workforce. Which means the women who feed us can't afford to feed themselves or their families," says Jayaraman. "The NRA has created a situation where restaurants can engage in de facto legal gender pay inequity because 60 percent of all tipped workers in America are women. . . . The industry has found a way to pay women in particular about a third of what they pay everybody else." She explains that these are "largely women who work at diners, IHOP, Applebee's, Olive Garden, working graveyard shifts and raising children. One in four restaurant workers are parents."

Jayaraman notes that restaurants have the "highest rate of sexual harassment of any industry in the United States." Many young women get their first jobs in the restaurant industry and "are introduced to the world of work in the situation where they can be paid less than $3 an hour, where they can be touched and spoken to inappropriately and it's completely normalized . . . where they can be yelled at and screamed at, where they have no benefits, and they have to work when they're sick. . . . This is the way we're introducing young women to the world of work."

ROC is pushing back on multiple fronts. The group has won more than thirteen campaigns against exploitation in high-profile restaurant companies. In 2008, ROC helped win $4 million from Fireman Hospitality Group, a large New York City restaurant owner, to settle claims of stolen tips and wages, sexual harassment, and discrimination. In 2012, Darden Restaurants, the world's largest casual dining company (it owns Red

■ **NEW DAY, NEW STANDARD. Marisa Morán Jahn for Studio REV, in collaboration with Domestic Workers United and MIT's Center for Civic Media, New York City, 2012** New Day, New Standard is a cross-media art project and interactive hotline that informs nannies, housekeepers, elder-care providers, and their employers about the landmark Domestic Workers' Bill of Rights, passed in New York State in November 2010. Domestic workers have been excluded from the protections of labor laws in the United States since the 1930s, when such laws were first enacted. More than 600,000 people in the New York City area are domestic workers suffering under racist, sexist, and anti-immigrant structures that prevent many from receiving respect and fair compensation for their labor. Domestic Workers United engages in political action and community activism and educates workers about their rights. Studio REV is a nonprofit art organization that combines sound research and bold ideas to produce creative media to impact the lives of low-wage workers, immigrants, women, and youth. MIT's Center for Civic Media partnered with the New Day, New Standard team to adapt VoiP Drupal, an open-source mobile tool kit, to the project.

Lobster, Olive Garden, LongHorn Steakhouse, and other national chain restaurants), announced that it would limit workers' hours in order to avoid paying for their health care under President Obama's Affordable Care Act. Two months later, the company canceled the plan after ROC and others protested and profits plunged 37 percent in response to the bad publicity generated by the protests.[16] This successful disruptive movement strategy reveals a vulnerability that business owners have to the power of direct action. Workers can leverage that power.

Today, ROC is working nationally to win paid sick days and raise the federal minimum wage, including for tipped workers. But does raising wages fundamentally change a system that exploits workers?

For Jayaraman, "structural change isn't just the Fair Minimum Wage Act. It's in the long term having a table . . . where workers have equal voice to employers and where workers are . . . setting the wages and working conditions for the entire industry at the national level. . . . It's about ongoing voice and power."

A COMMON ENEMY

One way ROC knows it is making a difference is that it is being attacked. "Every year the National Restaurant Association names ROC as one of their top five or six policy priorities to shut down," says Jayaraman, pointing to the anti-ROC website rocexposed.com, which launched in 2012 with funding from major restaurant owners. In 2014, *Salon* obtained internal NRA documents that revealed that the organization "provides $600,000 in additional support for the ongoing project to combat the tactics of the Restaurant Opportunities Centers, or ROC, and the new industry reputational campaign."[17] The NRA has also alerted its members to Jayaraman's book signings and media appearances.

Jayaraman indicates the keys to ROC's success: "You don't win big things by having small ambitions. We're focused on changing standards in some of the largest and fastest growing restaurant companies because they can set a different standard for the industry."

ROC sees its organizing in the context of a larger movement for social and economic justice. "The NRA plays such a huge role . . . on transparency [and] . . . corpo-

rate pay. . . . Bringing them down to size and reducing their role in our democracy does have much broader implications than just workers in our industry." The NRA is a member of the American Legislative Exchange Council (ALEC), through which it creates model legislative bills that are beneficial to corporate leaders and increase their power over workers (see Chapters 3 and 4 for more on ALEC). ALEC and the NRA are powerful lobbies through which corporations and billionaires get their will done in state legislatures and Congress. The consolidation of power of these CEOs and their attack on workers' rights has been very successful—at least for the personal fortunes of the CEOs. From 1978 to 2011, the annual pay for workers rose 5.7 percent. The annual income of CEOs during this period rose 726.7 percent.[18]

Of the broader fight, Jayaraman says, "Are we a nation that is going to roll over and let corporations control our democracy and our economy, and even our bodies as women? Is this what we're going to accept as a nation?" Her answer is clearly no. If you don't fight, you lose.

The NRA is also fighting the Service Employees International Union, which is aggressively organizing low-wage workers at fast-food restaurants such as McDonald's and Burger King. These workers are striking to demand a living wage of $15 an hour, which is nearly double the federal minimum wage paid at many fast-food restaurants

"We have common enemies in groups like the National Restaurant Association (NRA), which deal with the Monsantos and the Grocery Manufacturers Associations of the world," Jayaraman said. "When we target our common rivals and let our elected officials know that their obligations are not only to huge food corporations, that's when we demonstrate power and that's when we win."[19]

Jayaraman thinks and links big. As part of organizing low-wage workers, ROC has an active presence in the sustainable food and in the racial and gender justice movements, and many ROC workers participated in Occupy protests.

"This being the second-largest industry in the United States, we've partnered very closely to frame these issues as broader civil rights issues," says Jayaraman. "We definitely see ourselves as very much a part of a broader progressive movement for change."

NUESTRO LABOR MANTIENE LA ECONOMÍA DEL MUNDO
OUR LABOR DRIVES THE WORLD ECONOMY

عملنا يقود الإقتصاد العالمي

The Power of Our Love and Money can Sustain Transnational Communities
El poder de nuestro amor y dinero puede sustentar a comunidades transnacionales

■ **NUESTRO LABOR MANTIENE LA ECONO-MÍA DEL MUNDO. Favianna Rodríguez, Oakland, California, 2008** Understanding that workers of the world generate the profit of capitalists is a starting point for any critical analysis of the transformations needed in our economic system. Exploitation and ownership of the means of production by the capitalist class fuel a class struggle that is irreconcilable without a revolution of the economic and political systems that define our lives. This piece was originally developed for an international gathering of immigrant rights advocates that took place in Mexico City in 2008. It speaks to the imperialism of First World nations and workers, specifically immigrants, who are the engine of production in the world.

WHEN WE FIGHT, WE WIN!

What has the economic justice movement accomplished?

Ordinary people now talk openly about capitalism and inequality. As Occupy press team member Mark Bray wrote in the Occupy anthology *We Are Many:*

We have managed to initiate an unprecedented national conversation about economic justice and democracy, revive a long-dormant tradition of civic participation, and rejuvenate the American left. More "concretely," we've prevented foreclosures across the country and directly assisted successful labor campaigns.[20]

OWS participant and writer Ryan Harvey offered another view of the movement's accomplishments:

Occupy's greatest achievement might be that it declared, in a popular language and with great public support, that the financial system of unregulated capitalism and corporate control over life is the key political and economic problem we face today. That analysis existed before either in private or public only in what would be considered fringe circles. Now it's out in pop culture, and it's controversial to not recognize the problem.[21]

Sasha Costanza-Chock, an assistant professor at MIT who visited, trained, and surveyed Occupy encampments around the country as part of Occupy Research, observes, "I think that the most important impact of Occupy is actually in the radicalization of a new generation of activists inside the U.S. . . . in a similar way that the global justice movement ended up developing a whole generation from Seattle forward.

"I'm sure when people look back in a few years," he continues, "what they'll find is that there [were] a large number of people who came through Occupy and then moved on to become engaged in some other type of organizing effort." Occupy, concludes Costanza-Chock, is "sort of like a giant open university for social movement participation."

Steve Meacham of City Life/Vida Urbana says that the economic justice movement succeeds when it tackles bigger issues of injustice and inequality. "People like the idea that they're basing their struggle around building something larger than themselves. They'll more readily share their personal struggle if it's not just about their personal struggle."

Meacham says that in the anti-foreclosure struggle, "you can't fight rent increases and evictions (real estate firms and banks) without objecting to the capitalist market. If you accept market principles, if you say the fair rent is the market rent, then you might as well not even get into the battle because you've lost already.

"For people who are fighting to save their homes, they have to go through a process of radical transformation if they haven't already in order to do the most basic fight. They have to challenge the market. They have to struggle with what it means. The fight against the capitalist market grows organically out of the most basic struggle to save people's homes."

Challenging injustice is the beginning of change. Meacham recounts, "When I was working in the shipyard twenty-five years ago, we heard of a struggle in Germany where there was a big effort to propose other kinds of products to keep shipyards open other than for navy ships. The workers engaged in this radical act of taking over a shipyard that the owners wanted to close in Bremen, West Germany, and they hung this huge sign from the gate that said, 'If you fight, you may lose. If you don't fight, you've already lost.'

"That was the first time I heard something like, 'When we fight, we win.' We started using that phrase at City Life/Vida Urbana because it symbolized the fact that even though we don't win every battle and we don't win everybody's case, when we fight, we still win. Because people who even fight and lose would rather have fought than not fought. The movement always grows out of each fight." Other movements have used the powerful slogan as well.

Disruption and deep roots are key elements of the fight. Sociologist, Occupy activist, and author Frances Fox Piven observes that Occupy, in its brief history, lacked the reach in "diverse groups of workers and students and the poor" and lacked the "strategies of disruption that gave earlier movements some power" to effect transformative structural change:

The great movements of the American past did much more than communicate their point of view. They mobbed the house of the rich, helped steal the slave property of the south, shut down the mines and factories and even occupied them, rioted in the biggest cites.[22]

Piven takes the long view and is ultimately hopeful about Occupy and movements for economic power:

Evicted from the squares and parks it occupied, [activists under many auspices have] moved to connect with community and worker struggles, to demonstrate against banks, to block evictions resulting from foreclosures. . . . Numbers alone will not give this protest movement the leverage it needs to halt or slow down or turn around predatory financialized capitalism with global reach. More likely it will have to discover or rediscover the strategies of disruption that gave earlier movements some power. . . . They identified the leverage that people who are usually on the bottom side of cooperative relationship might have over the people on the top side.[23]

Economic justice struggles of today face similar questions: How can people transform society and create an economic structure that is not based on one class profiting and ruling over the many? How can activists respond to the violent crackdown of the state that occurs whenever the power of the ruling class is threatened? How can activists tear down the structures that enslave, exploit, and impoverish the majority?

The anti-foreclosure campaigns, the struggles by restaurant workers, Occupy Wall Street, and other movements in this book each suggest what a global mass movement centered on people, not corporate profits, might look like. Each of these movements critiques capitalism, sees a common enemy, and proffers paths for struggling families to gain economic power, changing how society configures power.

Their transformative visions echo Dr. Martin Luther King Jr.:

We must rapidly begin the shift from a "thing-oriented" society to a "person-oriented" society. When machines and computers, profit motives and property rights are considered more important than people, the giant triplets of racism, materialism, and militarism are incapable of being conquered.[24]

Bold visions that fight to win address the root causes of power and create opportunities for economic democracy and participation by all people in decisions that affect their lives, particularly the most historically excluded populations: the working class, people of color, and women. Transformative organizations advance visions of a generative economy that provides meaningful employment, with workers having democratic participation and control in their workplace and in society. Frances Fox Piven writes, "Social transformation in the pursuit of equality, inclusion, democracy, and social justice requires that we find ways to take back the wealth stolen from ordinary people here and elsewhere by capitalist elites, especially the wealth stolen from those who are the worst off among us."[25]

Twenty-first-century movements demonstrate that protest—fighting everything from foreclosures to unlivable wages to inequality to capitalism to racism—can catch fire and burn hot.

One night after a long session with Occupy Wall Street activists in Zuccotti Park, Manissa McCleave Maharawal biked home over the Brooklyn Bridge. "I somehow felt like the world was, just maybe, at least in that moment, mine—as well as everyone's . . . who needed and wanted more from the world. I somehow felt like maybe the world could be all of ours."

LILY
PAULINA

LILY PAULINA IS A FEMINIST, ACTIVIST, UNION ORGANIZER, AND MEMBER OF THE RUDE MECHANICAL ORCHESTRA (RMO), A NEW YORK CITY–BASED RADICAL MARCHING BAND AND DANCE TROUPE. THROUGH THEIR MUSIC, RMO STRIVES TO BRING JOY AND INSPIRATION WHILE PLEDGING TO FIGHT RACISM, SEXISM, HOMOPHOBIA, WAR, AND VIOLENCE IN ALL FORMS.

Photo by Erik McGregor

I play the trombone with the Rude Mechanical Orchestra (RMO), a consensus-based collective with a diffuse leadership structure. We support street actions by playing music and amplifying messages, drawing attention to social justice organizations and groups of people fighting oppression and exploitation in different ways. We do that by playing songs, supporting chanting, disrupting business, or by making people angry if that's what's needed. It's hard to get the attention of New Yorkers. A live band makes people stop and look.

You can send very strong messages with lyrics and songs of political content, but there are very few groups that actually commit to the political work. The RMO has taken on that challenge. What do you think should be the role of artists in twenty-first-century movements?

Like Toni Cade Bambara said, "The role of the revolutionary artist is to make the revolution irresistible."

Rude Mechanical Orchestra started in 2004 out of feminist organizing to try to get people in the street for the March for Women's Lives, and using music to express anger and draw attention.

We are in a time of crisis, especially economic crisis, of inequality in our world right now. As a band, getting people to find the energy and the places to get in the fight is really important. We hope it makes it more fun and helps people to get in the streets and stay there.

That's the feedback that the RMO gets after every action. Yesterday we were marching with families whose family members have been murdered by the NYPD. Hearing them say "Thank you so much, it's still good to dance and be angry" drives our work. We know that music makes it easier for people to do that march from Union Square to Times Square. We're happy to help boost energy. It makes a huge difference.

In the big picture, things are bad and getting worse in a lot of ways. It feels like we're losing. Low-wage workers, who are disproportionately women of color, are at the lowest rung of the white supremacy ladder and suffer the most. It feels like a bleak time right now, but the RMO is a solidarity organization and we see ourselves supporting groups that share our politics, helping them stay engaged and fight burnout and helping their voices be heard. When they win, that's success for us.

When did you decide to be clearer about messaging in terms of the visual work of the band?

Sometimes, especially when we're in a place where there are other bands, it just feels like a party and nothing else. We wanted to make sure that if you walk through a crowd, people are able to see our politics even if they don't listen to us. Really thinking about people being able to get our politics in a lot of different forms is important. We message in two ways: with our music and with the visual images we project as a band. We spend a lot of time thinking about which songs we play, who those artists are, and what their politics are. We think about what chants work best with each song, and what a given song can bring to a situation in terms of mood and energy—what people will think and how will they feel when they hear us.

In recent years we've gone back to the riot grrrl approach, where if someone takes a picture of you, you don't want them to be able to make that just a picture of a cute girl who's a musician, but that any visual would convey some of your politics. We've felt very pushed by the media. I actually ended up on the cover of a Harvard Square Business Association report one year. That was the moment for me personally where I was like, "Okay, I am going to make a glove that says, 'Fuck the profit motive,'" because if I had that on, I would not be on the cover of the Harvard Square Business Association as their poster girl.

JOINING A LONG LEGACY AS THE SOUNDTRACK TO THE REVOLUTION!

Honk! Festival of Activist Street Bands, Boston, Massachusetts, 2014. Photo by Jesse Edsell-Veter

6

ENVIRONMENTAL WARRIORS: GOING TO THE ROOT OF THE PROBLEM

■ **FIRST NATIONS PROTEST HARPER.**
#IdleNoMore protest on Parliament Hill, Ottawa, 2012 (Photo by Andre Forget, QMI Agency)
On December 21, 2012, more than a thousand First Nations demonstrators gathered at the Canadian Parliament to protest legislation that would erode indigenous sovereignty and environmental protections—an action that helped shut down a major downtown Ottawa street. Canadian premier Stephen Harper's economic agenda would fast-track the sale of their land to polluting extractive industries. The women-led movement demanded: "It is time to be Idle No More." The social media campaign has been driven by indigenous youth who are well connected and deeply committed to preserving their land, language, and culture.

PROTECTING OUR MOTHER FOR OUR UNBORN CHILDREN
STOP FRACKING ⚡ STOP DRILLING

■ **PROTECTING OUR MOTHER FOR OUR UNBORN CHILDREN. Gregg Deal, Washington, D.C., 2013**
This poster draws inspiration from a photograph of a First Nations anti-fracking protest in New Brunswick. A kneeling Amanda Polchies is seen raising an eagle feather to hold off heavily armed police. Polchies said her action represented a "wisp of hope." The photograph, by Ossie Michelin, went viral and became the image for the anti-fracking movement in Canada. Hydraulic fracturing, or hydrofracking, involves injecting noxious chemicals into the ground to break out oil and gas deposits. This practice has caused increased seismic activity and contamination of land and water supplies. Gregg Deal is an artist, activist, and member of the Paiute tribe of Pyramid Lake. Throughout his work the artist advances discussion and education about issues of decolonization.

In response to the climate crisis, communities, especially ones traditionally excluded from power structures, are organizing to create an unprecedented global movement to defend their rights to health and well-being and attack the root political and economic causes of the crisis.

Forging new alliances between mainstream environmental organizations, indigenous groups, and diverse grassroots activists and organizations, the currently evolving environmental movement has seen many successes: stopping construction of coal-fired power plants, blocking fracking for natural gas in numerous areas, stalling the construction of toxic oil pipelines, and challenging fossil fuel companies, and the banks that fund them, with a national divestment campaign. These transformers interrupt powerful economic systems, exposing those who profit as they destroy lives and homes. In addition to addressing problems, the environmental movement creates solutions: activists are developing practical energy systems, promoting large-scale renewable power, implementing local community-based sustainable structures that transition communities away from fossil fuels, and creating transformative visions.

The advances in the environmental movement take place against an increasingly urgent backdrop of worsening climate change. Still, polluters, governments, and international bodies—led especially by U.S. energy companies—fight hard to maintain the status quo.

The climate crisis forces much-needed questions. How can international environmental justice groups stop destructive, consumptive, undemocratic, corporate-driven, global economic and political systems? How will we create new systems to save the life of the earth? Can the world sustain capitalist society?

A new generation of creative change-makers is tackling these questions, disrupting power, and advancing alternative visions that uncover the root of our environmental destruction by linking with other issues. This chapter includes three inspiring stories: Idle No More, an indigenous group leading the fight against the destruction of native lands in Canada; the innovative "leader-full" resistance of 350.org; and the Los Angeles Bus Riders Union.

The group of marchers looked tiny against the backdrop of industrial-scale destruction. Chemical smells permeated the air as the marchers snaked slowly through the desertified landscape of the tar sands of Alberta. Huge towers belched black smoke that spiraled into the mouse-gray Canadian sky.

This apocalyptic landscape of mine tailings and denuded earth is the epicenter of the Canadian tar sands, where multinational energy companies are now prowling in search of the world's next big oil bonanza.

The dirty job of extracting oil from sand is so energy-intensive and toxic that renowned NASA climate scientists and activists on the front lines of communities devastated by the tar sands industry in North Dakota agree that our quality of life on this planet will be destroyed if the tar sands are fully exploited. It is ecocide.

This crowd of people had gathered for a Healing Walk. They assembled outside Fort McMurray, a tar sands boomtown, to reclaim and heal something precious to them: the earth. The indigenous women of Keepers of the Athabasca organized this effort to reclaim their community from environmental devastation. Many of these women were part of a native-led environmental justice group, Idle No More, which formed to fight climate change and environmental exploitation and to lead "a peaceful revolution to honor indigenous sovereignty, and to protect the land and water."

Clayton Thomas-Müller, a Native Canadian who is co-director of the Indigenous Tar Sands Campaign of the Polaris Institute, was master of ceremonies of this Healing Walk. He described the experience of walking through his homeland in *Yes!* magazine:

The landscape was unlike anything I had ever seen before. I walked past a tailings pond [an open pond of mining refuse and chemicals] so big that it covered the horizon for miles, fed by a 24 inch wide pipe spewing a yards-high flow of liquid hydro-carbon waste so toxic that water fowl who land in it die within minutes. We saw from up close the hellfires of the Suncor/Petro-Canada stacks, with their 50-foot flames shooting up into the sky. I wondered what madness allowed Suncor to build them 500 meters away from the precious Athabasca River, which so many First Nations, Metis, and Inuit communities depend on for water.

As we walked, I pondered all of the battlefields facing the emerging international movement to stop the tar sands. I was overcome by the magnitude of our undertaking, picking a fight with the most inhumane and wealthiest corporations on the planet . . . .

No, I thought, that cannot work. This beast must be smothered to death at the source.[1]

Smothering "the beast"—corporations and governments that are destroying the environment and accelerating climate change—has proven fiercely difficult. Thomas-Müller says that going to "the source," colonialism and capitalism, has been daunting, but it is a necessary part of our essential task to heal the earth and its people.

Indigenous people have taken a leadership role in the fight to address the underlying conditions that need to be changed for environmental and social justice. "We told the heads of every environmental organization in the continent and their funders that in the end, it's going to be First Nations asserting sovereignty and Aboriginal title over their land that's going to stop the tar sands. They laughed at us, they scoffed at us," Thomas-Müller recalls of his experi-

> "We told the heads of every environmental organization in the continent and their funders that in the end, it's going to be First Nations asserting sovereignty and Aboriginal title over their land that's going to stop the tar sands."

ence in 2006. Then in 2009, the American Clean Energy and Security Act (aka the Waxman-Markey bill), a legislative effort to reduce carbon emissions, was defeated in Congress. Environmentalists were stunned and demoralized.

"That's when Bill McKibben [from 350.org] called me up at the Indigenous Environmental Network and said, 'Hey, we heard you were organizing some Native American chiefs that are concerned [enough] about the Keystone XL Pipeline to go get arrested at Obama's house, the White House.' He said, 'We want to join you and support you,'" recounts Thomas-Müller.

In 2011, indigenous and environmental groups together organized what Thomas-Müller calls "the largest act of civil disobedience since the Vietnam War on the steps of the White House." Protesters called on President Obama to stop Keystone XL, the 1,700-mile-long pipeline that will open the floodgates of dirty tar sands oil from Alberta, Canada, and carry it to the Gulf of Mexico.

Following the White House protest, McKibben wrote, "A few months ago, it was mainly people along the route of the prospective pipeline who were organizing against it (and with good reason: tar sands mining has already wrecked huge swaths of native land in Alberta and endangers farms, wild areas, and aquifers all along its prospective route). Now, however, people are coming to understand—as we hoped our demonstrations would highlight—that it poses a danger to the whole planet as well. After all, it's the Earth's second-largest pool of carbon, and hence the second-largest potential source of global warming gases after the oil fields of Saudi Arabia."[2]

Thousands of protesters from all fifty states and Canada descended on the White House for the 2011 protest, and more than twelve hundred people were arrested, including Native American leaders. It was a momentous sign of civil disobedience and convergence. The once-isolated tar sands struggle, Thomas-Müller reflects, had "become the lightning rod of the U.S. climate movement."

"LED BY NATIVE PEOPLE ON THE FRONT LINE"

For Clayton Thomas-Müller, environmental justice is deeply personal and rooted in his community. A member of the Mathias Colomb Cree Nation in northern

Manitoba, Canada, he had been working on gang and poverty issues in his community. "It was a natural transition to go from working on the front line of human rights work into the environmental justice and eventually the climate justice movement. Because the answer [to] 'Why are we so damn poor and oppressed in our homeland?'—all roads lead to the same forces causing climate change: it's big oil, it's big mining companies, it's big timber companies that have decimated our land that put us where we are."

Thomas-Müller sees his work in the climate fight as part of a larger social justice mission. The Healing Walk "represented a very, very strong spiritual right hook into the check of those that are fanatical in their belief in the neoliberal free market agenda that is currently dominating our economic paradigm here in the so-called developed industrialized West. It represents a different phase of resistance . . . one that will see a very strong spiritual core . . . that cannot be defeated by the ridiculous propaganda that Big Oil, in partnership with the federal government of Canada and to a certain degree, the government in the United States of America, continues to put out to try and sell this dirty energy source across the planet.

"One of the beautiful things that the Indigenous Tar Sands Campaign has brought to the world—because it has become one of the most visible environmental campaigns ever—[is that] it's led by native people on the front line. No matter who's shaking hands in D.C. . . . native people have led this charge and we'll be the ones at the end to win this victory."

Thomas-Müller stresses that the climate justice movement will only advance if it forges links with other struggles in attacking the root political and economic causes of the environmental crisis. "The lesson here is that by converging struggles in a solidarity framework rooted in anti-racism, anti-oppression, and anti-colonialism—and by creating economic and political initiatives uniting urban and rural centers—as social movements, we can wield the power. That's never been seen by our oppressors.

"No matter what we do moving forward," he goes on, "we need to develop economies that don't force people to have to choose between clean air, water, and earth or putting food on the table."

BUILDING "LEADER-FULL" MOVEMENTS

"Why are we so damn poor and oppressed in our homeland?"

Bill McKibben has been thinking about tough choices, both personally and within the climate justice movement in which he is a leader—albeit an ambivalent one. McKibben was a staff writer for the *New Yorker* in the 1980s when he first researched and wrote an article about climate change. He was startled and disturbed by what he learned. In 1989, he went on to author *The End of Nature,* the first major book about the threat of climate change.

McKibben increasingly grew frustrated at the lack of action to address climate change. He had eloquently expressed the problem but had failed to move people to solve it. He decided to take action: he would undertake a long march to call attention to the issue, much as the Trail of DREAMs immigration activists and the Healing Walkers had. On Labor Day weekend 2006, McKibben was joined by enthusiastic students from Middlebury College and concerned local citizens and embarked on a climate march from his hometown of Ripton, Vermont, to Burlington, Vermont.

"Reading the story in the paper that said that the one thousand people we got to Burlington after five days of walking might have been the biggest climate rally in U.S. history—that was shocking," McKibben says. "I guess that must be one reason why we're losing."

Since that walk, McKibben has gone from astute observer to climate movement organizer. In 2008, McKibben and student activists founded 350.org with the goal of "building a global climate movement." The organization is named for 350 parts per million (ppm), the safe upper limit for carbon dioxide in the atmosphere if we are to preserve a livable planet, according to some climate scientists. The rising levels of carbon dioxide, currently 400 ppm, in recent decades are largely due to the increase in the use of fossil fuels.

On October 24, 2009, 350.org organizers in 181 countries staged 5,200 demonstrations to demand action on climate change. CNN called it "the most widespread day of political action in our planet's history."

It was a remarkable display of grassroots power. The protests were intended to bring pressure on international climate negotiators who were meeting in

**■ THE TRUE COST
OF COAL. Beehive
Design Collective,
Machias, Maine, 2010**
In 2008, the Beehive
Design Collective,
working with Appa-
lachian organizers
fighting mountaintop
removal coal mining,
designed *The True Cost
of Coal.* Mountaintop
removal is a practice
in which mountains
are destroyed to reach
thin seams of coal. This
poster is a storytelling
and educational re-
source that "depicts the
complex relationships
between industry,
commerce, society and
the natural world that
are inseparable from
the fight to end moun-
taintop removal. The
large-form pen-and-ink
image transitions from
scenes of undisturbed
wilderness to indus-
trialized madness."
Beehive Design Collec-
tive is a Maine-based
collaborative artists
group with a mission
of "cross-pollinating
the grassroots."

True Cost of Coal

■ **GREAT LAKES TAR SANDS RESISTANCE.**
Pat Perry, Grand Rapids, Michigan, 2013
For this poster, artist Pat Perry depicts four activists who locked themselves to construction equipment on July 22, 2013, to disrupt the expansion of Enbridge's Line 6B pipeline, which carries tar sands oil. This pipeline burst two years earlier into the Kalamazoo River, causing the largest land-based oil spill in U.S. history. Enbridge, an energy delivery company based in Alberta, Canada, is responsible for seven hundred other spills in the past decade. The artist worked with the Michigan Coalition Against Tar Sands, a direct-action coalition against the extraction, transportation, and refining of tar sands. Tar sands oil requires three times more energy to produce than conventional oil and discharges three times the amount of CO_2.

RESISTING TAR SANDS IN THE GREAT LAKE STATE

SAY NO WAY AS OIL JUNKIES TAKE NEW VEINS IN MICHIGAN

On July 22nd, 2013, four people locked themselves to construction equipment outside of Lansing, disrupting expansion of Enbridge's Line 6B pipeline, the same pipeline that burst into the Kalamazoo River in 2010 causing the largest land-oil spill in US history. Four actions took place over the summer; others involved skateboarding into a pipeline, tree sits, and soft blockades. The four arrested on the 22nd, are members of the Michigan Coalition Against Tar Sands (MICATS), and are now facing felony charges equivalent to that of "assaulting an officer" for their acts of nonviolent civil disobedience.

Enbridge's Line 6B carries tar sands oil, one of the dirtiest and most destructive fossil fuels on the planet. The tar sands process rapidly boosts carbon emissions and is quickly accelerating the climate crisis. Because of large gaps in oversight and accountability, Enbridge has successfully laid the groundwork for an explosion of new tar sands development in Canada that is being piped through our state as the tar sands are transported to the East Coast for export. This increase exposes the already threatened Great Lakes to larger and more toxic pipeline spills. In addition to the 2010 Kalamazoo River spill, Enbridge is responsible for 700 other spills in the past ten years.

The Enbridge extraction projects continue to jeopardize the health and safety of Michigan's citizens and Michigan's ecosystem, while the EPA estimates that 80,000-290,000 gallons of tar sands oil still remain in the Kalamazoo River. We can no longer let the state, and the fossil fuel industry decide our relationship to the environment and to each other. We can no longer wait for others to protect our state for us. Stand in solidarity with "the felonious four", take your own action, and learn more about MICATS at www.michigancats.org

ENVIRONMENTAL JUSTICE 101

Professor Antwi Akom, associate professor of Africana studies at San Francisco State University and the co-founder of the Institute for Sustainable Economic, Educational, and Environmental Design (I-SEEED), discusses environmental justice.

What Is Environmental Justice?

Environmental justice is the idea that climate change most adversely affects our nation's most vulnerable populations—the same people who are left out of our economic and political structures. It is embedded in social justice and public health and is intertwined with land use and transportation decisions.

Environmental justice activists know that where the ghetto begins bike share and Zipcar end.

Even though climate change is one of the highest-stakes transformative issues of our time, the climate change movement remains highly homogenous by race and class and significantly by gender in its leadership. Even in 2014, climate and sustainability conferences held around the world consistently feature mostly all-white male casts in leadership positions as well as mostly white people in attendance. The irony here is that people of color have always cared about climate change and, more often than not, are the first ones to most directly feel its impacts.

Environmental justice activists analyze the connections between the oppression of people with the least power—including the poor, immigrants, women, and people of color—and the degradation of the earth. They focus not only on the regeneration of nature but also on healing communities and innovating ways to transform educational, economic, and environmental ecosystems. Instead of viewing the impacts of global warming solely through the data gathered by scientific experts and portrayed by national policy makers, they perceive and analyze climate change through people's lived experiences, art, poetry, storytelling, and community-based research.

Environmental justice activists understand the power of local knowledge. And they understand that the experiences that people of color have about living with multiple environmental health hazards and chronic disease is one of the fundamental assets they can contribute to the movement against climate change. It is often a key resource the community organizes around to avoid being exploited and exposed to health risks and social toxins.

When communities of color engage in climate activism, their primary goal is often to help themselves and their communities by generating usable or actionable knowledge—information that goes beyond description and analysis and suggests proactive or precautionary intervention strategies. By taking action to transform the social and material conditions in their communities, community members build self-respect, self-confidence, and self-determination.

Although the environmental justice movement is evolving in the twenty-first century, there remain enormous barriers to collaboration between environmental justice activists and the climate change movement. These barriers—bred in corporate boardrooms, born on plantations, and reared in brownfields—underscore America's continued reluctance to invest in black and brown innovators and black and brown communities.

ENVIRONMENTAL JUSTICE 101 (continued)

What Is the Relationship Between Race, Gender, Class, and Climate Change?

Worldwide, poor people and people of color disproportionately suffer from higher morbidity and mortality rates from extreme water scarcity, heat waves, air pollution, and the "heat island" effect of urban areas. They are also disproportionately impacted by higher costs for food, transportation, land use, electricity, unemployment, underemployment, and seismic economic shifts. For example, in their 2008 report *A Climate of Change: African Americans, Global Warming, and a Just Climate Policy in the U.S.*, J. Andrew Hoerner and Nia Robinson wrote, "African Americans are 13 percent of the U.S. population and on average emit nearly 20 percent less greenhouse gases than non-Hispanic whites per capita. Though far less responsible for climate change, African Americans are significantly more vulnerable to its effects than non-Hispanic whites."[3]

Women, specifically women of color, are disproportionately impacted by disasters and environmental degradation caused by global warming. Women make up approximately 70 percent of those living in poverty, and low-income women, women of color, and immigrants will be most impacted by the severe weather events, heat waves, and increases in disease rates that will characterize the earth's changing climate.

We've known for a long time that there's been a gap between eco haves and eco have-nots. We've known that race and class have determined who gets left behind with respect to housing, health care, education, and all of the systemic ways that climate change really impacts our communities.

What we're really just seeing is the reproduction of structural and systemic inequality and the ecological impacts of that reproduction. I call it eco apartheid.

What Will It Take to Create a More Inclusive Climate Justice Movement?

The diverse and collective response necessary to counterbalance special interests in oil and coal will require the engagement and organizing of more people on the ground, from many different walks of life. We must forge new partnerships, build new frameworks, create new organizing models, and develop new technologies that connect seemingly disparate issues and address the systemic inequities and chronic dilemmas facing communities, people, and ecosystems across the planet. Those who are suffering the most should have a powerful voice in choosing how these issues are addressed. They should be involved at the individual and community levels, for without this on-the-ground community engagement, broad political power cannot be built and sustainable progress cannot be made.

The work of creating a climate justice movement for everyone is in large part about moving the margins to the epicenter. Poor people and people of color, who often live in the most toxic communities, are the first in line for the negative impacts of climate change, and therefore stand to benefit substantially from a more sustainable energy future.

It is critical for well-resourced organizations with the perceived authority on climate issues to step out of their comfort zones and engage poor people, people of color, and constituencies who bring different knowledge and assets to the shifting terrain of the climate crisis. Corporations and industries benefiting from the pollution-based economy will always have more money to tilt the scales in their favor with respect to political and regulatory issues. The climate justice movement's biggest counterforce is to engage everyday people from across the spectrum of U.S. society.

Copenhagen in 2009 to enact strict limits on carbon emissions. But the Copenhagen negotiations ended in disarray.

Copenhagen, says McKibben, "should have been the place, if this had been written by Hollywood, where the world comes together and agrees on fighting the aliens and goes to work. But none of that happened. It was a complete and utter bust . . . for me, redeemed by all the great kids that 350.org brought. They were wonderful."

This is the challenge: the climate justice movement has achieved remarkable success in getting out its message and mobilizing people to attend demonstrations. But it has failed to disrupt the production or use of fossil fuels or bring about meaningful reform that would turn the tide of the steadily warming planet.

Has the climate movement been transformative?

"Well, no—I mean, so far, we're losing," McKibben replies in his typically self-effacing manner. "The Arctic melted last summer. The temperature keeps rising." But he acknowledges the movement's potential power. "I don't think we're quite big enough yet to have turned the tide, but we're getting closer. And if I were the fossil-fuel industry, I'd be somewhat less confident."

McKibben says the biggest success of the climate movement is "education—finally getting the idea out there that this is a big problem."

McKibben has helped reframe the issue of climate change in everyday terms that people understand. Climate change is "a crime with a criminal, and that criminal is the fossil-fuel industry—getting that idea out has been very important," says McKibben. It "unites people at the local level . . . [from] someone who has a coal plant in their backyard and all their kids are dying of asthma, with people who have deep concern about the larger climate picture."

One of McKibben's contributions to this strategy was an article that he wrote in *Rolling Stone* in 2012, "Global Warming's Terrifying New Math." The article went viral and helped spark a brushfire of activism. "A third of summer sea ice in the Arctic is gone, the oceans are 30 percent more acidic, and . . . the atmosphere over the oceans is a shocking five percent wetter, loading the dice for devastating floods," McKibben wrote, citing these dire new developments to squarely focus movement energies on targeting the economic underpinnings of Big Oil. "The fossil fuel industry has become a rogue industry, reckless like no other force on Earth. It is Public Enemy Number One to the survival of our planetary civilization."[4]

McKibben quips that "the movement can take a certain amount of credit" for its global reach. But he adds with a soft laugh, "Mother Nature can take a large amount of credit for that. In one sense, it's a very difficult movement because it has a time limit. . . . If it doesn't get done what it needs to get done quickly, it won't matter. On the other hand, it has an ally like no other . . . in the sort of endless supply of teachable moments that nature is now providing."

A key problem for the movement is scaling up. "We're making it big fast, but whether that's happening fast enough is not clear," says McKibben.

The elephant in the room for climate activists is the perverse logic of capitalism: the fact that it's extremely profitable to pollute. "There can be no real answer to our climate woes that doesn't address the insane inequalities and concentrations of power that are helping to drive us toward this disaster," McKibben wrote in 2013.

McKibben sees a tandem effort to bring about climate justice and fundamental economic and political change. "There's nothing we could do as important as putting a really serious price on carbon. . . . The basic effect would be a rapid decentralization of power and wealth in this country because the logic of renewable energy is so different. . . . In a real world that ran on solar panels, a lot of things would look very, very different."

In 2012, McKibben traveled the country on a national Do the Math bus tour, spreading the word about the alarming speed with which climate change is happening, and pushing the case to ratchet up the tactics to confront it.

McKibben and others, including fellow author and activist Naomi Klein, decided to take their challenge

> "Mother Nature can take a large amount of credit for that. In one sense, it's a very difficult movement because it has a time limit."

YOU SHOULDN'T HAVE TO READ THIS POSTER. Rachel Schragis, Brooklyn, New York, 2012

You Shouldn't Have to Read This Poster is a flow chart about "the stuff we need to know about climate change besides the suffering that it causes—its history, politics and science. It's also about tactics for resistance to climate change." The image was designed for 350.org's Do the Math campaign of education and organizing. Launched in the fall of 2012, this nationwide divestment campaign targeted fossil fuel companies, recognizing that individual actions to reduce emissions are simply not enough to stop the climate disaster.

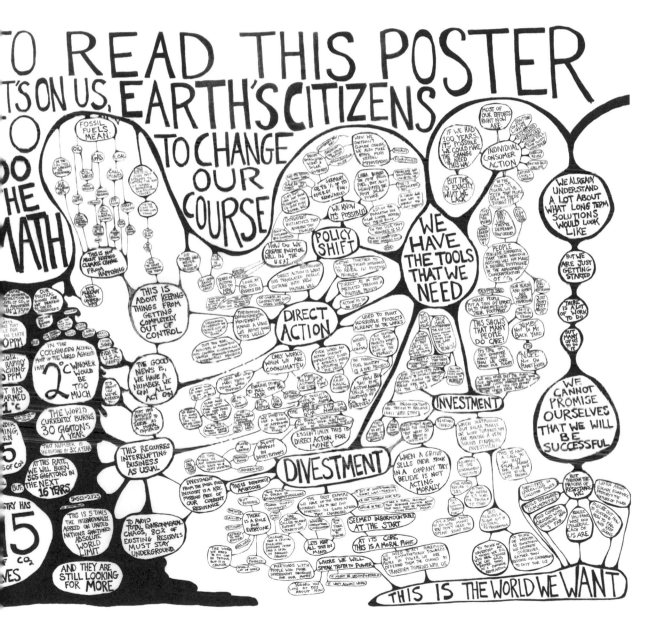

to the pocketbooks of the world's fossil fuel industry. They helped launch a national campaign calling for individuals, pension funds, universities, and others to withdraw their investments from the two hundred fossil fuel companies with the biggest carbon reserves. The campaign was modeled on a divestment effort a generation earlier mounted by a global anti-apartheid movement that pressured the racist government in South Africa to end apartheid.

The fossil fuel divestment campaign quickly gained traction. By 2014, more than three hundred college campuses had divestment groups, and universities, including Stanford, began divesting. Numerous cities—including Seattle, Washington; Portland, Oregon; Cambridge, Massachusetts; and San Francisco, Oakland, and Santa Monica in California—divested all or part of their stock portfolios of fossil fuel companies. Seventeen foundations with combined assets of nearly $1.8 billion committed to divest. And in a move rich with symbolism, the Rockefeller Brothers Fund, a philanthropy with almost $900 million in assets that was created by the grandchildren of the oil magnate John D. Rockefeller Sr., announced in September 2014 that it would divest its fossil fuel holdings.

"John D. Rockefeller, the founder of Standard Oil, moved America out of whale oil and into petroleum," said Stephen Heintz, president of the Rockefeller Brothers Fund. "We are quite convinced that if he were alive today, as an astute businessman looking out to the future, he would be moving out of fossil fuels and investing in clean, renewable energy."[5]

"Ultimately the divestment campaign has been very successful, partly because it started with a real burst of energy. Impatience helped drive that. I think a sense of urgency is very important in social change," offers May Boeve, executive director of 350.org.

> *"They put a refinery in the middle of a city full of poor people. They had an explosion there [in 2012] and they texted like five thousand people. Basically, the text was, 'Hold your breath. There's bad stuff leaking out.'"*

BREAKING DOWN BARRIERS OF RACE AND CLASS

McKibben spent much of the summer of 2013 on the road on a campaign that 350.org dubbed Summer Heat. The campaign evolved, making linkages between national environmental movements and local groups that are working on environmental and economic justice. The tour ended at a Chevron refinery in Richmond, California, a particularly potent symbol.

"This refinery in Richmond is a perfect example of environmental injustice on a massive scale," McKibben says. "They put a refinery in the middle of a city full of poor people. They had an explosion there [in 2012] and they texted like five thousand people. Basically, the text was, 'Hold your breath. There's bad stuff leaking out.' That's crazy, so that's reason enough to protest it. But Chevron also gave the largest corporate-campaign contribution post–*Citizens United* [the 2010 U.S. Supreme Court decision allowing corporations to make unlimited campaign contributions] before the 2012 election to make sure the House stayed in the hands of climate deniers. It was successful. Chevron also is the villain in this endless, ongoing fight in the rain forests of Ecuador. So from any perspective you look at them, it demands that kind of solidarity."

In 2014, Chevron spent more than $3 million in an effort to elect a pro-Chevron mayor and slate of candidates to the Richmond City Council. Chevron spent about $72 per registered voter, outspending their opponents twenty to one.[6] When the votes were counted, a slate of four progressive candidates claimed victory. Chevron had failed.

Richmond has lately become a model of how to challenge both climate change and economic injustice. Solar Richmond is a nonprofit organization self-described as being "committed to breaking down barriers of race and class as we promote the green economy."

"Solar Richmond is not only building solar panels, but building worker co-ops that produce solar panels . . . in an . . . economically viable and more sustainable way so that there's not the same level of pollution. They have a different model of capitalism, so that we're really creating communities that actually own the means of production rather than [just being] consumers.

■ **LIBERTY FOR ALL. Julio Salgado from Culture-Strike, in collaboration with Tina Vásquez, Oakland, California, 2014**
Liberty for All is a weekly online comic strip by Culture Strike artist Julio Salgado and writer Tina Vásquez. It features a queer, undocumented college graduate named Libertad Martinez, who cannot get a regular job because of her immigration status. In the strip, the artists reflect on the fact that, even though there is trendy rhetoric on "sustainability," green solutions are not new to communities of color. Sustainability, as a popular discourse in contemporary economics and politics, often ignores systemic problems of capitalism. Climate crisis must be understood as a product of the capitalist need to conquer new markets—including the "green" one—and does not offer effective solutions to planetary sustainability.

STORY-MEMES FOR THE PEOPLE'S CLIMATE MARCH. Joe Solomon for Energy Action Coalition, New York City, 2014

On September 21, 2014, 400,000 people took to the streets of New York City to demand action to end the climate crisis. The "story-memes" created by Energy Action Coalition featured the voices of New Yorkers, environmental justice activists, and allies who came together for the historic march. Each image features a photo of a community leader and their motivation for getting involved with the march. Energy Action Coalition consists of thirty youth-led social and environmental justice organizations working together to build the youth clean energy and climate movement. The memes produced by coalition youth are visual vehicles that carry messages of possibility and people power.

The green economy is going to have to move in that direction in order to not reproduce the same kinds of inequality that we've seen in the pollution-based economy," San Francisco State University professor Antwi Akom notes.

Bill McKibben has been finding commonality with broader and deeper networks of movements. "The Fossil Fuel Resistance looks more and more like Occupy—in fact, they've overlapped from the beginning, since oil companies are the one percent of the one percent," he wrote in *Rolling Stone* in 2013. "The movements share a political analysis, too: A grid with a million solar rooftops feels more like the internet than ConEd [the huge New York City electric utility]; it's a farmers' market in electrons, with the local control that it implies. Like Occupy, this new Resistance is not obsessed with winning over Democratic Party leaders."[7]

In late 2014, McKibben stepped down from the daily leadership of 350.org. He reflected in an essay for TomDispatch that removing himself as a leader of the climate movement may be just the kind of leadership that this and other movements need:

Most of the movements of the moment—even highly successful ones like the fight for gay marriage or immigrants' rights—don't really have easily discernible leaders . . . [who] the public at large identifies as the face of the fight. The world has changed in this way, and for the better. . . .

We may not need capital-L Leaders, but we certainly need small-l leaders by the tens of thousands. You could say that, instead of a leaderless movement, we need a leader-full one. . . .

It's our job to rally a movement in the coming years big enough to stand up to all that money, to profits of a sort never before seen on this planet. Such a movement will need to stretch from California to Ecuador. . . . It needs to remake the world in record time.

That won't happen thanks to a paramount leader, or even dozens of them. It can only happen with a spread-out and yet thoroughly interconnected movement, a new kind of engaged citizenry. Rooftop by rooftop, we're aiming for a different world, one that runs on the renewable power that people produce themselves in their communities in small but significant batches. The movement that will get us to such a new world must run on that kind of power too.[8]

ALL ABOARD THE BUS

The Los Angeles Bus Riders Union (BRU), comprising mostly public school students and low-income black and Latino workers, is leading a campaign to improve public transport with the vision of abolishing cars in L.A. Among other innovative strategies, the BRU has launched lawsuits against fare hikes, with the Natural Resources Defense Council emphasizing that raising fares results in more people driving and thus creates a health and environmental impact.[9]

Increased bus fares are also an obstacle for many students to get to school. Channing Martinez was elected in 2015 to the BRU's planning committee. "I first joined the BRU in 2007 when Metro proposed a major fare hike for the first time in ten years," he explained. "I still claim that to be one of the top five most exciting days with the Bus Riders Union. We filled the whole [Metro transit] boardroom, filled all of their overflow rooms, and *los estudiantes* rallied and filled their whole lobby so much that the Fire Department gave Metro a ticket that day for overcapacity. The movement was full of anger, hope, and excitement that day. It shows us what is still possible today."

Eric Mann is director of the Strategy Center and author of the book *Playbook for Progressives: 16 Qualities of the Successful Organizer*. The No Cars in L.A. campaign is intended to be "a challenge to the entire power and culture of the auto/highway industry, but also a challenge to the privatized, consumerized, alienated nature of public life for the great masses of people," he says. "People say, 'Why no cars in L.A.?' We say because that's the least we can do to stop global warming at

"We may not need capital-L Leaders, but we certainly need small-l leaders by the tens of thousands. You could say that, instead of a leaderless movement, we need a leader-full one."

> *"The organizers were teaching us how to think critically about the world we live in, and to recognize all the contradictions the system creates that are right in front of us if we just wake up."*

the present pace it's going. Imagining no cars in L.A. is no more difficult than envisioning an end to Jim Crow or the Vietnam War. It is historically possible to have no cars in L.A., but obviously people will have to make a political, moral, and cultural decision to move to a public transportation, not a private auto, society."

The BRU is building a large multiracial, multiclass movement. "The black and Latino communities are not just the ones suffering the greatest impacts" of privatization, says Mann. "They have historically initiated and modeled transformative organizing from the black liberation struggle and the Central and South American liberation movements."

The BRU offers practical solutions, such as improving public transport, using the collective power of bus riders as it illustrates the intersecting issues of buses, schools, climate change, immigration, and the rise of mass incarceration.

Channing Martinez and the BRU want a win that will benefit the community while addressing larger injustices:

> I'd been a bus rider for all 27 years of my life. . . . I got involved because I learned through my participation as a student organizer in [the Coalition for Educational Justice] that there was a system of oppression in place hitting from every direction. One of the first fights that I was involved in was a protest against the war in the Middle East [for oil]—the aha moment was questioning how the president justified budgets for a war when he couldn't afford to educate young folks in his own country. The organizers were teaching us how to think critically about the world we live in, and to recognize all the contradictions the system creates that are right in front of us if we just wake up. I was a very shy person back then, but the more I learned about how multiple facets of this society fed into that system, the more my voice lifted.

One of the things that always keeps me going is coming to the realization that it took us four hundred years to defeat American slavery. And it took the leadership of a few organizers, like Nat Turner and like Harriet Tubman and others, to not be afraid to stand up and fight back. [The BRU] planning committee is simply a modern-day form of that leadership that we desperately need in our community and in our organization to keep the fight going. One of the amazing things that many people don't talk about in terms of talking about Harriet Tubman is that she was a hell of an organizer. She was able to organize white abolitionists to stand in solidarity, and to use their houses and their resources as part of the Underground Railroad. . . .

Our eyes are open and they're all on the system. . . . There's a big chance that we will win a free student bus pass pretty soon [and] stop this MTA apartheid pass system. But that can only happen when we members are on the ground organizing at every chance we get.

The BRU is part of the Los Angeles–based Labor/Community Strategy Center's Fight for the Soul of the Cities campaign, which they describe as "an international vision for urban organizing" that calls for "the social welfare state not the police state, the environmental state not the warfare state." The campaign's demands include freeing 2.5 million U.S. prisoners, no cars in L.A., free public transportation, amnesty and open borders for immigrants, and stopping U.S. drone attacks.

These demands are ambitious, but Mann argues that radical critiques are the only way to capture the imaginations of people who are depressed about their own lives and even more depressed about the capitalist system under which they live. "Ultimately we have to totally transform the whole industrial, transportation, consumption, and production frame. It's a struggle against the system of capitalism in which the privatizing, polluting, policing classes dominate society and the cities."

■ **OUR CANTASTORIA OF THE SOUTH BRONX AND LA MADRE. Agit Arte/Papel Machete, in collaboration with South Bronx Unite and El Puente, New York City, 2014 (Photos by Osvaldo Budet Meléndez)** For the People's Climate March in New York City, AgitArte allied with community organizations in the South Bronx and Brooklyn to create visuals and performance to highlight how climate change affects most harshly communities of color. A *cantastoria* was developed to support South Bronx Unite's Boycott FreshDirect campaign. FreshDirect proposes to use taxpayer subsidies to occupy public waterfront land, which would impose two thousand daily vehicle trips through a community already facing asthma rates five times the national average. In Brooklyn, the artist troupe worked closely with CADRE artists and El Puente Academy to develop *La Madre*. The giant puppet, which represents both Mother Earth and working-class mothers of color, was an iconic image of the march and drew widespread media coverage.

MARCHING FOR A GENERATIVE FUTURE

Climate justice offers one of the best opportunities of any twenty-first-century social movement to bring about fundamental social and economic change.

Beginning in the 1960s, the United Farm Workers won huge victories for workers' rights and in stopping the use of toxic pesticides. In the 1980s, activists protested as part of a large movement to shut down deadly nuclear power plants; none have been built in the United States since then. Movements pushing for clean water in the United States largely succeeded: many of the same rivers that were once killing fish are now safe to swim in. In recent years, anti-fracking activists have succeeded in having the destructive and polluting practice of fracking banned in a number of cities, as well as in New York State.

These movements were successful in stopping the symptoms but not in curing the source of the problems; they never transformed the economic systems that drive our environmental and social ills. Today, climate change and toxic pollution continue to threaten our lives, our planet, and especially our children. Solving the climate crisis will require a shift that goes to the root of our politics, economy, and behaviors.

"I think climate is perhaps the best opportunity we have to address the larger ills of capitalism," observes Farhad Ebrahimi, who runs the Chorus Foundation in Boston and was part of the media team for Occupy Boston. "It's the greatest crisis of capitalism. It is the unchecked growth. . . . It is the way that money has bought and sold our democratic systems.

"More and more I'm seeing people who really care about climate come to really care about money in politics and really care about creating alternatives, both in terms of where our energy is going to come from [and also] what are the economic structures. How do we get away from this corporate power and move towards a system that's more equitable or more democratic and works for more people?"

Ebrahimi quotes a rallying cry at climate change protests: "We need system change, not climate change." He says, "The slogan speaks to how engaging on climate work can be really transformative." This has become more than just a slogan: System Change Not Climate Change is an "eco-socialist coalition" with thirteen chapters around North America. The group makes the case, now more and more broadly accepted outside of corporate news, that "capitalism is driving climate change and . . . a radical international grassroots movement can stop it."

Author and activist Naomi Klein drove home this point in an address to a new Canadian labor union in September 2013:

Climate change vindicates much of what the left has been demanding for decades. In fact, climate change turbo-charges our existing demands and gives them a basis in hard science. It calls on us to be bold, to get ambitious, to win this time because we really cannot afford any more losses. . . . Confronting the climate crisis requires that we break every rule in the free-market playbook— and that we do so with great urgency.[10]

Klein outlined what it will take to tackle climate change:

We don't just need new infrastructure. We need major investments in the old infrastructure to cope with the coming storms. For decades we have fought against the steady starving of the public sphere. . . . It is not hyperbole to say that our future depends on our ability to do what we have so long been told we can no longer do: act collectively. . . . I am not suggesting some half-assed token "green jobs" program. This is a green labor revolution I'm talking about. An epic vision of healing our country from the ravages of the last 30 years of neoliberalism and healing the planet in the process. . . . A democratically controlled, de-centralized energy system operated in the public interest.[11]

Climate visionaries are setting a path to fundamental transformation. They are offering systemic solutions—not just individualistic solutions such as green water bottles, green tech, organic gardens, or bike lanes, though these all contribute to change. The solution lies in confronting capitalism.

"Our entire economic paradigm is a threat to ecological stability," argues Klein. "Challenging this economic paradigm—through mass-movement counter-pressure—is humanity's best shot at avoiding catastrophe . . . . It makes the ditching of that cruel system in favor of something new (and perhaps, with lots of work, better) no longer a matter of mere ideological preference but rather one of species-wide existential necessity."[12]

On Sunday, September 21, 2014, many of the organizers featured in this book were in New York City along with 400,000 other concerned global citizens at the People's Climate March. This was more than an environmental march. An amazing array of activists—on immigration, prison rights, queer liberation, workers' rights, indigenous rights, education, and environmental justice—all marched together to call on world leaders at the UN to stop an ecocidal economy from destroying our collective home. While each of these activists may at times focus on a single issue, they see a connection between their problems and solutions. They see a holistic movement joined by fighting the same underlying causes.

There were thousands of presentations throughout the city that weekend. Frack-off included talks by indigenous women from North Dakota whose lives, land, and waters are being destroyed by the tar sands. There was a tour of the South Bronx, where the asthma rate is much higher than in the more affluent parts of the city, due in large part to the diesel fumes from trucks that are routed through this poor part of town. There, activists who closed down juvenile detention centers have also created successful restorative justice programs. Now they want to stop the building of an industrial park and use the area for recreational parks and green space. While surrounded by water, the residents of the South Bronx, who are mostly people of color, have no public access to the waterfront.

Favianna Rodriguez, whose art fills the pages of this book (see interview at end of Immigration chapter), talked about the life-giving force of Mother Earth and the two different paths ahead: the "generative" path, which creates and replenishes and generates life and beauty, and the "extractive" path, represented by the oil and gas industries, banks, and other massive corporations and militaries that take but do not replenish. That capitalist path is predicated on dominating nature and profiting from the labor of others. Rodriguez describes it as the "take and rape" culture versus the "give and nurture" culture.

Many of the stories told throughout that weekend (and in this book) have a consistent theme: certain people's lives are not valued. Families in the South Bronx spoke of feeling marginalized because they're black. Native people living near the tar sands of Canada and North Dakota told of how their governments treated the Indians as if they were better off dead.

People on the front lines of the crisis led the march. These are folks who have had family members die, who have been made homeless, and who are feeling the greatest impact of climate change. From New York to Puerto Rico, from Canada to Kentucky to Bangladesh, they reiterated how capitalism is the modern expression of colonialism. This ideology of supremacy asserts that colonial or capitalist rulers are superior while the "other" is inferior.

On Monday, September 22, the day after the march, many joined #FloodWallStreet to disrupt the powerful Wall Street banks that are funding and profiting from Big Oil and Big Coal.

It is time that every life is valued. It is time to replenish rather than extract. It is time to reclaim our planet, the home we all share, and build a new economy and global community.

■ THE PEOPLE SPEAK. Jetsonorama, Cow Springs, Arizona, 2014 (Photo by James "Chip" Thomas)

As part of his Painted Desert Project, street artist Chip Thomas (aka Jetsonorama) asked Navajo community members and activists their thoughts about a proposal to use reclaimed wastewater for snowmaking at a ski area in the San Francisco Peaks, considered sacred by local tribes. Their answers were painted across their faces, photographed and wheat-pasted in large format in the Navajo reservation in the fall of 2011. The text painted over their faces read: "Faces are sacred. Faces are beautiful. We walk on the face of the earth. The mountain is a beautiful, sacred place that needs to be protected. In beauty I walk." First Nations people face directly the issues around fossil fuel extraction and environmental destruction. The art celebrates the grace, strength, and myriad ephemeral beauties that arise even in the most difficult places. A Native of North Carolina, the artist is also a doctor who moved to the Navajo Nation in 1987 to work for the Indian Health Services.

ENVIRONMENTAL WARRIORS: GOING TO THE FOOT OF THE PROBLEM

RACHEL
SCHRAGIS

RACHEL SCHRAGIS IS A VISUAL ARTIST, FLOW CHART MAKER, EDUCATOR, AC-TIVIST, AND CULTURAL ORGANIZER WHO WAS ACTIVE IN OCCUPY WALL STREET ARTS AND CULTURE AND IS PASSIONATE ABOUT VISUALIZING AND ORGANIZING COMPLEX INFORMATION. HER MOST RE-CENT ENDEAVOR WAS HER ROLE AS ARTS COORDINATOR FOR THE HISTORIC PEO-PLE'S CLIMATE MARCH IN NEW YORK CITY.

Photo by Samuel Budin

I'm an artist and an art organizer working primarily in climate justice and economic justice. Working with organizers and activists, at times I am the one doing the artwork, and sometimes I am a liaison who goes between artists and activists and organizers to figure out how visual art can support the goals they're trying to reach.

The climate seems a concrete way in which we can show the inequality of our economic system. Our economy is tied up in how energy is produced. We have to change the system. The only actual climate solution is the radical democratization of both kinds of power. People have to be able to generate their own power and they have to have decision-making power.

How do you see the role of arts or cultural work and its transformative power in twenty-first-century political movements?

"Art" is the word that capitalism uses to reconcile itself with culture. That is art as the production of objects of commodities to be bought or sold.

Art is the tool that we have to impact how people feel and receive information, how people think of themselves and about the world. Art helps people reconcile facts and feelings.

With any issue that you're trying to move, you're trying to show people that they should feel invested in it and that it's urgent. Calling something an art project gives you permission to think intentionally about how it makes people feel. In the twenty-first century, we need to create authentic learning experiences to move people outside of consuming behind their computer screen. This kind of intentional design of emotional experience seems so critical. Art reminds us how thrilling participating fully in the world can be.

How does your political work relate to the collective, and how is it similar or different from your individual work aesthetically and content-wise?

That's the tension of collectivity and individuality. In my own practice, participation looks like organizing work and my individual expression looks like visual product.

Formalized organizations need to play a role in helping people have a sense of belonging. Politics are built through collaboration, and it's around the content, rather than the expression, that I've found myself collaborating.

For this reason, the organizations that I have been a part of in my creative and political life have largely been political organizations, where I exist within them as an artist. It's critical that our social movements have separate arts organizations with autonomy. I have incredible respect for people whose artistic practices are more collective than mine, and who form art collectives that can be their political and creative homes.

FIGHT FOR A NEW WORLD WITH YOUR WHOLE SELF!

People's Climate Sporatorium, Brooklyn Museum, Brooklyn, New York, 2014. Photo by Erik McGregor

EPI-
LOGUE
SOLIDARITY—A GATHERING

At the end of August 2014, the transformative organizers depicted in this book, most of whom had never met each other, came together. The intersection of people, organizations, and movements and our shared time shaped this book.

After weeks of wrestling with planning the agenda for the gathering, renowned meeting facilitator and my dear friend Gibrán Rivera, the book's editorial team (Jorge Díaz, Dey Hernández, David Goodman, Rinku Sen, and Antonia Darder), and I were all sitting at a table debating a final item. Gibrán addressed us: "We have amazing people, a great agenda, a great design team, and an experienced facilitator." He suddenly turned to me and added sternly, "At this point, it's ours to fuck up.

"Or," he continued, his gaze still locked on me, "we can become the hosts, welcome everyone, and smile. It can be an amazing gathering."

So began the two days where we broke bread and discussed our challenges, big questions, and what we all could do to make lasting social change.

Now, several months later, as I write this Epilogue, I feel the presence of the wonderful organizers, artists, and authors I have met along this journey. These visionary leaders—and their struggles, their progress, and the broad-scale social transformation they are working toward—fill me with a deep sense of awe. It is an honor to bear witness to all this energy, this huge force that represents the river of change, the evolution propelled by the daring and inspiring people whose stories are told in this book.

I end this journey with some observations about themes and commonalities shared by transformers. These are my takeaways.

MOVEMENTS CONSTANTLY CREATE CHANGE

One of the most remarkable things for me has been to experience many of the movements of our time as they are unfolding. Transformations are rapidly evolving all around us.

When I started writing in early 2013, fifteen states had legalized same-sex marriage. By June of 2015, same-sex marriage was legal in all states. The National Gay and Lesbian Task Force, which has fought long and hard for marriage equality, has evolved to embrace a broader vision, changing its name to the National LGBTQ Task Force in order to reflect the reality of a struggle that is larger than just gays and lesbians.

Hope and change are all around us—driven not by Barack Obama, who made that phrase a campaign slogan as a presidential candidate in 2008, but by dedicated grassroots activists like those in this book.

The world looks the way it does, in part, because past movements rose up. My faith in this evolution was beautifully captured by Gibrán at the close of the gathering:

There is a love that defines the evolutionary thrust, the evolutionary energy, and we can connect to that. . . . Evolution doesn't just happen to us. We can define it. . . . We're in the middle of it; we are a part of, and it's worth trying to find ways to align ourselves with, it. . . . If white men, in the middle of imperialist expansion, discover evolution, what they see is "survival of the fittest." But if you look at evolution for what it is and you look at the human species, you see that we couldn't have made it without connection, without empathy, without turning to one another, without caring for each other. These are the evolutionary traits that allow us to get anywhere that is good at all.

When I'm around people like you, I feel like I'm around evolutionaries. That's how I want to spend my time, so I am deeply grateful. . . . Let's keep this thing called evolution moving forward.

In this spirit, we ended the gathering.

"WE NEED SOLIDARITY"

The activists in this book have all harnessed the power of allies. As Jitu Brown said at the gathering:

People in oppressed communities don't need charity. We need solidarity. All we need to make change is time, space, and will. Our work must be driven and led by the people directly impacted.

The United States has 2.3 million people behind bars, mostly for nonviolent crimes and minor drug offenses. Mass incarceration has disproportionately impacted people of color: A black man in America today has a one in three chance of ending up in jail.

What does solidarity look like for our black and brown brothers and sisters who are in jail? It begins with exposing the racist and inhuman nature of the criminal justice system and repealing mandatory sentences and drug laws, but it would not stop there. What would radical change look like? It would begin with dismantling

social, political, cultural, and economic structures that exploit and alienate. In their place, as the transformative visions of the prison abolitionists describe, we can build new structures that support our full humanity.

Committing to confronting oppression in all forms is a key to solidarity. Indigenous activist Clayton Thomas-Müller explains:

We need an anti-oppression, anti-colonialism platform, [to] give space for people to express their differences, [and to provide] tools to address systems of oppression when they show up in our spaces.

By participating in organizations that embrace the fullness of the change we need, we create vast networks across movements and disrupt the "landscape of injustice."

We must commit to this full change and help steer away from the perilous direction of incarceration, deportations, the school-to-prison pipeline, and ecocide in which we are heading. We cannot go along with racism, sexism, homophobia, and capitalism. We can and must interrupt them!

The leaders in this book invite us to believe that humanity can change. They show we can all stand in solidarity because we see our fight as one, connected to each other through the larger quest for human liberation. Our futures are inextricably linked. As Rinku Sen says, "Solidarity implies that you stretch yourself to connect with another, with the other."

DISRUPT POWER

Communities and teachers in Chicago were transformed in 2012 when they confronted the mayor and launched the first teachers' strike in thirty years. Their defiance inspired students, parents, and teachers throughout the United States.

Similarly, strikes by California prisoners in 2013 and fast-food workers in 2014, the #BlackLivesMatter demonstrations to protest police brutality in 2014 and 2015, and AIDS activists' die-ins in the 1980s—all of these courageous and outrageous actions show that through the refusal to cooperate with unjust laws, we win our own humanity.

Don't go along with inhumane laws. As the son of immigrants who were forced to flee Germany as the Nazis came to power, I grew up with constant reminders from my parents that we had to speak up when we encountered injustices, "Don't think it can't happen here," they insisted, referring to the Holocaust. The Nazis were surprised that so much of the German populace acquiesced to anti-Jewish attacks. Compliance and collaboration emboldened the Nazis to escalate their brutal project of white supremacy, which eventually led to the death camps. Some, but not enough, stood in solidarity with the Jews, Communists, Roma, and queers who were sent to the camps. In 2001, my father pointed to the government expansion of domestic spying with the USA PATRIOT Act, the rollback of the rights of our own citizens, and the official propaganda during the buildup to the Iraq War, and warned, "This is how it all starts." He had watched it start similarly when he was growing up during the rise of fascism and Hitler.

Standing up is how we bear witness and signal that we are not just going along. True solidarity not only interrupts, it disrupts It says there is a limit.

As the history of the civil rights movement shows, sometimes white allies with privilege show solidarity with those who have historically been excluded by standing arm in arm with them on the front lines of struggles. Many have sacrificed in many ways. True solidarity requires allowing those most affected to lead and speak for themselves and for those with privilege to organize allies within their own communities of privilege. Too often, those who have a vested interest in systems that give them more opportunities are often reluctant to see class, race, or gender privilege and challenge it. By going along we signify consent. Transformative organizing requires privileged allies to stand in solidarity in social movements as they disrupt powerful entrenched systems.

Successful movements disrupt business as usual, utilizing tactics such as strikes, boycotts, occupations, and more. Sustained direct action that focuses on the vulnerabilities of oppressors, when brought to scale, forces a response to our demands. It forces public acknowledgment of what the issue is, even if we don't get what we have demanded.

When Gaby Pacheco struggled with immigration officials and wore a T-shirt proclaiming "Undocumented and Unafraid," she added her voice and body to the larger DREAMer movement—and by doing so she transformed and radicalized herself.

PREPARE FOR OPPOSITION

Opposition can be violent, as with the police eviction of Occupy Wall Street, the militarized response to the #Black Lives Matter protests in Ferguson, and the jailing of political prisoners. Or opposition can be subtle, such as the lobbying, political campaign contributions, and website and media attacks created by restaurant owners to oppose low-wage-worker campaigns or by the oil companies and banks to oppose change.

Schools have been resegregated and voting rights eroded since the victories of the civil rights movements of the 1960s and 1970s; labor and women's rights have been worn down similarly. Economic, political, and military forces are constantly finding new ways to maintain systems of exploitation and control. In all the movements in this book, a clear pattern emerges: when progress is made, it is actively attacked by those whose privileges are threatened. Movements will be co-opted or crushed. Understanding the opposition and building organizations with deep roots and broad solidarity can help us stand up to opposition, disrupt systems of privilege, and deal with them holistically at their roots.

Puppeteer Janelle Treibitz described organizing that resists cooptation and inspires her:

> I see people sell their own demands off piece by piece in order to get some sort of policy package through. Things that I identified that help prevent cooptation: an incredible job organizing . . . relationships built strongly with other groups, guiding principles for policies that they would fight for, incredible popular education—education with members about solidarity, anti-oppression and all.

CHANGE THE STORY

Paulina Helms-Hernández said at the gathering, "This book is a love letter to movements."

Make your own news. Transformers don't let the corporate media define who they are or who others are. We can counter the dominant negative images by re-telling stories like those in this book and seeing images that come from people in the struggle. Social media is an opportunity to put out our perspectives and make our own news.

Today the mainstream media refers to the "African American crime problem" and the "Hispanic illegal immigration problem," encouraging racial profiling and ignoring the root causes of deliberate policy choices and a system designed to punish, scapegoat, and control. Growing up in Germany in the late 1930s, my father often saw signs that declared, "The Jews are our misfortune." Such forms of propaganda can be subtle, but they are powerful and must be countered in order to make progress.

Derogatory myths are often repeated about the "other." How do we resist a society that underpays immigrants and insults their dignity by branding them as "illegal" or "ignorant" because they speak a second language with an accent? How do we take on subtly destructive attitudes of superiority?

We resist by creating new images. Artist Favianna Rodríguez does this when she depicts powerful Latina women. She celebrates female creativity and power, disrupting demeaning stereotypes of women. Her art agitates and moves us to action.

Create new language. This was done by the successful "drop the i-word" campaign that has helped stop much of the media from routinely describing undocumented immigrants as "illegal." In such a way we frame our messages so they are consistent with the paradigm we are shifting toward.

Alternative media goes where the corporate media won't and brings us movement voices and news from people who are traditionally excluded from the mainstream media, such as the prophetic young, women, people of color, and many others in this book.

HAVE A BIG VISION

Che Gossett shared a beautiful quote at the gathering from the Zapatistas, the revolutionary group in Mexico. It makes us rethink our entire paradigm of power:

The "center" [Mexican government] asks us, demands of us, that we should sign a peace agreement quickly and convert ourselves into an institutional political force, that is to say, convert ourselves into yet another part of the machinery of power. To them we answer NO—and they do not understand it. They do not understand that we are not in agreement with those ideas. They do not understand that we do not want offices or posts in government. They do not understand that we are struggling not for the stairs to be swept clean from the top to the bottom, but for there to be no stairs, for there to be no kingdom at all. We do not want to struggle for power, because the struggle for power is central to the world we reject; it does not form part of the world that we want.

What is so beautiful about the Zapatistas is that while they are resisting the dominant culture, they are creating a new society in Chiapas, Mexico. They are clear about the power that needs to be disrupted, and they focus on creating a more humane alternative.

Examine the roots of the problem, and become part of the solution. Housing activist Steve Meacham spoke about how the work of City Life/Vida Urbana is connected to a larger agenda:

You can't fight rent increases and evictions without objecting to the capitalist market. If you accept market principles, if you say the fair rent is the market rent, then you might as well not even get into the battle because you've lost already.

"Ultimately we have to totally transform the whole industrial, transportation, consumption, and production frame," asserted Eric Mann of the Labor/Community Strategy Center. "It's a struggle against the system of capitalism in which the privatizing, polluting, policing classes dominate society and the cities." It's a struggle toward community-driven participatory visions and solutions.

Many of the leaders frame an issue so that it connects them to other struggles. John H. Jackson, president of the Schott Foundation for Public Education, offered this example at the gathering:

> The goal has to be large enough . . . so people can see themselves as a part of that goal. In the work that we do, we talked initially about a high-quality education. So many movements don't see themselves connected to that. We needed to speak to a broader goal of "providing healthy living and learning communities." That brings in more levels of collaboration, more solidarity, [and] more people can see themselves in it. In that process, we're transformed, which sets us up for transformative change.

Thinking big means imagining new systems and countering the conventional wisdom that "there is no alternative" or "this is the price of freedom."

BUILD ORGANIZATIONS AND BELOVED COMMUNITIES

Lisa Owens, from City Life/Vida Urbana in Boston, said at the gathering:

> The times we're in are a chaotic place with no easy answers. . . . There is a magical thread that happens when people rise up. I believe the role of organizations can be to help create the conditions—so that when people rise up—there's a container for it. But we can't control the thing we call "magic." . . . It's a spiritual process. It has to do with love. . . . We can create the conditions for it to move unfettered and to drive our movement in ways we cannot even imagine.

Bring yourself, your ideas, and your passions forward. Gibrán Rivera coached us at the gathering to find inspiration and joy from an ever-widening circle of caring and committed people. Building such a beloved community gives meaning to life and sustains us while we do the hard work for liberation. Longtime activist and scholar Antonia Darder reflected:

> How do we help each other, how do we have each other's back, how do we have people in our life that support us? Because this work is hard. It's stressful. It kicks our ass sometimes, no matter how hard we're working. And more important, we don't need lone rangers. We need one another. We need to build community. And we can only do this together!

When you think differently from the dominant paradigm, it is crucial to connect with others. The progress in this country, in the history of the world, is the result of the fights waged by visionary organizers who dared to see the hidden injustice. But it is not easy to state hidden truths when you are alone. When Manissa McCleave Maharawal stood up at the general assembly of Occupy Wall Street to challenge the exclusion of women and people of color, she could do it because she was in a community of women and people of color. Join with people who are crying or similarly as pissed off as you. Create community, connectedness, belonging—we belong to one another in movement and we must care for ourselves and each other.

Anger at injustice can be used. It motivates us. But don't live in anger. Don't dwell there. As a proverb says, "It is better to light a candle than curse the darkness."

Take time for self-care and self-expression, for friends and laughs, as we work for serious change. Make music. Make art. Do what makes your heart sing. Dance. Perform in theater. Walk in nature. Keep mentally and physically fit. Take time to learn.

Building community-based organizations, with both local networks and broader ones, is fundamental for transformative change. Steve Meacham challenged us all at the gathering:

> What's the nature of an organization that unites people like us? That project has been put aside in the U.S. for lots of reasons—historic pragmatism and experience with sectarianism. But it should be on the table. We need

organization among dedicated activists like us. Let's not lose the bigger thing—dedication to broad transformative change.

THE RIVER OF STRUGGLE

This book is an invitation to join what historian, author, and civil rights activist Vincent Harding has called the "river of struggle, river of freedom [for] a transformed future" and "the right to develop our whole being." The organizers in this book have stepped into and become a part of that river of justice that has been flowing for centuries. The river of liberation that is democratizing power. Let us each step into the river.

Now is the time for us to create history and write our story.

Each of us can grow our capabilities and, like these transformative leaders, join with others and together develop our strength. Many have talked about how movements are "leader-full." As professor and environmental justice activist Antwi Akom said:

It isn't a matter of "Can we lead?" but "We should be leading!" We need to encourage each other to lead, remind each other of the power we have within ourselves and within our community.

We will fail. We will stumble. We will doubt and we will hesitate. Don't give up. Know that we are making a difference. Even if we make mistakes, we are testing out what is possible in our moment in history. We can reflect and adjust our theories. The visionaries in this book persevere and persist. They plan methodically. There will be many obstacles and many who are not ready to change. Join those who share your passion and sense of possibility. Join those who make a commitment and who you can learn from and who will learn from you. Together, we can build a world full of love, awareness, critical reflection, creativity, humanity, understanding, and meaning, bringing out each other's best.

My brothers and sisters, we are all meant to join this river of freedom. Our people need this change, they are ready for this change.

We are being called at this moment in history. When we fight, we win!

■■ **I WILL NEVER STOP REACHING (FOR YOU). Jess X. Chen in collaboration with CultureStrike, Mariposas Sin Fronteras, and End Family Detention, Los Angeles, California, 2015**
Women in detention centers often take risks by calling attention to the deplorable conditions they face by writing letters and participating in hunger strikes to highlight the deplorable conditions they face. Chen's piece was inspired by a letter written by a Honduran mother who is being kept in a detention center with her younger son after attempting to cross the border to be reunited with her family. The illustration is part of Culture Strike's *Visions from the Inside* project, a creative collaboration between women in Karnes Detention Center and fifteen artists from across the country. By illustrating their letters, the project aims to build awareness and expose the experiences that families face in for-profit immigration detention centers as well as shift ideas around criminalization. The image is a tribute to the undefeatable courage and resilience of the migrant spirit.

"It is not the unloved who initiate disaffection, but those who cannot love because they love only themselves. It is not the helpless, subject to terror, who initiate terror, but the violent, who with their power create the concrete situation which begets the 'rejects of life.'"
—Paulo Freire, *Pedagogy of the Oppressed*

AFTER-
WORD
STORIES OF LOVE AND FURY

ANTONIA DARDER

When We Fight, We Win! is a historical recounting of love and fury. The stories in unison echo the long-standing hardships and triumphs of everyday people and our communities. They are deeply resonant with past political struggles of working people everywhere. People who have had to find strength and fortitude collectively, in order to confront dehumanizing societal forces—*not of our own making*—that daily betray our common existence and trample upon our human rights. The works of activists in these spirited reflections are understood as never being the acts of masked lone rangers galloping in to rescue the poor unfortunate *rejects of life.* Instead, these contemporary political parables of love, though each different in their sociohistorical or geographic configurations and particular political focus, are nevertheless drawn together by the sacred thread of an underlying communal intent: to create a socially and materially just world where the dignity of our shared humanity, the power of our passion, the right to political self-determination, and the wisdom of our histories of struggle can thrive and evolve unfettered, despite the poverty and violence of oppression.

PERSISTENCE OF POVERTY AND VIOLENCE

> Poverty is the worst form of violence.
> —Mahatma Gandhi

The principles of struggle and lessons echoed through the many voices of those who persist in the arduous task of grassroots work are particularly striking, given this moment in history, when poverty and violence intermingle fiercely unchecked, both domestically and internationally. The greed, lack of accountability, and insatiable appetite of the ruling class in this neoliberal moment has devastatingly widened the gap between the rich and the poor, through draconian economic reforms that protect the privilege and wealth of the few, through the erosion of the commons and a whittling away of the public sphere. The consequence is that more children live in poverty today than when President Lyndon B. Johnson first declared a *war on poverty.* Fifty years after the Watts riots in Los Angeles and the release of the infamous federal report, *The Negro Family: The Case for National Action* (known colloquially as the Moynihan Report), working-class communities of color are more segregated and impoverished than in 1965.

However, this phenomenon does not persist because our communities are culturally inferior or caught up in "tangles of pathologies," as some would surmise. Rather, material inequalities and social exclusions persist because social and economic structures continue to reproduce racialized class formations that place the blame for society's ills squarely upon the most vulnerable populations. The large numbers of people at the margins of society are considered culturally or intellectually deficient or seen as pathological or criminal by nature. Impoverished communities are blatantly dehumanized, perceived as irresponsible, wasteful, and unaccountable for their lives. They are seen not only as undeserving of public resources or human compassion but also as easily disposable. Abandonment of responsibility for the social welfare of the nation under advancing capitalism has accelerated over the last two decades through a ceaseless drive toward full-scale marketization and deregulation.

The neoliberal privatization movement, in particular, has resulted in disastrous consequences to the human rights of working-class people, especially communities of color. The proliferation of charter schools, high-stakes testing practices, school closures, anti-immigration initiatives, the diminishment of worker rights, the privatization of prisons, mass incarceration, and an increasing presence of surveillance have all resulted in the erosion of civil liberties. Neoliberal policies of quantification and "evidence-based" reforms have inflicted a politics of bootstrap accountability while deceptively veiling the greed, lovelessness, and lack of accountability of the powerful to the broader ecological sustenance of life on the planet.

Despite all the hullabaloo of racial gesturing, neoliberal reforms have served well to manipulate, distort, and impede the voices and democratic participation of working people of color. Likewise, exacerbated neoliberal values of choice, competition, and individualism have coalesced to drown out the voices of collective dissent. Meanwhile, race problems are touted as the major source for societal ills, while the treacherous system of corporate exploitation and abysmal poverty required for capitalism to thrive remains veiled. The result is little room for movement outside the black/white binary of the dominant political psyche. This signals the need for interrogating the *orthodoxy of race* so prevalent in discourses across the political spectrum, including the Left, in order to engage more forthrightly with racism and its systemic role in the persistence of poverty and violence under capitalism.

RACISM IN CAPITALIST SOCIETY

I believe that there will ultimately be a clash between the oppressed and those who do the oppressing. I believe that there will be a clash between those who want freedom, justice and equality for everyone and those who want to continue the system of exploitation. I believe that there will be that kind of clash, but I don't think it will be based on the color of the skin.

—Malcolm X

This Afterword is being written amid the spectacle of media reporting on the police shooting of Michael Brown, an unarmed African American teenager who was gunned down by police in Ferguson, Missouri, in August 2014. The now-popular propensity to speak of race as something real and indisputable and as the root cause of the tragedy is well illustrated in the discourse that prevails. Many of the commentaries, particularly in the independent media, do provide a glimpse into how racism is enacted daily and made invisible in the United States—a phenomenon that is far more obvious to those of us who must contend daily with its debilitating social and material consequences. Yet, however real these commentaries make the idea of race appear, this still does not mean that race is an incontestable biological or sociological truth.

As a Puerto Rican child growing up in poverty in the United States, I came to learn, poignantly so, that Puertorriqueños exist racialized and impoverished not because of our skin color, culture, or language, but rather because of a politics of racism (enacted through an ideology of race) and a political economy of conquest. Puerto Rico was thrust violently into a state of colonization that restricted our struggle for self-determination and impeded our political participation as a people. A similar politics of conquest has existed historically for other racialized and subordinated populations in the United States and elsewhere, who to this day continue to endure the transgenerational trauma of genocide, slavery, patriarchy, and heterosexism.

The underlying problem must be understood as *racism in a capitalist society*. Effective struggle against racism can never be solely about gaining just and fair treatment in terms of race; rather, it must dismantle at the very roots the long-standing myth of race and its historical role in concealing staggering wealth inequalities and social exclusions. Such a myth effectively warps, distorts, and shrouds the truth about our interdependent humanity and disaffiliates us from the larger fight against all forms of human exploitation, domination, and violence. The tragic police shooting of

**KEEP AMERICA CLEAN.
Antonia Darder,
Pasadena, California, 1983**
Keep America Clean, by Antonia
Darder, speaks poignantly to
the manner in which bodies
of color have been racialized
in U.S. society and treated as
objects to be disposed of in
the wastebasket of history.
The painting emerged from
the frustration she felt working
in a grassroots community
organization during the
early 1980s—the ascent of
neoliberalism. The difficulties
experienced constantly with
school and city officials when
advocating for more resources
for poor working-class
communities of color echoed
the sense of disposability
portrayed in the piece.

Michael Brown, for example, is not a problem of black people or white people. It is a tragic *human* disgrace that sharply illustrates the racism that is embedded in the psyche of this nation.

DARING TO TRANSGRESS

> Our strategy should be not only to confront empire, but to lay siege to it. To deprive it of oxygen. To shame it. To mock it. With our art, our music, our literature, our stubbornness, our joy, our brilliance, our sheer relentlessness—and our ability to tell our own stories. Stories that are different from the ones we're being brainwashed to believe.
>
> —Arundhati Roy

Daily confrontation against debilitating forces that seek to render us intellectually inferior, emotionally passive, and materially bankrupt is indeed a grueling and persistent endeavor. A life committed to ongoing political struggle is not for the faint of heart nor the weak of will. Hence, we persist with our love and our fury because we know at our core that no one will serve us up liberation on a silver platter. We struggle because we know that we must. We struggle because we do not have a choice. And, for these very same reasons, the activists share their poignant tales, born of their refusal to surrender their humanity to the capriciousness of the wealthy and powerful. Instead, they make of their indignation beauty and of their truths hammers, daring to transgress injustice.

These stories, moreover, point to the need for a larger political movement, rooted in the full expression of our love and fury. Where our passion is activated in the name of freedom and justice. And where our collective and individual actions move us away from the alienation of a mode of production intended to thwart our political self-determination. Simultaneously, these stories of struggle speak to a decolonizing movement that must courageously relearn the power of communal survival and fundamental respect for the interdependence of all living beings. Also needed is a clear recognition that cultural and linguistic differences are absolutely vital and necessary to the perpetuation of human life, just as moments of political dissent are essential to the continuing evolution of our democratic existence.

Lastly, these powerful and passionate stories of struggle invite us to reignite our formidable capacity for human intimacy so that we can tangibly and intentionally expand our capacity to love and dream together, through the solidarity of our labor and the struggles we forge with community. Through bearing witness to moments of triumph and disappointment, the stories in *When We Fight, We Win!* also echo enduring faith in one another, personal political courage, commitment to struggle, profound respect for the world, and our deep yearning for social and material justice. In different and similar ways, the activists also bear witness to the powerful fury of the people—a fury born of love and woven into new possibilities for the making of an anti-imperialist, anti-colonial, and anti-capitalist future.

Dr. Antonia Darder is an internationally recognized scholar who has authored and edited numerous books including Culture and Power in the Classroom, After Race: Racism After Multiculturalism, A Dissident Voice *and* Freire and Education. *She holds the Leavey Endowed Chair of Ethics and Moral Leadership at Loyola Marymount University.*

DESIGNERS' NOTE BY AGITARTE

> Art is not a mirror held up to reality, but a hammer with which to shape it.
> —Bertolt Brecht

> Building a culture of faith in our species' ability to right the wrongs in our capitalism-corrupted culture—its ethics, concepts of human relations, falsification of what is our fundamental human nature and relationship to nature—is our task lest the human species not survive.
> —Herb Fox, AgitArte Co-Founder

Bombarded by oppressive narratives of capitalist hegemony, we are left without the stories of those engaged in the struggles of our times. From personal challenges of the status quo to mass organized actions for radical change, our stories are suppressed by the incredible power and resources of dominant institutions in our society. The media, schools and universities, political and civic organizations, and the government all play a critical role in producing and reproducing this alienating cultural reality. The study of these complex yet crucial ideas was developed into a theory of cultural hegemony by Marxist philosopher Antonio Gramsci. Lifelong activist and professor Stephen Duncombe writes about Gramsci's theory, in relation to the power that dominant ideas and practices have in defining our thinking and actions:

> The power of cultural hegemony lies in its invisibility. Unlike a soldier with a gun or a political system backed up by a written constitution, culture resides within us. It doesn't seem "political," it's just what we like, or what we think is beautiful, or what feels comfortable. Wrapped in stories and images and figures of speech, culture is a politics that doesn't look like politics and is therefore a lot harder to notice, much less resist. When a culture becomes hegemonic, it becomes "common sense" for the majority of the population.

The effects on our lives and community of this "common sense" are devastating. We face an incredible challenge against capitalist hegemony in a struggle for our own humanity. Nonetheless, cultural production by popular movements offers us a rich and powerful tradition of art as resistance, protest, and imagination to counter this hegemony. Emerging movements produce cultural workers, who in turn create a new culture of militancy and solidarity for liberation.

AgitArte, an organization of engaged political working-class artists, highlights projects of cultural solidarity with the movements featured in *When We Fight, We Win!* These organizations, activists, and artists create art to protest injustice and propose alternatives that, in turn, generate possibilities for fundamental transformations in our world.

Each chapter starts with art in action, "hammers" in the streets, as puppets, signs, performances, comics, posters, and viral images employed in effective and accessible ways to strengthen our collective actions. They are followed by other examples of visual art produced by and with the political and social movements of the twenty-first century that progress from current struggles to a broader analysis and possibilities beyond this reality. The book's design creates a dual narrative. Captions provide the context in which the artwork was created and introduce the artists who produced it. The result is a visual story in each chapter, a sample of the breadth of the cultural work being generated by our movements. Our alternative media, performance, street action, and artwork are committed to the front lines of the struggles against the terrible alienation of our times. We are out to prove that when we fight—engaging in cultural and political praxis with our people—we win.

Acknowledgments

• • • • • • • • • • • •

Five people made this book possible: Antonia Darder, José Jorge Díaz, David Goodman, Deymirie Hernández, and Rinku Sen. In the preface, I describe who they are and their pivotal roles on the editorial and design team. David Goodman was the steady, professional guiding hand throughout this process. He wrote, edited, and pushed me and helped me to write stories with cadence and drama. If I succeeded it is due to him. Dey Hernández's art choices, the stories behind the art, and the captions make this book sing and shout the brutal reality of our time. During our twenty years of friendship José Jorge Díaz has become my artistic, intellectual, and political teacher. If the book is precise and the analysis is clear, it is due to him. Profesora Antonia Darder has been my wise trusted sage who counseled me and helped me clarify my vision and my ideas on racism and what we are fighting against. Rinku Sen pushed me to make clear assertions in this book, role-modeled the ability to be forthright, and, like the others, introduced us to great activists and read and challenged us on every one of the chapters. I cannot recognize enough what these five people did to make this book a reality.

Many thanks to José "Primo" Hernández, who was integral to the art team, designed the cover, and partnered with Dey on the layout.

zakia henderson-brown, Julie Enszer, Diane Wachtell, Jed Bickman, Maury Botton, Ellen Adler, Julie McCarroll, and so many more at The New Press have helped guide this project, and participated in many parts of it. zakia was part of the August 2014 gathering of the visionary organizers in this book. I don't know of any other publisher that hires organizers or gets involved so heavily with activists. My thanks to Michelle Alexander for suggesting to The New Press that they reach out to me to publish this book.

Gibrán Rivera has been a deep friend and guide since way before this book was an idea, introducing me to many books and authors who shaped my thinking and then facilitating the August 2014 gathering of activists in this book.

My profound recognition goes to the visionary activists who joined together at that first gathering, most of whom are quoted and profiled in this book, all of whom have inspired and influenced me: Antwi Akom, Jitu Brown, Che Gossett, Paulina Helm-Hernández, John H. Jackson, Eric Mann, Manissa McCleave Maharawal, Steve Meacham, Lisa Owens, Clayton Thomas-Müller, Jackson Potter, Julio Salgado, and Janelle Trelbitz. Thanks also to the talented film crew of Osvaldo Budet and Carlos Pérez.

My deep thanks go to all the other activists who we profiled or interviewed for this book. Together with those who attended the gathering, they are my heroes. All took time from their important work and were generous with their insight. For the environment chapter: Bill McKibben, May Boeve, Farhad Ebrahimi, Van Jones. For the LGBTQ chapter: Rea Carey, Scot Nakagawa, Michael Bronski, Jay Michaelson, Evan Wolfson, Urvashi Vaid, Rashad Robinson, Andy Lane. For the incarceration chapter: Patrisse Cullors-Brignac, Walidah

Imarasha, Claude Marks, Michelle Fine, Rob Kampia. For the economic justice chapter: Ai-jen Poo, Saru Jayaraman, Sasha Costanza-Chock, Ted Howard. For the immigration chapter: Gaby Pacheco, Felipe Sousa-Rodríguez, Juan Rodríguez, Marshall Ganz, Carlos Saavedra, Deepak Bhargava, Miriam Ortiz, Renata Teodoro. For the education chapter: Karen Lewis, Jesse Sharkey, Pauline Lipman, Raul Botello, Barbara Ransby, Cassie Schwerner, and the entire team at the Schott Foundation for Public Education. Artists: Favianna Rodríguez, Lily Paulina of Rude Mechanical Orchestra, Kevin "Rashid" Johnson, and Rachel Schragis. You have all profoundly shaped our thinking and the content of this book.

I am deeply grateful to all the artists and culture organizations whose images and captions are featured in the book: Ernesto Yerena, Molly Crabapple, Sabelo Narasimhan, Jesús Iñiguez, Roan Boucher, CrimethInc., Cristy C. Road, Micah Bazant, Jeff Haynes, Papel Machete, Isamar Abreu, Youth Justice Coalition, Jason Killinger, Francisco Enuf Garcia, Overpass Light Brigade, Meredith Stern, Erik McGregor, Farhad Ebrahimi, Ricardo Levins Morales, Susan Wilmarth, LMNOPI, Gonji, Andrés "RHIPS" Rivera, Melanie Cervantes, Kris Krug, Pancho Pescador, Jesús Barraza, Salvador Jiménez, Kelly Creedon, Leonardo March, Christine Wong Yap, Mona Caron, David Solnit, Marisa Morán Jahn, Andre Forget, Gregg Deal, Beehive Design Collective, Jesse Edsell-Veter, CultureStrike, Joe Solomon, Osvaldo Budet, Jetsonorama, Samuel Budin, Jess X. Chen, The Real Cost of Prisons, Yollocalli Arts Reach and Radio Arte, Energy Action Coalition, *Colorlines*, Freedom Harvest, 67 Sueños, the Community Rejuvenation Project, #BlackLivesMatter, End Family Detention, and Mariposas Sin Fronteras.

A big shout-out to Adrienne Maree Brown, who suggested a large number of the organizers and artists in this book, participated in formative early discussions, and laid the groundwork for the web platform. I am indebted to Saulo Colón for being my teacher, introducing me to many authors, and setting me on this path.

Special thanks to Ann Beaudry for massive amounts of editing, cutting, sharpening, and for her strategic advice and encouragement through so many stages of this book with her good sense of humor and graciousness.

Warmest gratitude to my writing coach Sara Whitman for telling me when to start all over again and when I was done.

Huge thanks to Rose Gschwendtner for endless wisdom on movements and helping me over problems big and small. I thank my colleagues for their support with this project: Remona Davis, Margo Braithwaite, Andrea Garvey, Shawna Ellis, Pamela Muñiz, Joyce Litner, Sara Oaklander, Michelle Coffey, Patrick St. John, Kathy Peterson, Diane Franklin, Janet Grogan, Ike Williams, Paul Sennott, Kathryn Beaumont, Hope Denekamp, Maisie Chinn, Deborah LaBelle, Alvin Starks, and Ian Enaba.

Thanks to author Judith Nies who planted the seeds of this book. Nies's wonderful book of stories, *Nine Women: Portraits in the American Radical Tradition* gave me a model and inspired me as it cut across movements and centuries. Thanks to Deborah Frieze, author of *Walk Out Walk On*, for reading drafts and showing me it was possible to write a movement book filled with images. Additional thanks to Noam Chomsky, Stephen King, Otto Scharmer, Tim Wise, Peggy McIntosh, Resource Generation, Jean Hardisty, Rosa Smith, Juan Leyton, and Noelle Hanrahan of Prison Radio for your inspiration.

For editorial advice and content, a big thanks to Cassie Schwerner, my colleague and comrade for thirty years, and to Penn Loh, Victor Wallis, Claude Bruderlein, Deepak Bhargava, Alexie Torres-Fleming, Si Kahn, Stephona Stokes, Dayna Cunningham, Tarsos Ramos, Jeffrey Wolfman, Chris Tinson, Aron Tanaka, Steve Early, Adria Goodson, Josephine Auciello, Michael Fogelberg, Andrew Yarrow, Michael Holzman, Chris Willard, Hannah Baron, Carol Rosen, Vanessa Green, Terri Shuck, Dana Rae Warren, Maya Wiley, Gordy Fellman, Jim Green, Nakisha Lewis, Kelly Bates, Bryant Muldrew, Omo Moses, Ali Tinku Ishtiaq, and Matthew Shapiro.

Huge thanks to Damon Douglas, who pushed me to get this book done in half the time I thought it would take and guided me to develop that capacity.

Family is central to this project and to my life. My eighty-six-year-old mother, Lilo Leeds, has been a warrior of the women's rights, civil rights, and educational struggles for over sixty years. I have worked side by side with her for almost thirty of those years. She read every word, pushed me to be courageous, reminded me of important lessons, and added her stories, which became mine.

My dad, Gerry Leeds, died while I was writing this book. Through the mourning process, his powerful presence and principles came alive once again, and he role-modeled for me the importance of reinventing myself, taking a stand, following my passions, doing what is right, doing everything with great quality, and respecting the integrity of those with whom I work.

My activist father- and mother-in-law, Bill Jobin and Sally Fritz, both role-modeled daring courage and encouragement. My brother, Dan Leeds, read many chapters and provided insight into the structure of the book. My brother Richard Leeds and sister-in-law Anne Kroeker advised me on the climate chapter and marched with my other sister-in-laws Sara Jobin and Laura Jobin Acosta at the People's Climate March. My brother Michael Leeds gave me management coaching. My sister Jen fed me with great ideas. My thanks to Camille and Eliza Jobin-Davis for their enthusiasm and design advice.

My children have been constant loyal readers, helping sharpen the text with probing questions and edits, and always calling me to my highest ideals. Several of their eighteen- to twenty-three-year-old friends were readers who participated in campaigns, theater, and marches with us, brought in fresh connections, and helped clarify terms that we took for granted. Their enthusiasm has been contagious, and their insights helped make the book more relevant and readable. My thanks to Aviva, Zander, Oscar, Jake, Rosa, Karina, Matilda, Cal, and many others for enjoying the book so much.

My last and greatest shout-out goes to Maria Jobin-Leeds, who has been a tireless activist, organizer, and visionary partner with whom I have worked, loved, and grown for over three decades. Together we have celebrated victories and mourned the loss of colleagues doing AIDS activism and working on Central American solidarity movements, South Africa divestment campaigns, and many of the movements in this book. Maria was a reader and a coach for me during the writing of this book. But more than anything else, she is my life partner in creating change and building a home and family from which we go out and explore the farthest reaches of this world and our imaginations.

To everyone else, named and unnamed, this book comes out of a deep bond of love, community, and networks of committed people. My words on these pages emerge out of the scene that you and I are immersed in together. You know who you are, and my cup runneth over with your brilliance, comradery, and the blessings you bring to me and our beloved community. Thank you. You are the hope of our future.

The Gathering
First row, standing from left to right: John Jackson of The Schott Foundation for Public Education, David Goodman, zakia henderson-brown of The New Press, Eric Mann from LA Bus Riders Union, Steve Meacham of CityLife/Vida Urbana, Jitu Brown of Journey for Justice Alliance, Antwi Akom of Institute for Sustainable Economic, Educational, and Environmental Design (I-SEEED) and José Jorge Díaz Ortiz of AgitArte. **Second row**, standing from left to right: Manissa McCleave Maharawal from Eviction Free San Francisco, Aviva Jobin-Leeds, Rinku Sen of Race Forward, Janelle Treibitz, Antonia Darder of Loyola University, Paulina Helm-Hernández from Southerners on New Ground (SONG), and Deymirie Hernández of AgitArte. **Third row**, kneeling from left to right: Jackson Potter from the Chicago Teachers Union, Gibrán Rivera, Greg Jobin-Leeds, Che Gossett and Julio Salgado of CultureStrike.

WHEN WE FIGHT, WE WIN! TEAM

Greg Jobin-Leeds is founder and board co-chair of the Schott Foundation for Public Education, whose mission is to develop and strengthen a broad-based, representative movement to achieve fully resourced, quality public education. He is a writer, a high school and adult literacy teacher, a teach er trainer, and an activist. A son of refugees who fled war, Jobin-Leeds has been engaged in struggles for racial, gender, and economic transformation in Boston, New York, Spain, Puerto Rico, and Central and South America. He has launched and nurtured high-impact social justice organizations that have won milestone victories for underserved children and families. He lives in Cambridge, Massachusetts.

Rinku Sen is the president and executive director of Race Forward: The Center for Racial Justice Innovation (formerly the Applied Research Center) and the publisher of the award-winning news site *Colorlines*. Race Forward brings systemic analysis and an innovative approach to complex race issues to help people take effective action toward racial equity through research, media, and practice. She is co-chair of the board (with Greg Jobin-Leeds) of the Schott Foundation for Public Education. Rinku is the author of *Stir It Up: Lessons in Community Organizing and Advocacy*, and the *Accidental American*, and an editor of *When We Fight, We Win!*. She wrote the foreword for this book and has been an important guide and source of characters and resources.

Antonia Darder is an internationally recognized scholar, who has authored and edited numerous books in the field, including *Culture and Power in the Classroom*, *Reinventing Paulo Freire: A Pedagogy of Love*, *After Race: Racism After Multiculturalism*, *A Dissident Voice*, and *Freire and Education*. Her scholarship over three decades has sought to interrogate questions of inequalities and social exclusions in ways that make a critique of capitalism and class struggle central to her critical theory of cultural democracy and biculturalism. Over the years, she has also been active in community struggles related to the eradication of poverty and racism, bilingual education, gender inequalities, immigration rights, and community projects that seek to integrate art as a political force. Antonia holds the Leavey Endowed Chair of Ethics and Moral Leadership at Loyola Marymount University and is Professor Emerita at the University of Illinois Urbana-Champaign. She wrote the afterword for the book and has been a consistent editor, mentor, coach, and source of stories and lessons.

Deymirie Hernández is an architect, multimedia artist, and educator. Issues of race, identity, language, and community are fundamental to her work. She experiences first-hand the power of the creative process in the lives of youth as a teaching artist throughout the city of Boston. She designs and directs art workshops with AgitArte, a nonprofit organization dedicated to artistic and popular education projects in marginalized communities, where she is also a board member. Dey is also a puppeteer of the radical workers' theater collective, Papel Machete, which is based in Puerto Rico. Her work and performances most recently have been exhibited at the Mills Gallery of the Boston Center for the Arts, and Loisada Center, Lower East Side, New York City. She is the art director and curator of this book.

Jorge Díaz Ortiz is a cultural worker/popular educator, community organizer, puppeteer, and DJ (Cano Cangrejo) from Puerto Rico with over twenty years of praxis in the field. Jorge is deeply committed to working class struggles that challenge patriarchy, white supremacy, imperialism, and capitalism in all of its forms. He is currently the artistic director of AgitArte, a nonprofit which generates workshops and projects in communities in Boston and San Juan. He is actively engaged in struggles for liberation and an active member of the Movimiento Socialista de Trabajadores. Jorge is also a founding member and co director of Papel Machete, a collective of radical artists and street theater/puppetry dedicated to education, agitation, and solidarity work in twenty-first-century Puerto Rico and its Diaspora. He has been a political advisor, mentor, and developmental editor of the book and gathering design.

David Goodman is an award-winning independent journalist, a contributing writer for *Mother Jones*, and the author of ten books, including three *New York Times* bestsellers co-authored with his sister Amy Goodman, host of *Democracy Now!* His work has appeared in the *New York Times*, the *Washington Post*, *Outside*, the *Boston Globe*, *The Nation*, and numerous other publications. Goodman has appeared as a guest on national radio and television shows, including PBS *NewsHour*, *Democracy Now!*, NPR's *Fresh Air*, and CNN. He also hosts a public affairs radio show, *The Vermont Conversation*. David was an editor, writer, and an advisor in the interviews and in creating the stories in this book.

NOTES

INTRODUCTION

1 Attributed to Pastor Martin Niemöller, as stated in Franklin H. Littell's foreword to *Exile in the Fatherland: Martin Niemöller's Letters from Moabit Prison*, ed. Hubert G. Locke (Grand Rapids, MI: William B. Eerdmans, 1986), viii.

1: RECLAIMING WHOLENESS

1 "Half of Americans Support Legal Gay Marriage," Gallup, May 8, 2012, www.gallup.com/poll/154529/half-americans -support-legal-gay-marriage.aspx.

2 "Testimony of 12-Year-Old with Two Moms Moves Some Vermont Legislators to Support Gay Marriage Bill," *Democracy Now!*, April 8, 2009.

3 David Goodman, "Vermont's 'Happily Ever After,'" *Mother Jones*, April 8, 2009.

4 Martin B. Duberman, "The Stonewall Riots," *The Martin Duberman Reader: The Essential Historical, Biographical, and Autobiographical Writings* (New York: The New Press, 2013), 91.

5 "Poll Indicates Majority Favor Quarantine for AIDS Victims," *New York Times*, December 19, 1985.

6 "State Sodomy Laws Continue to Target LGBT Americans," Equality Matters, August 8, 2011, http://equalitymatters .org/blog/201108080012.

7 Elizabeth Sheyn, "The Shot Heard Around the LGBT World: *Bowers v. Hardwick* as a Mobilizing Force for the National Gay and Lesbian Task Force," *Journal of Race, Gender and Ethnicity* 4, no. 1 (2009): 2.

8 George Chauncey, "The Lesbian Baby Boom," *Why Marriage? The History Shaping Today's Debate over Gay Equality* (New York: Basic Books, 2004).

9 Evan Wolfson, "Freedom to Marry's Ladder of Clarity: Lessons from a Winning Campaign (That Is Not Yet Won)," *Columbia Journal of Gender and Law* 29, no. 1 (2015): 236–43.

2: GROUNDED IN COMMUNITY

1 Eric "Rico" Gutstein and Pauline Lipman, "The Rebirth of the Chicago Teachers Union and Possibilities for a Counter -Hegemonic Education Movement," *Monthly Review*, June 2013, 2.

2 "Civil Rights and Education Justice Groups File Title VI Complaints in Chicago, New Orleans and Newark," Advancement Project, May 13, 2014, www.advancementproject.org/news/entry/civil-rights-education-justice-groups-file -title-vi-complaints-in-chicago-n.

3 "Amazing 9 Year Old Asean Johnson Brings the Crowd to Their Feet at Chicago School Closings Rally," Catalyst Project, May 20, 2013, https://www.youtube.com/watch?v=oue9HlOM7xU.

4 "National Charter School Study 2013," Center for Research on Education Outcomes, Stanford University, 2013, http://credo.stanford.edu/documents/NCSS 2013 Final Draft.pdf.

5 Ibid.; Pedro Noguera, "Why Don't We Have Real Data on Charter Schools?," *The Nation*, October 13, 2014.

6 Diane Ravitch, "The Secret to Eva Moskowitz's 'Success,'" *The Nation*, September 24, 2014.

7 For the New Orleans example, see Beth Sondel and Joseph L. Boselovic, "'No Excuses' in New Orleans," *Jacobin*, July 24, 2014, www.jacobinmag.com/2014/07/no-excuses-in-new-orleans. For the Michigan example, see Jennifer Dixon, "Michigan Spends $1B on Charter Schools but Fails to Hold Them Accountable," Michigan.com, June 22, 2014, www.freep.com/article/20140622/NEWS06/306220096/Michigan-charters-1-billion-taxpayer-dollars.

8 Robert Barlett, "Creating a New Model of a Social Union: CORE and the Chicago Teachers Union," *Monthly Review*, June 1, 2013.

9 Alexander Russo, "Political Educator," *Education Next*, Winter 2003.

10 Gutstein and Lipman, "The Rebirth of the Chicago Teachers Union."

11 Michael Fullan, "Choosing the Wrong Drivers for Whole System Reform," Centre for Strategic Education, Seminar Series Paper No. 204, May 2011, www.michaelfullan.ca/media/13436787590.html.

12 Michelle Fine and Michael Fabricant, "What It Takes to Unite Teachers Unions and Communities of Color," *The Nation*, September 24, 2014.

13 Gutstein and Lipman, "The Rebirth of the Chicago Teachers Union."

14 Jerusha Conner and Sonia Rosen, "How Students Are Leading Us: Youth Organizing and the Fight for Public Education in Philadelphia," *Perspectives on Urban Education*, Graduate School of Education, University of Pennsylvania, Summer 2013, http://urbanedjournal.org/archive/volume-10-issue-1-summer-2013/how-students-are-leading-us-youth-organizing-and-fight-public-.

15 "Attorney General Eric Holder Delivers Remarks at the Department of Justice and Department of Education School Discipline Guidance Rollout at Frederick Douglass High School," news release, U.S. Department of Justice, January 8, 2014, www.justice.gov/opa/speech/attorney-general-eric-holder-delivers-remarks-department-justice-and-department-education.

3: TRANSFORMING VISIONS

1 "*The New Jim Crow* Author Michelle Alexander Talks Race and Drug War," *Drug War Chronicle*, Issue 825, March 10, 2014, www.stopthedrugwar.org/chronicle/2014/mar/10/new_jim_crow_michelle_alexander_talk.

2 The Sentencing Project, "Report of the Sentencing Project to the UN Human Rights Committee," August 1, 2013, http://sentencingproject.org/doc/publications/rd_ICCPR Race and Justice Shadow Report.pdf.

3 National Center for Transgender Equality, "National Transgender Discrimination Survey," September 11, 2012, 163, http://transequality.org/issues/resources/national-transgender-discrimination-survey-full-report.

4 Michelle Alexander, *The New Jim Crow: Mass Incarceration in the Age of Colorblindness*, rev. ed. (New York: The New Press, 2011), 11

5 The Sentencing Project, "The Sentencing Project News Racial Disparity," www.sentencingproject.org/template/page.cfm?id=122.

6 The Sentencing Project, "Women in the Justice System," www.sentencingproject.org/template/page.cfm?id=138; Julie Ajinkya, "Rethinking How to Address the Growing Female Prison Population," Center for American Progress, March 8, 2013, www.americanprogress.org/issues/women/news/2013/03/08/55787/rethinking-how-to-address-the-growing-female-prison-population.

7 Andy Kroll, "This Is How Private Prison Corporations Make Millions Even When Crime Goes Down," *Mother Jones*, September 19, 2013.

8 Laura Sullivan, "Prison Economics Help Drive Ariz. Immigration Law," NPR, October 28, 2010.

9 Adam Gopnik, "The Caging of America," *New Yorker*, January 30, 2012.

10 Patrisse Cullors-Brignac, *Stained: An Intimate Portrayal of State Violence*, http://www.wherevent.com/detail/Patrisse-Marie-Cullors-Stained-An-Intimate-Portrayal-of-State-Violence.

11 Angela Davis, *Are Prisons Obsolete?* (New York: Seven Stories Press, 2003), 107.

12 Ibid., 108.

13 "What Is Transformative Justice?," *Philly Stands Up!*, www.phillystandsup.com/tj.html.

14 David Goodman, "Hard Time Out," *Mother Jones*, August 2008. Reprinted here by permission of the author.

15 Sylvia Rivera Law Project, "'It's War in Here': A Report on the Treatment of Transgender and Intersex People in New York State Men's Prisons," 2007, http://srlp.org/files/warinhere.pdf.

16 "'Black Trans Bodies Are Under Attack': Freed Activist CeCe McDonald, Actress Laverne Cox Speak Out," *Democracy Now!*. February 19, 2014.

17 Shaena Fazal, "Safely Home," Youth Advocate Programs, June 24, 2014, www.safelyhomecampaign.org/Portals/0/

Documents/Safely%20Home%20Preview/safelyhome_es.pdf?ver=2.0.

18 Ian Lovett, "Inmates End Hunger Strike in California," *New York Times*, September 5, 2013.

19 "*The New Jim Crow* Author Michelle Alexander Talks Race and Drug War."

20 Steve Holland and Andrea Shalal, "Obama Orders Review of U.S. Police Use of Military Hardware," Reuters, August 23, 2014.

21 "Michelle Alexander: Locked Out of America," *Moyers & Company*, December 20, 2013, http://billmoyers.com/segment/michelle-alexander-locked-out-of-the-american-dream/.

22 "The Campaign to End the New Jim Crow," brochure, http://nationinside.org/images/pdf/CENJC_Brochure.pdf.

4: THE POWER OF STORIES

1 Jose Antonio Vargas, "My Life as an Undocumented Immigrant," *New York Times*, June 25, 2011.

2 "The Immigration Spring," editorial, *New York Times*, March 31, 2013.

3 David Bacon, "How US Policies Fueled Mexico's Great Migration," *The Nation*, January 4, 2012.

4 Ibid.

5 Ibid.

6 Juan González, "Immigrant Workers Point the Way to a Better World," *Imagine: Living in a Socialist USA* (New York: HarperCollins, 2014).

7 "The 'Secure Communities' Illusion," editorial, *New York Times*, September 5, 2014.

8 Elise Foley, "Deportations Continue as Congress Seeks Immigration Reform," *Huffington Post*, April 24, 2013.

9 "Immigrants in Solitary," editorial, *New York Times*, April 1, 2013.

10 Detention Watch Network, "The Influence of the Private Prison Industry in Immigration Detention," www.detentionwatchnetwork.org/privateprisons.

11 Ibid.

12 "Profit Motive Influences Immigration Detention Policy, Says Report," Fox News Latino, May 13, 2011.

13 Peter Wallsten, "President Obama Bristles When He Is the Target of Activist Tactics He Once Used," *Washington Post*, June 10, 2012.

14 Peter Wallsten, "Marco Rubio's Dream Act Alternative a Challenge for Obama on Illegal Immigration," *Washington Post*, April 25, 2012.

15 González, "Immigrant Workers Point the Way to a Better World."

5: "WHEN WE FIGHT, WE WIN!"

1 National Poverty Center, University of Michigan Gerald R. Ford School of Public Policy, www.npc.umich.edu/poverty.

2 Oxfam, "Working for the Few," January 1, 2014, www.oxfam.org/sites/www.oxfam.org/files/bp-working-for-few-political-capture-economic-inequality-200114-en.pdf.

3 Ben Stein, "In Class Warfare, Guess Which Class Is Winning," *New York Times*, November 25, 2006.

4 Laura Shin, "The 85 Richest People in the World Have as Much Wealth as the 3.5 Billion Poorest," *Forbes*, January 23, 2014.

5 Manissa McLeave Maharawal, "So Real It Hurts," in Kate Khatib and Mike McGuire, eds., *We Are Many: Reflections on Movement Strategy from Occupation to Liberation* (Oakland, CA: AK Press, 2012), 174–75.

6 Ibid.

7 Joel Olson, "Whiteness and the 99%," in Khatib and McGuire, eds., *We Are Many*, 46.

8 Occupy Research and Data Center. "Research By and For the Movement," in Khatib and McGuire, eds., *We Are Many*, 70.

9 New York Civil Liberties Union, "Stop and Frisk Facts," www.nyclu.org/node/1598.

10 Noam Chomsky, "America Hates Its Poor," *Salon*, December 1, 2013.

11 Naomi Wolf, "Revealed: How the FBI Coordinated the Crackdown on Occupy," *Guardian*, December 29, 2012.

12 Stan Humphries, "Getting to Know Underwater Homeowners," *Forbes*, August 4, 2012.

13 Laura Gottesdiener, "The Backyard Shock Doctrine," TomDispatch.com, August 1, 2013, www.tomdispatch.com/post/175731/tomgram:_laura_gottesdiener,_the_backyard_shock_doctrine.

14 Alan J. Heavens, "$25 Billion 'Robo-Signing' Settlement Reached with Five Banks," *Philadelphia Inquirer*, February 9, 2012.

15 David Dayen, "Bank of America Whistle-blower's Bombshell: "We Were Told to Lie,"" *Salon*, June 18, 2013.

16 Jillian Berman, "Darden Restaurants Profit Plunges 37 Percent After Bad Publicity over Attempt to Skirt Obamacare," *Huffington Post*, December 20, 2012.

17 Josh Eidelson, "Private Documents Reveal How Big Restaurant Lobby Monitors Fast Food Protests," *Salon*, May 5, 2014.

18 Lawrence Mishel and Natalie Sabadish, "CEO Pay and the Top 1%: How Executive Compensation and Financial-Sector Pay Have Fueled Income Inequality," Economic Policy Institute, May 2, 2012, www.epi.org/publication/ib331-ceo-pay-top-1-percent.

19 Michael Halper, "Five Questions with Saru Jayaraman of Restaurant Opportunities Centers United," Goldman School of Public Policy, University of California, Berkeley, January 22, 2015, https://gspp.berkeley.edu/news/news-center/five-questions-with-saru-jayaraman-of-restaurant-opportunities-centers-unit.

20 Mark Bray, "Something That Takes Time," in Khatib and McGuire, eds., *We Are Many*, 370.

21 Ryan Harvey, "Occupy Before and Beyond," in Khatib and McGuire, eds., *We Are Many*, 124.

22 Frances Fox Piven, "Is Occupy Over?," in Khatib and McGuire, eds., *We Are Many*, 378–79.

23 Ibid.

24 Martin Luther King Jr., "Beyond Vietnam: A Time to Break Silence," April 4, 1967, World History Archives, www.hartford-hwp.com/archives/45a/058.html.

25 Frances Fox Piven, "Welfare in a New Society," in Frances Goldin, Debby Smith, and Michael Steven Smith, eds., *Imagine: Living in a Socialist USA* (New York: HarperCollins, 2014).

6: ENVIRONMENTAL WARRIORS

1 Clayton Thomas-Müller, "A Healing Walk Through Canada's Tar Sands Dystopia," *Yes!*, June 6, 2013, www.yesmagazine.org/planet/a-healing-walk-through-canada-s-tar-sands-dystopia.

2 Bill McKibben, "Jailed over Big Oil's Attempt to Wreck the Planet," TomDispatch.com, August 24, 2011, www.tomdispatch.com/post/175435/tomgram:_bill_mckibben,_jailed_over_big_oil's_attempt_to_wreck_the_planet.

3 J. Andrew Hoerner and Nia Robinson, "Climate of Change: African Americans, Global Warming, and a Just Climate Policy in the U.S.," July 1, 2008, http://rprogress.org/publications/2008/climateofchange.pdf.

4 Bill McKibben, "Global Warming's Terrifying New Math," *Rolling Stone*, July 19, 2012.

5 Suzanne Goldenberg, "Heirs to Rockefeller Oil Fortune Divest from Fossil Fuels over Climate Change," *Guardian*, September 22, 2014.

6 Carolyn Jones, "Chevron's $3 Million Backfires in Richmond Election," SFGate, November 5, 2014, www.sfgate.com/bayarea/article/Chevron-s-3-million-backfires-in-Richmond-5873779.php.

7 Bill McKibben, "The Fossil Fuel Resistance," *Rolling Stone*, April 11, 2013.

8 Bill McKibben, "A Movement for a New Planet," TomDispatch.com, August 18, 2013, www.tomdispatch.com/blog/175737/.

9 "MTA Bus Fare Increases Challenged in Court by Environmental, Community Groups," press release, NRDC, June 26, 2007, www.nrdc.org/media/2007/070626.asp.

10 Naomi Klein, "Why Unions Need to Join the Climate Fight," September 3, 2013, www.naomiklein.org/articles/2013/09/why-unions-need-join-climate-fight.

11 Ibid.

12 Naomi Klein, "How Science is Telling Us All to Revolt," *New Statesman*, October 29, 2013, http://www.newstatesman.com/2013/10/science-says-revolt.

INDEX

Note: *Italicized*, **boldface** page numbers represent photographs, artwork, and the information in captions.

INDEX

INDEX

INDEX